LAST NIGHT AT THE VIPER ROOM

ALSO BY GAVIN EDWARDS

VJ: The Unplugged Adventures of MTV's First Wave (with Nina Blackwood, Mark Goodman, Alan Hunter, and Martha Quinn)

Is Tiny Dancer Really Elton's Little John?: Music's Most Enduring Mysteries, Myths, and Rumors Revealed

Deck the Halls with Buddy Holly: And Other Misheard Christmas Lyrics

When a Man Loves a Walnut: And Even More Misheard Lyrics

He's Got the Whole World in His Pants: And More Misheard Lyrics

'Scuse Me While I Kiss This Guy: And Other Misheard Lyrics

itbooks
AN IMPRINT OF HARPERCOLLINS *PUBLISHERS*

LAST NIGHT AT THE VIPER ROOM

RIVER PHOENIX

AND THE HOLLYWOOD HE LEFT BEHIND

GAVIN EDWARDS

HarperCollins books may be purchased for educational, business, or sales promotional use. For information please e-mail the Special Markets Department at SPsales@harpercollins.com.

FIRST EDITION

Designed by Shannon Plunkett
Photo research by Laura Wyss and Wyssphoto, Inc.

Library of Congress Cataloging-in-Publication Data has been applied for.

ISBN 978-0-06-227315-4

13 14 15 16 17 OV/RRD 10 9 8 7 6 5 4 3 2 1

FOR JEN, WHOM I LOVE MORE DEEPLY
WITH EVERY PASSING YEAR

CONTENTS

INTRODUCTION

I t ends outside a nightclub called the Viper Room, on a Hollywood sidewalk. The young man convulsing on the pavement is named River Phoenix. His brother is on a nearby pay phone, pleading with a 911 operator. His sister is lying on top of his body, trying to stop him from injuring himself as his muscles twitch and his limbs flail against the concrete. River Phoenix has overdosed on a speedball of heroin and cocaine, and has only minutes to live.

It begins twenty-three years earlier, on a peppermint farm. A young woman from New York City had quit her secretarial job, become a hippie, and wandered all the way to Oregon. Now, in a small house with an upside-down horseshoe over the front door, she is in labor, trying to push another life into the world. She declines medical professionals, drugs, a drive to the nearest hospital—but she is surrounded by friends. And when, at last, her first child is born, the infant's arrival on planet Earth is greeted with the sound of applause.

Between applause and agony, between the farm and the Viper Room, between peppermint and heroin, there hangs a life: the twenty-three years of River Phoenix. Documenting River's time on earth are fourteen feature films, one season of a TV show, and a handful of commercials, including spots for cars and cranberry juice. The movies range from excellent to unwatchable; one of them (*Running on Empty*) yielded an Oscar nomination for River and two others (*Stand by Me, My Own Private Idaho*) are generally considered classics.

As an IMDb page, it's not a huge ledger: a legacy of steady work over a decade as River grew from an adorable tyke with a bowl haircut into a strikingly handsome young man. But River had impact that far exceeded the number of films he made; he seemed like he had the chance to be the brightest light of his generation. Not long after his death, Brad Pitt mused, "I think he was the best. Is. Was. Is the best of the young guys. I'm not just saying that now—I said that before he died. He had something I don't understand."

Ethan Hawke said, "River was one of those people that had that strange magic glow around them; he could drive you crazy, or make you fall in love with him, sometimes in the same minute."

Even considering that he was an actor, River had a remarkable number of identities in his short life: Child star. Pinup. Proselytizing Christian. Icon to gay men. Street performer. Drug user. Vegan. Singer/songwriter. Rain forest activist. Hollywood scenester. Oscar nominee. These were skins he lived in, or masks he wore for a while. Depending on your point of view, the number of them meant that he had a life full of lies and contradictions, or that he compartmentalized the different aspects of his existence with remarkable success—or that, like many twenty-three-year-olds, he was still discovering who he was, trying on different identities and figuring out how they connected to his fundamental self.

The people who knew him, in whatever context, agreed on one thing, even if they fumbled for the vocabulary to describe it—River had a special quality, they said. Some called it a spark, some called it a light, some called it a soul.

He was the kind of guy, said one friend, "that if you walked outside and it was snowing, you knew the first thing on his mind was making a snowball."

River loved to embrace friends in massive bear hugs, sometimes surprising them by lunging at them from behind. But if somebody hugged him, he'd quickly squirm away. He wanted any embraces to be on his terms.

Dermot Mulroney, who acted in two movies with River, thought that River's lazy right eye expressed a fundamental dichotomy in his spirit. He said, "His eyes made him the focus of energy in every scene, the centrifugal force so strong you didn't even try to duel him for control. The off-center eye read as madness, and the other read pure sanity. In a close-up, from one side he was the guy next door, and from the other he was absolutely insane."

Cinematographer Bobby Bukowski spent weeks filming River for the movie *Dogfight*. He vividly remembered their initial encounter: "He had very long hair and he struck me—as he came out of an elevator—as an angel, some kind of supernatural being. An angel could be Gabriel, but an angel could be Lucifer too. He would as readily delve into the deep, dark recesses as he would fly up to the lofty, illuminated places."

On October 30, 1993, actress Patricia Arquette—then best known for *True Romance*—was at home with her younger brother Richmond, who was staying with her. When he asked her who she most wanted to work with, she said River Phoenix. The next morning, Richmond was woken up by Patricia, who tearfully told him the news: while they were sleeping, River had died on the Sunset Strip. The world had changed overnight, and its possibilities had diminished.

THE VIPER ROOM WAS A small club: a black box with a stage in the corner. It could hold a couple of hundred people comfortably—more if the fire marshal didn't pay a visit. But it had the highest celebrity quotient this side of a red carpet, because Johnny Depp was an owner. In the Viper Room on the night of October 30, 1993 (and the early morning of the next day), people in attendance included River; his girlfriend, Samantha Mathis; his sister, Rain; his brother, Joaquin; John Frusciante of the Red Hot Chili Peppers; Christina Applegate of *Married . . . with Children;* and Depp himself, who was playing with his band P, which also included Flea of the Chili Peppers, Al Jourgensen of Ministry, Benmont Tench of Tom Petty's band, and Gibby Haynes of the Butthole Surfers. One of their songs that night was about going to parties in the Hollywood Hills—it name-checked Michael Stipe, Sofia Coppola, and River Phoenix. River had never heard it, and never would.

When Depp walked off the Viper Room stage, a bouncer told him that a friend of Flea's was having a medical situation on the sidewalk. Depp stepped out of the club's back door and surveyed the scene: paramedics treating a young man he didn't recognize, surrounded by a cluster of onlookers in Halloween costumes. Late that night, Depp found out that the young man had been River, and that he had died.

Depp and Phoenix had met, but they weren't close. On a professional level, Depp admired Phoenix's work; "there was a specific road he was on that I respected," he said. He recognized a fellow performer eager to get off the Hollywood highway and hack through the undergrowth.

Depp reflected, "The guy was having a good time but he made a big mistake and now he's not here. He doesn't breathe anymore and his mom doesn't get to see him anymore." Depp struggled for words. "The thing is, he came with his guitar to the club. You could cut me open and vomit in my chest because that kid . . . what a beautiful thing that he shows up with his girl on one arm and his guitar on the other. He came to play and he didn't think he was going to die—*nobody* thinks they're going to *die*. He wanted to have a good time. It's dangerous. But that's the thing that breaks my heart, first that he died, but also that he showed up with his guitar, you know? That's not an unhappy kid."

Years later, actress Samantha Mathis ("his girl") said, "It was completely shattering. It was hard to conceive of your mortality at that age. It's really strange now, to think that I'm not twenty-three, and he'll always be twenty-three."

In 1980s Hollywood, Tom Cruise and Michael J. Fox drew the showbusiness road map: a relentless path to stardom. At the same time, the Brat Pack demonstrated how fleeting that pursuit could be. In the 1990s, River taught a generation of young actors that there could be a different approach, one that placed greater value on artistic integrity and personal politics. Even today, when a young performer advocates for environmentalism or vegetarianism, it's a ghostly echo of River's life. His absence got filled by other performers—Brad Pitt, Leonardo DiCaprio, his own brother Joaquin. Looking at them, we can see the ectoplasmic outline of what sort of man River might have become—and looking at him, we can better understand the world he left behind.

PART ONE

"WHEN YOU'RE YOUNG, YOU JUST ACCEPT WHAT GROWN-UPS TELL YOU"

1
SKYLARKING

River Phoenix stands high in the hills of Malibu, facing west. On a clear day, he would be gazing at the Pacific Ocean: sparkling blue, full of possibility all the way to the horizon. Today, the marine layer has rolled in, meaning that clouds have come right up to his feet.

On one side of River stands a friend of his, a beautiful young dark-haired woman. On the other side is another friend, William Richert, almost three decades his senior; Richert has directed him in one movie (A Night in the Life of Jimmy Reardon) and acted with him in another (My Own Private Idaho). They are all standing outside Richert's house, which is currently full of River's young Hollywood friends, including actress Ione Skye. Keanu Reeves rolled up to the party on his motorcycle. River has adopted Richert's house as a second home, sometimes sneaking in during the dead of night.

"Take my hand," River says, and the woman and the man both comply. They stand on the edge of a platform, and although clouds swaddle the house, making it look like Shangri-la in a Maxfield Parrish painting, Richert knows all too well that underneath the clouds, there is a thirty-foot drop down a steep hill.

"We're going to jump," River tells his friends. They aren't sure this is a good idea, but he continues, "And as we go through these clouds, all our past sins, and everything we ever did that we thought was wrong, will all be forgotten. All new things will happen to us, and we'll be filled up forever."

River jumped into the clouds, and his friends leaped with him.
River always jumped.

2 THE SEARCHERS

River Phoenix's mother changed her name piece by piece, but her life all at once. Born Arlyn Dunetz in the Bronx (on New Year's Eve 1944), by age twenty-three she had settled into a cozy, dull domestic life: married to a computer operator and employed as a secretary in a Manhattan office. Her destiny as a mother and housewife seemed preordained, as inevitable as *Gunsmoke* and *The Carol Burnett Show* on Monday nights.

"I just wanted to be loved," she said, "and find somebody to love. I wanted to do what I saw in movies and television: get married and live happily ever after. I found it immediately—and within two years, I was like, 'Oh my God, this is not the way they said. I have to start all over.' So I did."

The sounds in the air were psychedelic: the national mood oscillated between embracing love and advocating revolution. Dunetz didn't know what she wanted to do with her life, but she knew it exceeded the boundaries of a Bronx apartment. In the summer of 1968, she put some clothes into a backpack and, with just a few dollars in her pocket, started hitchhiking west.

Left behind: her astonished husband and parents. Her mother, Margaret Dunetz, knew that Arlyn was going to become a hippie: "I wasn't thrilled, but what could I do? I didn't try to stop her because she was a grown woman already."

RIVER PHOENIX'S FATHER GOT A head start on running away from home, but he was never able to run away from himself. John Lee Bottom was born on June 14, 1947, and grew up in Fontana, California—part of the "Inland Empire" east of Los Angeles. Fontana was a hot, desolate slice of desert suburb, home to a Kaiser Steel plant and famous as the birthplace of the Hell's Angels motorcycle club.

John didn't have an overabundance of parental attention: his father, Eli, was too focused on his glass business to spend time with him. And as John entered his teen years, his mother, Beulah, was in a terrible car accident: after being in a coma for a year, she was sent home from the hospital as a brain-damaged husk of her former self. Overwhelmed by a failing business and a failing wife, Eli started drinking heavily and staying away from home. One day, without warning or explanation, he left. (Eli headed up to San Francisco, and ultimately relocated to Perth, Australia, where he would die on September 23, 1993—five weeks before the death of River, the grandson he never knew.) Beulah was sent to a home; John stayed with his seven-years-older brother, Bobby. But when Bobby joined the navy, John ended up in a private Methodist orphanage.

John tried to escape: "I ran away from home to become a songwriter in Hollywood," he said. The freedom was short-lived, and not marked by a hit single: he was soon sent back to Fontana. John also ran away to Long Beach, south of L.A., where his aunt Frances and uncle Bruin lived, and begged them to take him in. They told him that they couldn't look after him, and he sadly returned to the orphanage.

John Bottom turned from a gentle child full of daydreams into an unhappy, wounded teenager. He drank heavily, smoked pot, and started riding motorcycles, with what he said were serious consequences: "When I was sixteen, a drunk lady ran head-on into me and I spent one and a half years in the hospital." His relatives, such as Aunt Frances, don't remember that accident, and think that he suffered his lifelong back injury while working as a carpenter.

Some possibilities to consider that might explain that discrepancy, none of them happy: John was trying to make sense of his mother's tragic accident by folding the narrative into his own life. Or he couldn't distinguish between reality and his own fables. Or he was so abandoned by his relatives that they didn't know he was hospitalized.

5

John left the orphanage and floated around California with his guitar, picking up jobs gardening and refinishing furniture. At age fifteen, he got a girl pregnant, resulting in a daughter named Jodean (aka "Trust"). Like his own father, he didn't stick around. In 1966, worried about the draft— Lyndon Johnson was starting to ramp up the Vietnam War—John headed up to Canada.

A year later, he drifted back into the United States and drove down to Los Angeles in his battered Volkswagen minibus. On Santa Monica Boulevard, he saw a hippie chick sticking her thumb out for a ride. She was short (five foot two), beautiful, radiant. John Bottom stopped to pick up Arlyn Dunetz.

"It's very interesting that my mom and dad met at all," River mused years later. "I feel they were meant to be together."

John invited Arlyn to his place; two nights later, she accepted the invitation. They stayed up all night, finding common ground in the tie-dyed verities of the day: the insanity of the Vietnam War, the shallow values of the materialistic world, how everybody's problems could be solved with peace and love. By dawn, they were already falling in love.

In that VW minibus, they spent the next few years floating up and down the West Coast, staying in various communes. They never got legally married, but they did have a commitment ceremony in April 1968. As they wandered, seeking new friends and new truths, they became eager consumers of mind-expanding drugs, particularly LSD, which Arlyn described as a "gift from God."

The couple treated tabs of acid as religious sacraments. "Acid was the truth serum," Arlyn said. "It was the thing that was going to get you above the world to a level of consciousness where you could feel the power of God. That was the only reason we took it."

For John, the drug reframed his perceptions of American society. "I just instantly saw that I was living in a pit," he later told River. "There were a lot of lost people and the president wasn't necessarily the nicest guy in the world."

("Maybe you didn't need drugs to know that," River riposted.)

Looking to build a society where "nicest guy in the world" might actually be a job qualification for the presidency, John and Arlyn collected a dozen fellow seekers in a traveling commune. "We were flower children," John said. "We were full of faith and we loved everybody."

Intending to work their way across the United States to Florida, they started by heading north. In early summer 1970, they ended up in the flat scrubland of Oregon, specifically a small town called Madras. Arlyn was in an advanced state of pregnancy when they arrived; the group needed to stay in one place until she gave birth. None of the local farmers had ever hired hippies, but John convinced a young farmer named Roy Nance to take them on. The band of hippies moved into a small two-story house on the farm, and did the manual labor of a peppermint farm, growing a crop that would end up in America's toothpaste and chewing gum. They hauled sprinklers and hoed the mint—and befuddled Nance by taking unannounced breaks whenever they felt the impulse, sitting down in the middle of a field if necessary.

"They were a rather strange lot," said Nance, who was bewildered but tolerant. "One time, I was driving the tractor. The hippies all were supposed to pick the rocks off the ground and put them in the trailer I was pulling. All of a sudden, it got quiet. I looked back, only to find that they all decided to just lay down on their backs and look up at the sun. One of them did that too many times: I still know him, and today he's nearly blind."

The hippies did some freelance agriculture, planting marijuana seeds on Nance's land and trying to grow their own crop. What they didn't know: to reduce weeds, Nance had treated the soil with a "preemergence spray." "Every time the plants got about an inch high, they would die," Nance said with a chuckle. They never did figure out why they were doing so poorly with such fertile land.

Although Nance, then around twenty-five, wasn't much older than his guest workers, he had a more conservative outlook. "They just didn't have the morals that the rest of us had," he said. The women worked in long skirts, and delighted in shocking him by letting them ride up over their waists, revealing that they weren't wearing any underwear. They would regularly strip to go skinny-dipping in the farm's creek, and then splay their nude bodies spread-eagled on the grass, laughing at his reaction. "Once I was on the tractor when they did that," Nance said. "I nearly wrecked several rows of potatoes."

The hippie contingent kept to themselves, but were well liked by their fellow workers, who considered them to be courteous if unconventional. After long days in the fields, the hippies spent their nights by themselves in that two-story house, listening to music by candlelight and taking turns reading books out loud, including Hermann Hesse's *Siddhartha*.

The novel, set in India, is about a young man's quest for enlightenment: he experiments with various instructors and identities (like many college sophomores) until he discovers wisdom by working as a ferryman (unlike most college sophomores). Sample dialogue: "The river has taught me to listen; you will learn from it, too. The river knows everything; one can learn everything from it. You have already learned from the river that it is good to strive downwards, to sink, to seek the depths."

Arlyn kept working until the hot, dry summer day when she went into labor. She refused to go to the hospital in Madras or to have a doctor present, although Nance arranged to have a nurse around. In later years, the story of this birth would become mythologized as a three-day delivery in a log cabin. (Nance said there was no log cabin on his property and that the labor went on for "three and a half hours to five hours at most.") On August 23, 1970, at three minutes after noon, Arlyn gave birth to her first child.

Years later, she told a story about another birth she had attended: "When the baby came out, they said, 'Please don't tell us what it is.' For the first half hour, we just held the child in the birthing tub, and nobody looked. Let's just hold this being as a being, without labeling him right away. If it's a boy, it won't be long before people will be buying him only blue clothes. It was so interesting, because you're dying to know. But why does it matter so much? Why are we obsessed with the difference?"

Her own child was a boy. Later that afternoon, John rushed into the nearby town of Metolius and bought some candles at the hardware store, excitedly telling the clerk that he needed them for a naming ceremony for his newborn son. By candlelight, John and Arlyn christened the child River Jude Bottom. "River Bottom" might be evocative of catfish and mud, but the name "River" was intended as a tribute to a cleansing force of nature, flowing through all of existence.

The name was prompted by the commune's recent choice of reading material, Arlyn explained: "The book *Siddhartha* talks about the river being an answer to life's many questions, as looking into it you can see the reflection of everything."

And "Jude"? The name had biblical overtones: Jude was one of the twelve apostles of Jesus Christ, sometimes believed to be his brother (but not to be confused with his betrayer, Judas Iscariot). The actual inspiration, however, was more immediate and suffused with a "na na na na" chorus: one of John and Arlyn's favorite songs was the Beatles' "Hey Jude."

The name laid out their hopes and expectations for the newborn child: a shimmering reflection of the entire world who could salvage any lost cause, taking a sad song and making it better.

As summer turned into fall, the peppermint was harvested and work on the farm dried up. Arlyn was wan and sickly after the birth, so she and John lingered in Madras with River, even as the other members of their commune hit the road without them. Winter in Madras can be harsh: the high altitude means heavy snowfalls and impassable roads. The family decided they wanted to head back south to warmer climes. The problem was that the VW minibus had stopped running, and neither John nor Arlyn was capable of fixing it. Although Nance was concerned that Arlyn and little River weren't healthy enough to be traveling, he nevertheless towed the bus fifty miles to the south, where a friend of John's repaired it.

For the next couple of years, the family continued their nomadic journey through the American West and Southwest. Greeted with antipathy by straight American society, John and Arlyn would bond briefly but intensely with fellow long-haired travelers. They continued to get high with pot and various hallucinogens, but eventually two stoned visions, separated by one year, sent them looking for actual religion.

Arlyn's: She was in the void, until a golden hand seemed to rip away the darkness.

John's: Lying in a field, he was surprised by a disembodied voice asking, "Why don't you receive me?" When he asked for proof that the voice was real, a "tall fellow" materialized, holding two Bibles and proclaiming, "I'm a Christian." One of the Bibles was antique—a touch that John believed was intended to appeal to his interest in history. John wept. Then he resolved to stop using drugs and smoking cigarettes.

"Spirituality has changed," Arlyn reflected years later. "It's not in the box it used to be in, when you *had* to be in this religion. There's a new understanding that we are all a part of this creation. There's no getting away from it. It's a miracle, and it's magic, and nobody understands it. And there's a great power that comes from that."

John and Arlyn's aimless voyage of self-discovery was transforming into a quest for the divine. Their faith was like a body of water searching for a vessel that would give it a shape. They found it, or it found them: a sect called the Children of God.

3 DEAR GOD

Only ten miles away from the Viper Room, just three weeks before River Phoenix died on the sidewalk, the Los Angeles Sports Arena was decorated with golden columns and torches. The building was usually home to the hapless L.A. Clippers, not simulations of the excesses of Roman emperors. But on this night, the Church of Scientology was having a party.

Ten thousand Scientologists gathered under the arena's roof—the largest such gathering ever—to celebrate a historic moment in the church's history.

After twenty-five years of legal wrangling and corporate espionage, the IRS had officially classified Scientology as a religion, not a commercial enterprise. "There will be no billion-dollar tax bill which we can't pay," declared church leader David Miscavige, looking natty in a tuxedo. This ruling made all the difference: if a language is a dialect with an army, as philologists say, then a religion is a cult with a tax exemption.

In 1993, the streets of Los Angeles were punctuated by Scientology buildings: the Dianetics Testing Centre, the L. Ron Hubbard Life Exhibition, an array of Celebrity Centres. Behind the scenes, Miscavige was living lavishly, with $5,000 suits, a $100,000 stereo system, a car collection, and a staff that included two full-time chefs making him dual entrées for every meal so he could reject one.

Miscavige was not the first religious leader with an extravagant lifestyle financed by the contributions of his followers, or even the first in Los Angeles. Before Miscavige (or his predecessor, Scientology founder L. Ron Hubbard), the city of angels seemed to attract as many religious leaders as it did aspiring actresses. Aimee Semple McPherson, for example, drove into town in 1922, arriving in a beat-up car with two small children and one hundred dollars. Three years later, she had collected a million dollars in donations from tens of thousands of followers and had another quarter-million dollars' worth of land. Soon she built the five-thousand-seat Angelus Temple, at a cost of $1.5 million, where she staged elaborate religious pageants. She had beauty and charm, and consorted with movie stars like Charlie Chaplin. But her glamour was eroded after she disappeared for a week in 1926—she said she had been kidnapped, but the newspapers soon reported that she had been shacked up in a "love cottage." McPherson led her diminished church until 1944, when she died of a drug overdose.

Katherine Tingley, the "Purple Mother," built the Point Loma Theosophical Community, featuring a bugler hidden behind the Egyptian-style gates to herald the arrival of any visitors. Albert Powell Warrington bought fifteen acres of Hollywood real estate and dubbed it "Krotona," a sanctified colony on "magnetically impregnated" ground. The "I AM" cult was based on a vision Guy W. Ballard had while hiking: the Ascended Master Saint Germain materialized, tapped Ballard's shoulder, and let him drink a cupful of "pure electronic essence." Arthur Bell, founder of Mankind United, promised a future age of luxury, thanks to the revelations of miniature metallic supermen living in the center of planet Earth. The "New Thought" movement originated in New England—it was known as "the Boston craze"—but migrated west until Los Angeles became its home.

The American story is a westward journey, looking for new frontiers as a way to leave one's troubles in the rearview mirror. It's not an accident that the movie studios are located in Hollywood: studio heads wanted to be as far away as possible from Thomas Edison, inventor of the motion picture camera, and his patent lawyers. And so many new religions—or sects, or cults, depending on their tax situation—kept heading west until they found a place to settle. For the Mormons, the Utah desert sufficed. For some other infant religions, the only thing stopping their continued travels west was the Pacific Ocean.

In Southern California, they found a ready pool of followers—Los Angeles has traditionally been a city of recent arrivals. Separated from their families and the churches they grew up in, but seeking some spiritual solace, many Los Angelenos have ended up joining fringe sects.

Sometimes the religions, like successful TV shows, have developed in L.A. and then been released across the globe. The Pentecostal movement had its origins in Texas, but became an evangelical blockbuster at the Azusa Street Mission in L.A., under the guidance of a one-eyed preacher named William Joseph Seymour, the son of former slaves; it now has over 250 million adherents worldwide.

The term *cult* suggests not just that a religion is new and small, but that outsiders see its unfamiliar beliefs and rituals as nefarious. Even a few thousand worshippers in a new sect can seem threatening to old-time religions. Sometimes, those sects can take wrong turns.

Living in and around Los Angeles in 1968 and 1969, Charles Manson got his acolytes to believe in "Helter Skelter," the apocalyptic race war that would be coming soon—and to hasten its arrival through a campaign of brutal murders. A more benign cult in that era was the Source Family, whose members, under the guidance of "Father Yod," lived in a commune, practiced free love, played in psychedelic rock bands, and ran an incredibly lucrative organic vegetarian restaurant at 8301 Sunset Boulevard—just one mile east of the building that twenty years later would host the Viper Room.

4 ONE NIGHT AT THE VIPER ROOM

The staff of the Viper Room—bartenders, bar backs, security—is gathered around a table. Club co-owner Johnny Depp stands there, as does his girlfriend, British supermodel Kate Moss, and his best friend (and Viper Room general manager) Sal Jenco. On top of the table is a towel. On top of that towel is a toilet, at which they all gaze intently, trying to puzzle out how to remove a toilet-paper roll that has gotten firmly lodged in the plumbing.

Finally, Moss asks Depp, "Would you give me $100 if I stick my hand in and take it out?"

Depp immediately agrees. His logic: "I can get $400 from the National Enquirer *for a picture of you with your hand in a toilet."*

5 SUFFER THE CHILDREN

Flower children who discovered that the flowers had wilted: that was who David Brandt Berg wanted in his church. As he told the story, "One dark night, as I walked the streets with those poor drugged and despairing hippies, God suddenly spoke to my heart and said, 'Art thou willing to go to these lost sheep to become a *king* of these poor little beggars? They need a voice to speak for them, they need a shepherd to lead them, and they need the rod of My Word to guide them to the Light."

In 1968, Berg—"Father David," or later, "Moses" or "Mo"—turned forty-nine and brought his Teens for Christ ministry to Huntington Beach, California. In this sleepy seaside town, just a little south of Los Angeles, the Teens for Christ traded in their neckties for groovy threads and took over a local coffeehouse. The message: praise the Lord and fight the system.

By 1971, renamed the "Children of God," their numbers had grown from fifty disciples to fifteen hundred, with sixty-nine religious communes scattered around the United States and Canada. And Berg had found the spiritual cornerstone of his church in Scripture, specifically First Corinthians 6:12: "All things are lawful to us." In Berg's reading, all forms of sexual freedom were encouraged, if they were motivated by love. This was only a cubit's distance from "Do what thou wilt shall be the whole of the Law," the credo of British occultist and black magician Aleister Crowley.

Sexual libertinism became the rule at the Children of God, practiced first by Berg, then condoned among the rank and file, and ultimately, encouraged as a sacrament—or as Berg put it, a "come-union." Former members of the Children of God have called it a "Christian sex cult."

Berg became steadily more reclusive, communicating with his followers through epistles called "Mo Letters." In 1973, the letters began to read like *Playboy* editorials: "It was not until I kicked over the traces, thumbed my noses at old-fogey churchianity and all of its old-bogey inhibited sexual superstition and really let myself go and enjoy sex to the full, wild and free, to the absolute utmost, it was only then that God also helped me to achieve this spiritual and mental and physical freedom that I have since had, to completely explode in a total orgasm of psychological, social, economic, political, religious and sexual freedom and liberty and worldwide accomplishments."

Or more succinctly (in a Mo Letter titled "Come On Ma!—Burn Your Bra"), "We have a sexy God and a sexy religion with a very sexy leader with an extremely sexy young following! So if you don't like sex, you better get out while you can."

While male homosexuality was forbidden by the Children of God (underscoring that its tenets were just reflections of Berg's personal mores), they believed that the Bible approved of adultery and incest. Children should be raised as sexual beings, Berg wrote, and encouraged to bathe together, play in the nude, and experiment sexually. But not, Berg emphasized, in front of outsiders unfamiliar with "the revolutionary sexual freedoms."

What did this mean in practice for children born into the cult? With missions scattered across the globe, the implementation of Berg's principles varied somewhat by location, but in the personal stories and testimonials of the Children of God's actual children, unmistakable patterns emerge. Children were separated from their parents and raised communally, with an emphasis on apocalyptic teachings and conformity. With the adults bed-hopping, fatherhood could be uncertain, or nominal: some mothers of large families had multiple children who only vaguely resembled one another.

Children as young as three were encouraged to "play" sexually with their parents and other adults. But even greater emphasis was put on the children stimulating each other; they could pair off for sexual exploration at night, after prayers but before bed.

Rose McGowan, the actress famous for *Charmed* and *Grindhouse,* was born three years after River Phoenix, and, like him, grew up in the sweaty

15

embrace of the Children of God. Her community was fifty hippies, living on the property of a duke just outside Florence, Italy.

"Like most cults, you were cut off from your family" outside the religion, McGowan remembered. "There were no newspapers, no television. You were kept in the dark so you would obey." She learned to read at age three, but didn't have anybody around who would teach her to tie her shoes. "The group encouraged you to have a lot of kids as fast as you could," she said. "Then if you made plans to leave, they would lean on you. You know . . . maybe your kids would disappear."

While her father happily drew illustrations for Children of God comic-book pamphlets, McGowan never bought into their philosophy. "When I was five, we had a complete wall of Bibles, and I burnt that down," she said. "I think I had some anger." McGowan decided that she didn't want to live like the women she saw around her: not only were they subservient (some men, including her father, had multiple wives), they had hairy legs.

McGowan's father could see that the Children of God were about to start more actively proselytizing for sex between adults and children: he was instructed to draw cartoons about it. He took that as a sign it was time to leave. The family escaped, fleeing through a cornfield in the middle of the night during a thunderstorm.

"Their whole thing was that children are very sexual beings," McGowan said. She remembered Berg declaring that God wouldn't have made children capable of enjoying sex if he hadn't expected them to engage in it. She concluded, "I was not molested because my dad was strong enough to realize that hippie love had gone south."

16

6
FOLLOW THE LEADER

Like sheep looking for a shepherd, John and Arlyn wandered around the Southwest until they got shorn. Their hippie ramblings were now imbued with a sense of providence—so in 1972, when they encountered the Children of God in Crockett, Texas, they were eager to join the flock. They disavowed their previous worldly existence, pledged their devotion to Christ, and donated their possessions to the Children of God. (The church's communes sometimes looked like pawnshops or garage sales: a jumble of used stereos and TV sets donated by new members, waiting for resale.)

With thirty other true believers, the Bottom family then trekked over eight hundred miles in a converted school bus to Colorado Springs, Colorado, where they founded a new commune on the site of an abandoned vacation resort near Pike's Peak: they recruited new members by visiting Denver and Boulder, where they distributed pamphlets and sang Children of God hymns in the street. The Children of God songbook included selections such as "Mountain Children," "You Gotta Be a Baby," and "God's Explosions," which placed religious faith halfway between a volcanic eruption and an orgasm: "We'll blow like Krakatoa / If you try to shut us up / 'Cause we're filled with God's hot Spirit / And exploding with His love."

After a few months, they moved back to Texas for "Leadership Training" classes at the cult's Texas Soul Clinic ranch. The ranch was in Thurber, Texas, a deserted coal-mining town west of Fort Worth—but not completely un-populated, as drunk cowboys would sometimes come by with rifles to take potshots at the hippies. John and Arlyn picked new Old Testament names for themselves: Amram and Jochebed, the parents of Moses. By extension, River was Moses; already, they were casting him as a future prophet. On November

21, 1972, John and Arlyn (or Amram and Jochebed) had a second child: a baby girl they named Rain Joan of Arc, after the weather during her birth and the French religious martyr. John delivered the baby himself.

Having established themselves as loyal members of the Children of God, the Bottom family were sent south to proselytize. "We moved around a *lot*," River said later. They went first to Mexico, then to Puerto Rico for almost two years, where River's younger brother was born on October 28, 1974, and given a Spanish-language name, Joaquin Rafael. Young River quickly became fluent in Spanish and acquired the nickname "Rio" (the Spanish word for "river"). The family then headed even farther south, living in multiple South American countries before landing in Caracas, Venezuela. For his devotion to the Children of God, John was named "Archbishop of Venezuela and the Caribbean."

John the Archbishop was basically left alone to run things in Venezuela: John and Arlyn had oversight of nine or ten Children of God homes in Venezuela. Underneath archbishops in the Children of God hierarchy were "regional shepherds," "district shepherds," and "colony shepherds." The only guidance came in the form of Mo Letters, which regularly arrived in the mail with Berg's latest pronouncements on matters theological and sexual. The family was expected to set an example of adherence to the Children of God creed.

The Bottoms established a Children of God colony and lived in a house in Mariposa Hill in Venezuela's capital city of Caracas—the property, previously owned by one of their new converts, had been donated to the cause. The Children of God provided no financial support to the colonies, which meant the children of John and Arlyn Bottom were constantly at risk of going hungry.

Some families might have gotten paying jobs, or returned to the United States. The Bottoms' solution was to have the children beg. River and Rain had already been helping their parents "witness," trying to convert Venezuelans to the sect. They sang in the street, performing the Children of God songbook and becoming known as Los Niños Rubios Que Cantan: "The Blond Children Who Sing." "The kids grew up going out on the street, telling people God loved them," Arlyn said. "They gave their lives to God." Now the tossed coins they received had become their family's primary source of income.

On nights when River was restless or overwhelmed, Arlyn would lull him to sleep by singing "You've Got a Friend." Soon he had memorized the words and was singing along with her.

"They were devoted parents," said another member of the Children of God, called Ado. "We took many camping trips together with our kids." He remembered John and Arlyn telling him that one reason they had joined the Children of God was to stay off drugs.

The family befriended Alfonso Sainz, a local doctor who had previously been a Spanish pop star, cofounder of the band Los Pekenikes. The group had started in the 1960s by doing Spanish-language covers of the pop hits of the day, and eventually began recording their own material. Although none of their work broke out of the Spanish-speaking market, they became a footnote in Beatles history: in July 1965, weeks before the famous Shea Stadium show, they opened for the Fab Four at their concert in Madrid's Plaza de Toros de Madrid.

By 1975, Sainz was living in Venezuela, and had become improbably friendly with the gringo missionaries. River spent hours talking with him about music, and on Christmas of that year, Sainz gave him a real guitar. River took the instrument everywhere, practicing incessantly, undaunted by how disproportionately large it was compared to his five-year-old body and hands. Within a few months, he could play simple songs; Sainz was impressed enough to offer to record him at his studio in Orlando, Florida.

The Blond Children Who Sing performed everywhere: hospitals, jails, the streets. "We did it because we needed money, but we also wanted to pass along love," River remembered later. "A lot of people would gather and listen to us. It was really a novelty. We had a whole act together. I'd be strumming on a guitar that was taller than I was at about a hundred miles an hour. I knew about five chords. That was where I learned to give a lot of joy and happiness, from singing."

19

Around the age most children attend kindergarten and are entrusted with blunt-tipped scissors, River had the massive responsibility of supporting his family. If he didn't come home with enough money after serenading the citizens of Caracas, then they wouldn't eat that night. He and Rain learned which locations were the most lucrative: hotels and the airport.

On July 5, 1976—one day after the American Bicentennial—the family grew again with the birth of another girl, Libertad Mariposa (which translates into English as "Liberty Butterfly"). July 5 was Liberty Day in Venezuela; "Mariposa" came from the name of the hill where the Children of God colony was housed.

Under John's leadership as archbishop, the Children of God were thriving in Caracas. The sect found an ally in "Padre Esteban"—Father Stephen Wood, who was director of the Catholic Church's local youth ministry. Presumably unaware of the more outré beliefs of the Children of God, he tried to incorporate them into his work, reasoning that they were fellow travelers. If he was doing youth outreach, he might invite a Children of God contingent along to sing. When the Children of God population expanded beyond the limits of their Mariposa house, Wood even provided lodgings for a dozen of them in the basement of the Cathedral of Los Teques.

Wood, who died in 2010 (stabbed in his Venezuela home), remembered the Children of God as being so spontaneous that it was impossible to make any plans with them: "It was what God told them to do that day," he said. He also discovered he had theological differences with them in regard to the Bible. "Their interpretation tended to be rather fundamentalist Protestant and very apocalyptic," Wood remembered. They ultimately went their separate ways, although he would sometimes spot Children of God missionaries as far afield as Colombia or Costa Rica.

Arlyn, hoping to make more of River and Rain's musical act, entered the children in local talent shows, without any particular success. The family lived with empty pockets but good cheer. "I've been through some pretty desperate times," River admitted as a teenager. "I've lived a lot even though I'm still young. But I feel that when you're born into a way of life—and that's all you know—you don't mind it. The good times and the bad are all part of the experience."

Then, in 1976, the mailman brought an international delivery that changed everything. The latest Mo Letter was advocating the benefits of "flirty fishing." The term was derived from Jesus Christ's message to his disciples (in Matthew 4:19): "Follow me, and I will make you fishers of men." Now, Berg told his female followers, they should bring new men into the Children of God by sleeping with them.

"What greater way could you show anyone your love than to give them your all in the bed of love?" Berg wrote. "How much more can you show them the Love of God than to show them His Love to the uttermost through you?"

Flirty fishing was the official policy of the Children of God for a full decade, until 1987, when it was curtailed because of AIDS and other sexually transmitted diseases. Apparently, it did bring thousands of men into Berg's flock, but it also transformed many of his female disciples into prostitutes—or, as some nicknamed them, "Hookers for God." Some women established long-term sexual relationships with locally powerful men who could offer political protection for their commune, or with wealthy men who provided funds to keep the commune going. In other locations, the transactions became even balder, as the women were hired out to local escort services.

The Bottom family didn't stick around for these developments. Arlyn's summary of the Children of God experience: "The guy running it got crazy. He sought to attract rich disciples through sex. No way," she said. "The group was being distorted by a leader who was getting very full of power and wealthy. We were serving God; we weren't serving our leader. It took several years to get over our pain and loneliness."

John looked back at Berg ruefully, unable to condemn his onetime spiritual guide: "He may have been a sexual pervert, but he is still a better man than a lot of people."

Without money or a place to stay, the Bottom family turned to their friend Padre Esteban—Father Stephen Wood was now pastor of his own parish in Caracas. They told him that the twin lodestars that guided their conduct had long been the Bible and the Mo Letters. Now that they found these two sources to be in conflict, they had opted for the Bible.

Concerned for their four children, Wood invited the family to stay at his church for a few weeks, in return for singing at Sunday services. During the week, the Bottoms kept proselytizing at the shopping malls of downtown Caracas. "They tried to evangelize and entertain at the same time," Wood said. "I got the feeling that all the parents in the Children of God were exploiting their kids' talents, aware that the kids were more effective beggars than them."

Later in life, River would describe his seventh birthday—August 23, 1977—as a day spent in squalor. As he told it, his family at that point was living on the beach in a rat-infested shack with no toilet, surviving by scavenging coconuts and mangoes from the trees. In fact, Wood said, while River may have availed himself of the local fruit, there was always food available at the mission. "While they were definitely poor, it was never quite down to the level of Venezuelan poverty," Wood said. "They were struggling, and they didn't have much money, and they didn't know where they were really going to go."

The family did stay on the beach—not in a shack, but in the caretaker's cottage at the back of a large property unused by its owners except on weekends. So during the week, the family had access to the main house's swimming pool.

UNDER THE HOT VENEZUELAN SUN, River jumps into the swimming pool, his limbs skinny and his hair a golden bowl crowning his head. A jet airplane flies overhead, leaving from the nearby airport at La Guaira for someplace far away. The family has put the Children of God behind them; an uncertain future lies before them. But a salty breeze is blowing in from the ocean, and for the moment River is free.

LATER IN LIFE, RIVER WOULD treat interviews as opportunities for spontaneous fiction: he would give answers that were at variance with other things he had said, or with reality. George Sluizer, who directed him in his last movie, *Dark Blood,* remembered, "When a journalist would come, he'd say, 'Oh, George, let's see how much I can lie to him.'" This wasn't pathological; mostly, it seems to have been a young actor enlivening the sometimes dull work of talking about himself with some improvisation. But it was also a defense mechanism: when River described his parents as having been "missionaries" during their time in Venezuela, rather than "cult members," he was being misleading if not quite untruthful, both out of consideration for them and out of a desire not to unwrap part of his life that he had boxed up and put away.

For public consumption, River was usually casual about his unusual childhood, even glib: "It was a neat time growing up in Venezuela in the late seventies." But once, his shell cracked, in a 1991 interview with *Details.*

> Q. *Is there anything you did at an early age that you wish you had waited for?*
> A. *Yes—make love.*
> Q. *How old were you?*
> A. *Four.*
> Q. *With whom? Another four-year-old?*
> A. *Kids. But I've blocked it out. I was completely celibate from ten to fourteen.*

23

"Yes, yes, yes, he was molested," a good friend said. "It began with other friends in the same commune/cult, and it escalated."

Some people have drawn a straight line from the sexual abuse of River as a child to later aspects of his life: in this narrative, acting and drugs were both parachutes that let him escape from his own damaged self, while his philanthropy and veganism were attempts to negate the guilt he felt over being abused. Another possibility: despite being repeatedly molested, he ended up a joyful person anyway, full of love for the world. He was certainly self-aware enough about what had happened—he told good friends about it, although he chose not to share it with the world.

Even if River were alive today, he might not be able to explain how his experiences in Venezuela formed his adult self. The human spirit is a mysterious thing: traumas that flatten some people bounce off of others. Pain and hope get tangled into uncuttable Gordian knots.

One would hope that leaving the Children of God and getting out of Venezuela put an end to this chapter in River's life where his young flesh served as the raw material for the sexual desires of others. By his own telling, however, he was active sexually between the ages of four and ten—meaning that it continued for three years after the family left the cult.

Once, when River was eighteen, somebody asked him if he had had a happy childhood.

"Happy?" he replied, as if the idea had never occurred to him. "Well, it was interesting."

24

ANOTHER NIGHT AT THE VIPER ROOM

Down the rabbit hole: the Viper Room is hosting an Alice in Wonderland *night. Bartenders have dressed up as playing cards at the Queen of Hearts' croquet match; bar back Richmond Arquette is kitted out as the White Rabbit. Two different women are in pinafores, acting as Alice. The onstage entertainment is sixties icon Timothy Leary, LSD advocate and godfather of Winona Ryder, reading excerpts from* Alice *and discussing the life of its Victorian author Lewis Carroll, the stammering Oxford mathematician with a taste for absurdity and the company of little girls. (Nonsexual, by all accounts, but still unusual.)*

While Leary speaks, an audience member lights a joint and passes it up to the stage. Leary takes a long pull from it—when he's done, the Viper Room staff promptly disposes of it. The last thing they want is another drug-related incident.

At the end of the night, Arquette stands outside the Viper Room, getting some fresh air and flirting with one of the Alices. A couple walks out—they look like tourists who had come to the Viper Room hoping to spot a celebrity. Arquette hears the guy say to the girl, "You know, these people sure do party strange in L.A." Arquette isn't irate that they haven't appreciated a historic evening, or even dismayed that mainstream American culture will never understand what the Viper Room is trying to do. He's happy to be in the minority.

8 MEAT IS MURDER

After a year living in the caretaker's cottage and swimming in that pool, John and Arlyn were eager to get the family back to the United States, not least because Arlyn was pregnant again. Six international plane tickets, however, seemed as unattainable as seats on a rocket to the moon.

Arlyn's parents might have been able to afford the airfare, but she refused to ask them for money. Wood had a church fund for needy people, but didn't feel he could tap it to send some Americans home. Then he had an epiphany: "An airplane is not the only way to get them there." He went to a member of his parish who was a maritime captain and the owner of a small shipping line. Wood explained that he was trying to get Los Niños Rubios Que Cantan and their family to Miami: "All of them are U.S. citizens with passports, so we're not smuggling anybody."

Arrangements were made; in October 1978, the family got on a cargo ship for the thirteen-hundred-mile journey north. In later years, River liked to claim they were stowaways—"the crew discovered us halfway home," he said. But although the accommodations were Spartan, they were welcome guests: the ship's cook even brought along the ingredients for a birthday cake, because Joaquin turned four during the journey. The ship was carrying a shipment of Tonka Toys and the crew gave some damaged trucks to Joaquin as a birthday present.

While the family lived in Venezuela, the United States had become a land of polyester, disco, and Farrah Fawcett posters. Number one singles that fall were Exile's "Kiss You All Over" and Nick Gilder's "Hot Child in the City," while the *Grease* soundtrack dominated the album chart. The top shows on TV were the sitcoms *Laverne & Shirley* and *Three's Company,* followed by the Robin Williams vehicle *Mork & Mindy.* As River and his family plowed north to the United States and its colorful, tacky, vibrant culture, they made another major life choice.

Some of the crew were fishing off the side of the ship; when they reeled in a catch, they would unhook the fish from the line and then impale it on a board that had nails sticking out of it, so it wouldn't flop back into the water. The Bottom children had never seen anything like that before, and were horrified. "These weren't bad people, but they'd become totally desensitized to the pain they were causing," River said. "It was the first time that I really saw that meat wasn't just a hamburger or a hot dog or some disguised food on your plate, that it was an animal, it was flesh. It seemed very barbaric and kind of cruel, and me and my brother and sister were all crying and were traumatized. The reality just hit us so hard."

River, Rain, and Joaquin told their parents that they didn't want to eat meat anymore. "Our parents were very sensitive to our feelings," he remembered. "I mean, they were obviously immune to it themselves—meat-eating is so much a part of society as a whole and how people eat—but they were very interested in our sensitivity to it, so they were open to us becoming vegetarian."

The lighter ecological impact of vegetarianism was appealing to the parents. "I tell my kids to celebrate the Earth," Arlyn said. "We're living creatures who should live as gently and lovingly as we can on the Earth."

Within months, the family was not only eschewing meat, they—led by River, and encouraged by Arlyn's vegan sister—had sworn off eggs and dairy.

At the time, vegetarianism was further out of mainstream American culture than it is today; veganism (where one avoids not only meat, but animal products in general) was so fringe that magazine articles about River sometimes just called it "ultravegetarianism." "It was hard to give up dairy for a while for a lot of people in my family," River said. "My mom and dad were so used to eating cheese, and it was so convenient. But I said, 'Hey, if we're doing this thing, let's go all the way with it.'"

"Every child starts out loving animals, identifying with them," River declared later. "But early on, adults start sending them contradictory messages. They'll give a kid a stuffed animal to hug and love and sleep with. But at the same time, they're serving them animals for dinner every night. It's crazy, if you think about it. But when you're young, you just accept what grown-ups tell you as the truth."

Now that River's family had left the Children of God and street-corner evangelism behind, veganism became the central tenet of his philosophy: not just a way to be kind to animals, improve the environment, and better one's health, but the root of enhanced planetary consciousness.

"Vegetarianism is a link to perfection and peace," River said when he was seventeen, after years of considering these beliefs (and acting on them). "But it's a small link. There are lots of other issues: apartheid, vivisection, political prisoners, the arms race. There's so much going on in this world today, so much ignorance among people. That's not to say I'm not standing amongst everybody. But the point is, What can we do now? That's the thing about vegetarianism; it's an individual's decision and it's something you have control over. How many things do we really have control over?"

RIVER PHOENIX WALKS DOWN A wooded path, accompanied by two large dogs, a German shepherd and a Doberman/German shepherd mix. He calls for the dogs, Justice and Jupiter, to come along. The camera cuts to a close-up: River rubs a dog's neck, and kisses it on top of its nose.

"Hello, I'm River Phoenix," he says, and swallows uncertainly, as if he's trying the name out for the first time. He's wearing black jeans, black boots, and a white

27

People for the Ethical Treatment of Animals sweatshirt with a microphone clipped to it. His hair is long but tucked behind his ears. He's glowing as if there's a forty-watt bulb concealed in his esophagus. "And if you care about animals, here's some good news: People for the Ethical Treatment of Animals can show you some easy ways to help out."

The camera pulls back to reveal that River is sitting cross-legged on the ground, holding his dogs, surrounded by fallen leaves. "It's up to us to take care of all our friends," he says as we dissolve to footage of him wrestling and playing with one of the dogs. "Write for a free brochure: PETA Kids, Washington, D.C., two-zero-zero-one-five. Thank you." The camera dissolves back to River on the ground, although one of the dogs has wandered off for a nap. He smiles so winningly that you want to buy whatever it is he's selling, whether it's cranberry juice or animal liberation.

In another take, River sits on a bench, his right arm draped around one of the dogs as if he's a high school quarterback on a date. "Are you a kid who cares about animals?" he asks. "There are lots of us. Come join us and find out how you can help." River turns to the dog. "Hope to hear from you soon. Right, Jupiter?"

Outtakes from the PSA reveal the work that goes into letting River Phoenix chat casually with his fans for thirty seconds. He tries talking while walking toward the camera, but the wire for his microphone gets snagged. He trips over his lines and rolls his eyes. Cue cards are offered to him, but he objects, "If I read it, it'll just look like I'm reading it!"

River pushes his hair back, but then it falls into his face again, revealing how long it actually is. With one hand on each dog, he casually jerks his head clockwise, flipping his hair so it goes sailing over and back, a fleeting blond waterfall.

"People for the Ethical Treatment of Animals can show you—" River stops short. "You're not filming this, are you?"

PART TWO

"I'M GOING TO BE FAMOUS"

BACK IN THE U.S.A.

Delivered to the docks of Miami like a cargo package, the Bottom family returned to the United States with few possessions beyond River's acoustic guitar and some battered Tonka trucks. They headed to Winter Park, near Orlando; Arlyn's parents had retired and moved from the Bronx down to Florida. They were delighted to see their grandchildren, but there wasn't room in their house for six more people. Fortunately, the family found a place in the Orlando area where they could stay: Alfonso Sainz, their friend from Venezuela who had given River his guitar, had a mansion nearby. John agreed to serve as handyman for Sainz's property, and the family moved into another caretaker's cottage.

River was having 120-volt culture shock. After four years away from the States—half his young life—he thought of Spanish as his native tongue. And like millions of children before him, he discovered television, which he found alluring and confusing. He saw a western movie and, not realizing it was fiction, thought "that companies paid people's families money to kill them."

River's grandparents were shocked to discover that he had never attended school. Since he was now eight, they insisted that he enroll right away. He entered the first grade but felt hugely out of place: the older kid who didn't get anybody's jokes. It wasn't just that River didn't understand American cultural references—he had never really developed a sense of humor and was unfamiliar with the format of a joke. Director and friend Gus Van Sant remembered

River saying "that he never really got its logic, the surprise of the unexpected. You know: an elephant and a hippo go into a bar, something is introduced, punch line. And he'd be like, 'Yeah? So what happened then?'"

It wasn't just his lack of punch-line comprehension: young River Bottom stood out in every way possible, starting with his name. "When I was in first grade, everybody made fun of my name, of course," he said later. "I think it's kind of a big name to hold up when you're nine years old. It seemed goofy. I used to tell people I wanted to change the world and they used to think, 'This kid's really weird.'"

Within his own family, it had long been expected that River would carry the weight of the world like a pint-size Atlas. Now he was discovering that other kids cared more about recess and *Star Wars*.

Arlyn and John had their fifth child on December 10, 1978. Ignoring the calendar, they named her "Summer Joy." Four-year-old Joaquin, dismayed at being the only child in the family with a mundane name, asked his mother if he could change it.

"Ask your father," Arlyn said.

Joaquin went to John, who was earning the family's keep by raking leaves. "Pick another name," John assented. With a pile of leaves in front of him, the boy chose "Leaf." As writer Michael Angeli later observed, the names of the children (River, Rain, Leaf, Liberty, and Summer) sounded like "generic items you'd find on the *Family Feud* tote board if the subject were Emerson."

A few years later, River considered the personalities of the five children. "We all look completely different and we all have our distinct things. Leaf was the family clown, the comedian—very witty and smart." Rain (who would later modify her name to Rainbow) "was the older sister and trendsetter. Mom had to work a lot, so she took her place." About himself, River said, "I played the guitar." Although he thought that was a sufficient summary of his personality, he continued, "I went off to my room a lot and had a real goofy side to me, really corny—laughing about stupid things, making fart noises with my mouth. A lot of inside jokes. Liberty was always the most physical, like an acrobat: nimble, strong, slender, a really beautiful girl. And Summer was

32

the youngest, the baby of the family, with big brown eyes and blonde hair. She looks WASPy. Liberty and Rainbow have more of an ethnic look, Israeli or Italian."

John and Arlyn strived to speak with their children as if they were peers. "We never treated them like children, but like extra added friends," Arlyn said. "It was never like, 'We know better because we're the parents.' It was more like, 'This is the first time we've ever done this, too. What do you think?' And the children were so wise. If we made a mistake, we made it together."

The family wasn't big on table manners, or on taking turns in a conversation, but John did have one rule of family comportment: "The youngest gets to yell the loudest because they're never listened to!"

The Bottom kids played with other neighborhood kids, and became friendly enough to have sleepovers. Decades later, one of their child guests still remembered the bedtime stories: "They were really trippy—about the *stars*." After tucking in the kids with celestial tales, John and Arlyn would sneak out of the house to visit other neighbors, fearlessly leaving the children alone. "I just remember the parents were major hippies," River's friend said. "His mom had this crazy curly hair, and his dad had a beard, and they smoked a lot of pot."

Even with a place to stay, finances were tight for a family of seven. The kids were well dressed, but only because they received a large donation of upscale clothes from a wealthy local family. "They were the best clothes we ever had," River said. "We were these pure, naïve, poor children," he said. "The rich kids called us a lot of names but it never bothered us because we didn't know what the names meant," he insisted.

John started a landscaping business, with the kids helping him haul plants and sod, but before it could take off, he threw out his back, his old injury recurring. The business went kaput, and when John stopped acting as caretaker on the Sainz property, the family had to leave. They moved about eighty miles west, to Brooksville, in a rural corner of the county. While John recuperated, Arlyn got a job as executive secretary for the director of the Hernando-Sumter Community Action Agency.

Feeling that the family's fortunes had hit bottom, John decided that the way to change them would be to abandon the surname Bottom. He chose a replacement: "Phoenix," the glorious firebird of Greek mythology, periodically reborn from its own ashes. Although the name is entirely suitable as a symbol of resurrection and rejuvenation, John might have gotten the idea from a source other than classical mythology: in the spring of 1979, the "Phoenix Saga" was in full swing in the pages of the *Uncanny X-Men* comic book. (The telepath Jean Grey transforms into the godlike Phoenix and becomes corrupted by power, killing billions of aliens when she annihilates a solar system. To stop the rise of Dark Phoenix, she commits suicide.) Joaquin was a fan of the *X-Men* comic book—even if John wasn't reading it, the Phoenix character was regularly featured on the cover and a stray sighting could well have sparked the idea. (If it did, then River and Joaquin Phoenix would end up as two of three Oscar-nominated actors whose last names were drawn from Marvel Comics characters, the other being Nicolas Cage, who traded in his Coppola family name for the surname of Luke Cage [aka ghetto muscleman Power Man.])

34

Meanwhile, River and Rain were retooling their act, with more emphasis on popular songs and less on Children of God hymns. Arlyn dubbed the family Team Phoenix, emphasizing that they were focused on show-biz success, but River later insisted that she was not the driving force behind his music and acting. "We all wanted to be entertainers," he asserted, "and our parents did whatever they could to help us out." Alvin Ross, part of the management team for the rock band Kiss, expressed interest in the act, but nothing came of it.

River and Rain were no longer spending their days busking; instead, they performed at every talent contest and county fair they could find. On April 25, 1979, they entered a contest at the "Hernando Fiesta" in Spring Hill, Florida. Also entering were a belly dancer and a snake charmer, sent over by the Busch Gardens amusement park. "Those girls were moving parts of their bodies I didn't know existed," said one female spectator.

Second place went to a mime, but first place went to River and Rain, performing their old Children of God showstopper, "You Gotta Be a Baby." "Except a man be born again, he cannot enter into the Kingdom of Heaven," they sang, first rendering the biblical quotation in English, and then in French, Spanish, German, and Japanese. They won fifty dollars. More importantly, they caught the attention of Gayle Guthman, the reviewer from the *St. Petersburg Times,* who wrote a full article about the Phoenix family three weeks later.

The article, appearing on the same page as "Murdered Man's Pickup Truck Found" and "Lutherans to Sponsor Ice Cream Social," featured John Phoenix's cleaned-up version of the family history. As John related the family history, they had been working as "independent missionaries" in Latin America; River and Rain first performed with a Venezuelan band John was leading when he lost his voice; Liberty was actually born one day earlier, on the Fourth of July, making her name a tribute to America rather than Venezuelan independence.

One thing that couldn't be concealed: the precocity of River, who told Guthman, "I hope to be famous one day, not to be proud of myself because I thank God for giving me my powers."

"This was an 8-year-old talking," an astonished Guthman wrote.

Team Phoenix proudly touted the article, sending it to friends, family, and anyone they thought could help the kids get famous. One copy was mailed to Penny Marshall in Hollywood: the star of the top-rated TV show *Laverne & Shirley* was an old school friend of Arlyn's in the Bronx. The letter ended up in the hands of the Paramount Pictures casting department, which sent Arlyn a form letter. As River described it, "They answered, 'Yeah, we'd be happy to see your children. If you're ever in California, by all means, look us up, but don't make a special trip.' And so, of course, we just threw everything into the old station wagon and drove out to Burbank."

The Phoenix family wasn't just chasing stardom: they thought this was all part of a divine plan in which the children, especially River, could be instrumental in changing the world into a better, holier place. The family sold their possessions, loaded up another battered VW minibus (which John had converted into a camper), and drove three thousand miles west: seven people and a dog, looking like *Grapes of Wrath* reenactors. "Things went wrong for us all the time," Arlyn said. "One night, it was freezing—but we didn't have a back window in the camper. It got so cold, we stuffed Pampers in the window."

Jacked up on hope and naïveté, River resolved that acting rather than singing was his path forward, and announced this destiny to anyone who would listen. "We'd roll into gas stations," River said, "and I'd tell the attendant, 'I'm going to be an actor!'"

The family kept moving west, looking through the windshield with the optimism of a nine-year-old, and doing everything they could to block out the view of what lay behind them.

10 JOHNNY CAME FROM MIAMI F-L-A

Around the same time, farther down the peninsula, in a Miami suburb called Miramar, a sixteen-year-old Johnny Depp was considering his future. Determined to be a rock star, he had just quit high school, and now worried that he had made a huge mistake.

Depp grew up in Kentucky watching his uncle play guitar with his gospel group: "These hillbillies, for lack of a better description, playing guitar right in front of me—that was where the bug came from." When a young Depp was listening to *Frampton Comes Alive,* his older brother grabbed the needle off the record and turned him on to Van Morrison's *Astral Weeks* instead.

At age twelve, Depp talked his mom into buying him a Decca electric guitar for twenty-five dollars; he taught himself songs from a Mel Bay chord book that he had shoplifted by stuffing it down his pants. Depp locked himself in his bedroom and learned to play chords: soon he could hammer out Deep Purple's "Smoke on the Water" and Chicago's "25 or 6 to 4."

With some other neighborhood kids, he started a band called Flame and played backyard parties: "This one guy had a bass, we knew a guy who had a PA system, it was ramshackle and great." They even cobbled together a home-made lighting system. Depp knew he had found his calling in life.

"There's a big change from thirteen to fifteen," Depp noted. "You start out with super-innocent names, and then by the time you're fifteen, you're a guitarist in a band named Bitch." He laughed. "Kind of ludicrous." Depp never considered being lead singer: ironically, he didn't want to be the guy that everybody looked at.

The band got popular enough to play local clubs—which is when Depp dropped out of school, reasoning that he was on the fast track to stardom. After two weeks, reality set in: he wasn't ready to be an adult. He considered joining the marines, but instead, went back to his school to talk to his dean.

"Listen, I've realized that I've made a terrible mistake, and I'd like to come back and try again," Depp told him.

The dean gazed at him, not unkindly, and said, "Johnny, you can do what you want, but I don't think that's such a good idea. You love your music—that's the only thing you've ever applied yourself to. You should go out there and play."

"He wasn't nasty about it," Depp remembered. "He was giving me what he felt to be very good advice. I wouldn't say that this is right for everyone, certainly not, but in my case at that time, it was exactly the right thing for me. That was the proper medicine."

After Bitch came Bad Boys ("very original," Depp notes of the name) and then a new-wave group called the Kids, who became local superstars, opening for the Ramones, the Pretenders, Iggy Pop, and the Stray Cats.

In 1983, when Depp was twenty years old, the Kids packed up a U-Haul trailer and moved to Hollywood, intent on getting a record deal. On the way, they changed their name to Six Gun Method. They soon discovered that gigs were few and far between—and that L.A. clubs worked on a "pay-to-play" system, where you had to sell a certain number of tickets or make up the financial gap yourself (sometimes with confiscated musical instruments). "Suddenly," Depp remembered, "we're not big fish in a little pond. We're like guppies and we're nearly destitute." They needed to eat, so they got day jobs.

Depp found a gig in phone sales. He tried to convince people to buy a gross of customized pens, with incentives such as a grandfather clock or a trip to Greece. "Oddly, that's kind of my first experience with acting," he said. "There was a whole spiel. You had the lines right in front of you." On the phone, Depp called himself Edward Quartermain, a character on the soap opera *General Hospital*.

Despite working on commission, Depp would torpedo his own sales. "People only bought the pens because they wanted the grandfather clock," he said. "When the supervisor wandered off, I'd say, 'Listen, don't buy these pens. The grandfather clock is made of corkboard. I'm a thief—we're ripping you off.'"

On Melrose Avenue, Depp was filling out a job application at a video store when he ran into Nicolas Cage, who had already starred in *Valley Girl*. They knew each other through Depp's first wife, Lori Anne Allison: Cage dated Allison during a break in her relationship with Depp before they got married (they got hitched when Depp was twenty, and divorced when he was twenty-two). Cage suggested that Depp meet with his agent: "Why don't you try acting? I think you could do it."

Motivated by the desire to pay rent and buy groceries, Depp auditioned for a horror movie, *A Nightmare on Elm Street*. For playing the role of Glen Lantz, he received the unthinkably large sum of $1,200 a week for eight weeks. He told the band they would take a short break, but when he came back after two months, everybody had gone their separate ways. The movie turned out to be a huge hit, launching a franchise with nine sequels and spin-offs. "I never wanted to be an actor," Depp said. "It was a good way to make easy money, it seemed. I didn't care what the movies were—if you're going to pay me, fine. So I just kept going forward."

11

SHOW-BIZ BABIES

The Phoenix family arrived in California, unheralded and unwanted. Lacking any other options, John drove to Orange County (the semi-urban sprawl south of Los Angeles), the home of the Becks: his aunt Frances and uncle Bruin. Twenty years earlier, when he was a runaway from the orphanage, they had declined to take him in, but now they welcomed his whole family. Frances offered them dinner, but was flummoxed by their dietary restrictions. They ate only fruits and vegetables and wouldn't even mix the two.

She recalled, "I put a bowl of fruit on one side, a bowl of vegetables on the other. River came in the kitchen. He said, 'Aunt Frances, we can't eat but one.' I said, 'Okay, well, eat the one, and then you can take the other home.'" (There's no reason vegans couldn't mix fruits and vegetables, other than personal preference.) The Phoenixes slept in their camper; the next morning, they drove up to Hollywood.

When their cross-country journey ended at Paramount Studios, they were rebuffed. "We were really naïve," reflected River. "I figured I'd play guitar and sing with my sister and we would be on television the next day." Instead, they found themselves living in the camper. They couldn't afford apartments at L.A. rents, but sometimes they talked their way into one anyway. After a few months, they'd be evicted and head back to Orange County to visit Aunt Frances and Uncle Bruin again.

"We schlepped forever in L.A.," River said. "Moved every three months, being evicted regularly for late rent, for kids, for whatever. We just kept it so we'd rather be poor than owe anybody money. So we didn't have any debts, but we had no money whatsoever—it was just day-to-day." He particularly remembered a "shitty little apartment" in North Hollywood. Kids were prohibited, so when the landlady came around, all five Phoenix children had to hide in the closet.

The family returned to their busking ways. Aunt Frances said: "When they went to L.A., they started playing on the streets. They'd put out the pan, and they'd get money. They kept doing that, then the police would make 'em leave, and they'd go to another spot." The younger siblings were now incorporated into the act, singing, playing tambourine, and wearing matching Western-style costumes (complete with fringe).

"That's the way I understood they got their money to live on," Aunt Frances said. "Johnny claimed he was hurt—hurt his back or something—and never could work. I think he was too lazy to work."

Around 1980, Arlyn remembered, the family appeared on a local NBC news segment. The reporter interviewed them about their street performances and asked Leaf, "So what's been the happiest day of your life?"

Somewhat baffled by the question, Leaf shrugged and asked his siblings, "What am I supposed to say?" Finally, he settled on an answer: "It hasn't happened yet."

"Oh," the reporter said. Before he could ask the next question, Leaf interrupted, shouting, *"But it's coming soon!"*

Recognizing that donated loose change wasn't paying the bills, Arlyn found a secretarial job, working for Joel Thurm, head of casting at NBC. This was a savvy move on her part: it let her suss out the mechanics of Hollywood and network with people in the business. She brought her kids to audition for the brassy Iris Burton, one of Hollywood's leading talent agents for children.

"I'm a groomer. A talent scout," Burton said of her relationship with her juvenile clients. "I watch their weight. Hair. Nails. And most of all, I watch their parents. By the time a kid walks through the door, I know if he or she's a winner or a loser. If they jump in or slouch in, if they're biting their nails and rocking back and forth, I don't want 'em. If I don't see the hidden strength, feel the energy, then the magic isn't there. I can smell it like a rat."

Burton, born in 1930 to a Ziegfeld Follies showgirl, entered show business as a dancer: on Broadway in the 1940s and on Milton Berle's TV show. She moved to Hollywood and played a seductive Egyptian dancer in Cecil B. De-Mille's 1951 biblical epic *The Ten Commandments*. After stints selling dishes and working as a waitress at the Playboy Club, she found a job at a talent agency. Discovering that nobody wanted to handle kids—the stage parents were too big a headache—she left after a year and opened her own agency, working out of her home (as she did for her whole life).

Her first star client was Andy Lambros, star of Oscar Mayer TV ads for b-o-l-o-g-n-a, but she went on to represent a huge swath of actors in their childhood years, including Henry Thomas circa *E.T.*, Kirsten Dunst, Drew Barrymore, Jaleel "Urkel" White, Kirk Cameron, and the Olsen twins. In a town where the agent archetype became a young CAA rep in an Armani suit, she was old school: a five-foot-two fireplug who would never take no for an answer. When the mother of one client called to tell Burton that they would miss an audition because a windstorm was blowing sand across the highway and there was no visibility, Burton's response was "Throw a white sheet around you, grab a camel, and pretend like you're Lawrence of Arabia. I don't care how you do it—just get to the call."

Burton's philosophy: "Kids are pieces of meat. I've never had anything but filet mignon. I've never had hamburger. My kids are the choice meat." Despite this unvegan point of view, she signed up all the Phoenix offspring. "River was the most beautiful child you've ever seen, like a little Elvis," she said. He started going on casting calls for commercials, accompanied by his dad. Even with hundreds of kids competing for each job, he landed several spots, including ads for Ocean Spray cranberry juice, Mitsubishi cars, and the toy Star Maker electric guitar.

After only a year, River announced that he didn't want to do any more commercials. He felt like a fraud, and he had difficulty smiling on demand. "Commercials were too phony for me," he explained later. "It was selling a product, and who owns the product? I mean, are they supporting apartheid? I just didn't like the whole thing, even though it helped us pay the rent. How could I tell anybody to drink canned cranberry juice? I didn't drink it. I didn't believe in what I was saying. I guess what I was zeroing in on was that performing was more about telling the truth through a different character's eyes. I felt that the constant lying, the smiling on cue, and the product naming was going to drive me crazy or numb me to a not-yet-developed craft that I was beginning to feel staring me in the face."

Remarkably, the adults around ten-year-old River supported his decision. If Arlyn was captain of Team Phoenix, John was the family's hippie idealist, worried that they would have to compromise their values in Hollywood. His son's refusal to be the smiling pitchman for American society must have felt like a victory for John.

Burton was perplexed—she wasn't accustomed to clients turning down work—but River was a prime enough piece of steak that she accepted his decision and focused her efforts on getting him cast on a TV show.

Meanwhile, the Phoenix kids kept performing on the streets of Los Angeles. Video from 1982 captured all five children, in yellow tank tops and matching satin shorts, doing a choreographed routine as they sang, "Straight to the top / Gonna make it, gonna make it." They were all young enough that it was hard to figure who was a boy and who was a girl—but River was unmistakable. He was the blond front man wearing sneakers without socks, expertly playing the guitar, finishing the song with a spin and bathing in the applause of passersby. The star of the show, even if the show was still on a Westwood sidewalk.

12

LET'S WORK

Bright colors. That's what many people remember about the 1980s: neon fashions, the jumbled faces on a Rubik's Cube, Duran Duran videos on MTV. But the real spirit of the decade was the valorization of work: relentless industry as the supreme virtue. Gym culture went mainstream; people traded in bell-bottoms for gym shorts. Bruce Springsteen had the biggest album of his career when he changed his image from scrawny street poet to muscular laborer wielding a guitar. Ronald Reagan was elected president twice with bromides about hard work and American strength. The drug of the decade was cocaine, or, as some called it, "Bolivian Marching Powder": a stimulant that let you keep partying all night. It was an illegal drug with a Calvinist work ethic.

The two emerging stars who best embodied the sweaty spirit of the eighties were Michael J. Fox and Tom Cruise. Starring as Alex P. Keaton on *Family Ties,* Fox was the very symbol of generational change: he played a money-minded young Republican whose supply-side values were consistently at odds with those of his parents, former hippies. Fox's winning smile made Reaganism go down easy. "What are your goals?" Fox jokingly asked himself in an interview, and then answered, "Women, money, and world domination."

Fox capitalized on his fame with hit movies such as *Teen Wolf* and *The Secret of My Success.* But the project that put him over the top was *Back to the Future,* the inventive time-travel comedy produced by Steven Spielberg and directed by Robert Zemeckis. Fox's character, Marty McFly, traveled from 1985 to 1955 in a souped-up DeLorean—reflecting the mood of the times, the movie was set in the presidencies of Reagan and Eisenhower. To make the movie, Fox pulled double shifts, shooting *Family Ties* during the day and *Back to the Future* during the night, filming until 2:30 A.M. "I averaged about four hours of sleep a night," Fox said. "Working such long hours really taxes your sanity. But what was I going to do? The movie had to get done." It grossed over $200 million in the United States and spawned two sequels.

Tom Cruise, meanwhile, became a star by playing a junior capitalist run amok in *Risky Business*—when his parents go out of town, he not only dances around the living room in his underwear, he runs a brothel out of their suburban home. The movie was originally intended as an exploration of the underbelly of American go-go capitalism in the eighties, but with Cruise's megawatt charisma and a new happy ending where he gets the girl (Rebecca De Mornay)

43

and secures admission to Princeton, it became a sales pitch for the virtues of entrepreneurship. Soon after, Cruise also played a hotshot pilot called Maverick in *Top Gun,* which similarly glorified Reaganite military muscle—it played as a de facto recruiting film for the military.

Cruise became known for his unblinking intensity, on-screen and off. His relentless work habits and focus earned him the nickname "Laserhead." He found himself drawn to Scientology, one of the most capitalist religions around: it promised that all problems could be solved with sufficient applications of work and money.

THE MAGNIFICENT SEVEN

44

In the fall of 1982, Americans could choose from just three broadcast television networks. Wednesday nights at eight, NBC was broadcasting *Real People,* their hit hour of human-interest stories (a man who walks everywhere backward!), which alternated between heartwarming and bizarre. ABC offered *Tales of the Gold Monkey,* a *Raiders of the Lost Ark* ripoff about a seaplane pilot in the South Pacific in 1938, featuring Roddy McDowell as a dapper French magistrate. And CBS had a modern update of the 1954 frontier musical *Seven Brides for Seven Brothers*—this version was about a family of ranchers in Northern California. The oldest brother was played by Richard Dean Anderson, soon to be famous as MacGyver, while the youngest brother was played by newcomer River Phoenix.

The series featured a musical number each week, so River brought his guitar to the audition and did his Elvis Presley impersonation. Executive producer David Gerber said, "He had that clean, fresh, wholesome young look and a really ingratiating smile. He was a natural. I always thought he was the peach-fuzz kid."

When River found out he had the part, he said, "I just leaped five feet into the air." Or more honestly: "I got all red and freaked out."

The Phoenix family relocated to the Northern California town of Murphys, in the foothills of the Sierra Mountains. John and Arlyn took turns supervising River on the set and homeschooling the rest of the family.

Almost immediately, River's veganism came into conflict with the production: he wouldn't wear leather cowboy boots or a leather belt. After some wrangling, the costume department found plastic cowboy boots (and River went without a belt). But the incident provided fodder for the actors playing River's six older brothers: they would razz him about his veganism and generally condescend to him. Twelve-year-old River didn't know how to cope.

Cast member Terri Treas, who played Hannah (a bride), remembered, "He would burst out crying, which only made things worse. River had been isolated, and he did not have the social skills to know how to be with other boys. He had never had to go out and defend himself on the playground." Unsure how to fit in, River spent most of his downtime on the set by himself, playing guitar.

The pilot episode was cowritten by Sue Grafton, later the author of the best-selling Kinsey Millhone series ("A" is for Alibi, etc.). In keeping with her book titles, the brothers were named in an orderly alphabetic fashion: Adam, Brian, Crane, Daniel, Evan, Ford, and (River's role) Guthrie. In the pilot's opening scene, an extremely young River, wearing a baseball cap and a denim jacket, pops open a beer. An older brother confiscates it, telling him, "Hey, not until you're fourteen."

On-screen, River's most obvious qualities were his soup-bowl haircut and his eager-to-please puppy-dog quality. His offscreen desire to be considered a peer of the older actors came through all too strongly. Where he really came to life was during the musical numbers, where he could play guitar and hop around on one foot.

45

> *A dinnertime scene:*
> RIVER PHOENIX: *Pass the damn bread.*
> RICHARD DEAN ANDERSON: *Guthrie, watch your mouth.*
> RIVER PHOENIX: *Pass the damn bread, please.*

As the season progressed, River was astonished to get fan mail, and insisted on responding to each letter personally. He got to sing "Rock Around the Clock" while trapped during a cave-in, and to star in an episode where his character was abducted by gold prospectors. Stripping River to the waist in that episode may have been intended to make him seem more vulnerable, but it made him look like the star of an inappropriate Calvin Klein ad.

There was even an episode, "The Killer," that played off River's vegan beliefs: brought on a hunting trip, Guthrie finds himself unable to shoot a deer. By the end of the episode, he decides that he is willing to shoot a mountain lion to save his brother's life. That episode's featured song was a ballad about the mountain lion, rhyming "a warrior brave and bold" with "a wonder to behold."

Judy Marvin, the owner of the property where the show was filmed, thought of River as "a sad little child." And not just because of his failed efforts to fit in with American teenagers and adults, she said. He seemed "as if he had the weight of providing for his family on his little shoulders."

The last new episode of *Seven Brides for Seven Brothers* ran in March 1983—the show was on the air for twenty-two episodes and just one bride.

14

TV EYE

Rain, now eleven, decided her name was "kind of dreary" and changed it to Rainbow. The Phoenix family moved back to Hollywood, and River resumed the lather-rinse-repeat life of a working actor, even a teenage one: lots of auditions, lots of rejections, occasional breakthroughs. Over the next two years, he collected credits and gained experience.

River and Rain sang on *Fantasy,* an NBC daytime variety show that fulfilled the dreams of people who appeared on it, whether that meant paying for medical procedures or letting a teenager perform with a professional ventriloquist. Their number went well enough that the show hired River to be the "Kid News Roving Correspondent," joining the team alongside variety-show veteran Leslie Uggams.

On the NBC miniseries *Celebrity,* he played Jeffie, the son of movie star Mack Crawford (played by Joseph Bottoms) and spent an inordinate amount of screen time building a sand castle on the beach. His big scene came when Jeffie discovered that his dad was gay—by finding him in bed with another man.

Next was an *ABC Afterschool Special,* "Backwards: The Riddle of Dyslexia." River played Brian Ellsworth, a bright junior high kid doing poorly in school because neither he nor his family realizes he suffers from dyslexia. Although the script mainly called for River to look frustrated (and for some reason, to run in slow motion through a flock of pigeons), he began to display actual acting talent, convincingly portraying a class clown who was frantically masking his own insecurities. And if he was sometimes wooden—well, the adult cast wasn't any better.

In retrospect, the most charming aspect of "Backwards" is the appearance of ten-year-old Leaf as River's on-screen little brother. Leaf looked young enough to be convincing as a kid just learning to read—and the brothers were utterly at ease together, whether they were roughhousing or reading cereal boxes. Leaf gazed at River adoringly, while River regarded Leaf protectively as he threw him up in the air and told him bedtime stories. It was the only time they acted together.

River appeared in the pilot for *It's Your Move,* a sitcom starring Jason Bateman as a teenage scam artist; River played a minion helping out with the annual term-paper sale.

On *Hotel*—an Aaron Spelling show that was like *The Love Boat,* except at the landlocked location of a luxury hotel—River played a preppy gymnast whose sportscaster father (Robert Reed) turns out to be bisexual. The repetition of the plot from *Celebrity* suggests that either forty percent of prime-time programming in 1984 was about closeted gay husbands or that River had found an unusual niche as an actor.

Next up: the miniseries *Robert Kennedy and His Times*. If it wasn't critically acclaimed, at least it was nominated for an Emmy for Outstanding Achievement in Hairstyling. A slew of top child actors played RFK's children, including River, Shannen Doherty, and Jason Bateman again.

River turned fourteen. His teenage years were rolling by in a procession of sound stages; he never attended a conventional high school. In September 1984, when he might have been entering his freshman year, he instead flew to Oklahoma City to film the television movie *Surviving,* about teen suicide. Director Waris Hussein said, "River was very much part of the Hollywood auditioning scene at the time, but he stood out from the others."

Molly Ringwald (after *Sixteen Candles* but before *The Breakfast Club*) and Zach Galligan played the star-crossed lovers who kill themselves; River was cast as Galligan's younger brother, with Ellen Burstyn and Len Cariou playing his parents, too shattered by the death of their older son to see how it's affecting their other children. River won the obscure but nonfictional "Young Artist Award" for his raw performance in *Surviving*—there wasn't much nuance in his acting yet, but he was learning the trick of slipping into somebody else's skin.

ECHO #1: *SURVIVING*

Tina (Ellen Burstyn) has just discovered that her son Philip (River Phoenix) has taken a handful of sleeping pills in a copycat suicide attempt. In a clean beige polo shirt, he is slumped over the desk in his bedroom, about to die from a drug overdose. "How could you do this?" she demands, and slaps him. "Damn you! Damn you, Philip! Damn you!"

Heading for the hospital, she lugs him down the stairs with his arm draped over her shoulder, angrily asking how he'll do it next time, and whether she'll be the one to find the body. At the car, he starts sobbing, explaining that he was jealous of how his older brother had gotten all the attention, and that he had even wished he was dead: "He was always better than me. It was my fault, it was my fault."

Burstyn hugs him tightly. River survives his overdose and lives to see his family another day. On the TV screen, anyway.

16
UNMAPPED TERRITORY

While on location in Oklahoma City, River got a hall pass: the shooting schedule of *Surviving* was rearranged so he could fly back to L.A. for an audition. Director Joe Dante, fresh off the success of *Gremlins,* was putting together another family-friendly sci-fi action comedy. This one, called *Explorers,* was about three suburban kids who make first contact with an alien race, using the information they receive in dreams to build their own spaceship.

"I got a thrill just from reading the script," said River, who landed the part. He declared his first feature film to be "a movie kid's dream." River was cast as Wolfgang Muller, the nerdy brainiac inventor of the trio. The regular-kid hero was played by Ethan Hawke, also making his film debut, while Jason Presson was the tough kid. The movie shot in Petaluma, California, just north of San Francisco, and on the Skywalker Ranch, George Lucas's production facility. The cast stayed in a motel outside of San Francisco. A few days into the shoot, Hawke realized that River wasn't your average teenager: "I saw him practicing his character's walk in the parking lot," Hawke said. "Uncommon behavior for a thirteen-year-old."

Over the previous couple of years, River had phased out his bowl haircut, but for Wolfgang, it was back in all its symmetrical glory. Plus, he had to wear

49

a particularly bookish pair of glasses—which he removed as soon as he got off camera, or if a pretty girl walked by. River had been many things in his life, but never a dork. "River had to do the most acting of all the kids, since he was playing against type," Dante said.

"Although River liked to be cool and act cool, there was a geek inside him that would come out and embarrass him," Dante added. "He did not enjoy watching himself in that part—I think that he saw a lot of things about himself that he wished he didn't have. There were childish things that he was trying to change."

By law, the teen actors could work only four hours a day, so the three of them had lots of off-duty time together, and soon became fast friends. "It was the longest shoot I've ever had," Hawke said a decade later. "Six months with River Phoenix. Man, it was intense."

River and Hawke both pretended to be more mature than they actually were—and both strived to attract the interest of their beautiful costar, Amanda Peterson, a contest that Hawke won. "We competed for the attention of girls like crazy," Hawke said. "In fact, we competed over everything. We bragged and boasted continually about sex. The truth is, we were both virgins. I guess it's touching to look back on two teenage boys struggling with hormones." (River actually hit puberty on the *Explorers* set.)

Dante added that "getting laid was a major goal" in River's life. "It was one of the things that was most important to him." (Neither Dante nor Hawke seems to have known of the Children of God's sexual practices.)

On the set, through his headphones, Dante could hear River and Hawke talking between takes. "River had a very doctrinaire set of ideas that he had been taught by his parents," Dante remembered. "Ethan, who was a far more worldly boy, would often challenge River—and I don't think he was used to that. He was suddenly confronted with a whole lifetime of thinking one way and finding out that it wasn't the way the mainstream of the world thought. It was probably the first time that River had spent time with people who weren't necessarily agreeing with everything that he had heard at home. It was a great experience for him and very mind-expanding."

Although Hawke liked River, he thought his defining quality was "naïve pretentiousness." Hawke said, "To me, education helps you see that your weirdness is not unique. I doubt, though, that River, at age fourteen, had read a book. He thought his ideas on life and the environment were original. Because he'd never been to school, he had no social skills, and lacked a sense of what was appropriate conversation. And he had this peculiar way of anecdotalizing his past, living his life in the third person. You had the sense he was making his own mythology. I suppose we all do that, but River went to the extreme."

River's lack of formal education frequently tripped him up on the set. He would mispronounce words or names that would be familiar to most other teenagers, betraying his lack of familiarity with them: past presidents; famous actors, writers, and singers; major historical events. "River didn't have a lot of material knowledge of the world because of the way he had been brought up. The meaning of things often had to be explained to him and it put him in a difficult position," Dante said. "Considering River had been somewhat deprived of an education, he was a very bright kid and very smart and knowledgeable about things. He just didn't have a lot of facts at his command because he'd never been walked through history and literature."

Television was also a largely unknown landscape to River. He had spent more time in his life making TV than watching it. "Television wasn't really one of the things that was in our house," Arlyn said, in an understated description of the family's itinerant lifestyle. When River, on a break from shooting *Explorers,* stumbled across a TV set playing MTV, he was immediately hypnotized and spent the next several hours inhaling clips by the likes of Van Halen, Prince, and Night Ranger. When he was introduced to the Three Stooges, he couldn't understand why anybody thought they were funny; he started asking random people if they liked the Three Stooges.

Dante encouraged his young actors to improvise, and was pleased by the spontaneous rapport they developed. "We got along exceptionally," River said. "It's like having foster brothers and sisters that you just move in with for a while and get to know. Ethan, Jason, and Amanda are good personalities,

51

very easy to work with. There are some Hollywood kids who are really brats, and it's just hard to deal with them. I've been lucky that I haven't been such a brat; I'm trying my best not to be . . . When we get hyper, we can get on adults' nerves, and we get tired of just hanging around the set. And maybe we, like, light people on fire and stuff."

One night, River asked Hawke a direct question that most actors, of any age, would dance around: "Are you going to be famous?"

Hawke tried to play it cool, and act more humble than he actually was. "I don't know—I don't care much," he lied.

River was straightforward: "I'm going to be famous. Definitely. Rich and famous."

"Why? What's so cool about fame?"

Hawke didn't expect River's answer: "I'm doing it for my family."

"After that night, I really saw the heavy trip his family had laid on him. To them, he was the Second Coming, the man of the house at age fourteen. Maybe that's why River always took himself so seriously," Hawke said. "I also think he made a myth out of his parents. Incessantly bragging about his father, he'd say, 'My father is the coolest guy with the deepest philosophy.'"

John's behavior could fall short of his son's claims. "One day, John showed up at a looping session obviously drunk," an eyewitness reported. "River tried to laugh it off, saying, 'My dad, well, he gets funny sometimes.' But you could see the kid was hurt and embarrassed."

Explorers flopped at the box office. It was hindered by being released on the heels of another kids' adventure, *The Goonies,* and further hurt by not being a good movie. "It's charmingly odd at some moments, just plain goofy at others," opined Janet Maslin in the *New York Times.* The first two-thirds of *Explorers,* when the kids build and test-drive a spaceship, mouths agape with a sense of wonder, played like warmed-over Spielberg. But the final third went off the rails: the kids reach an alien spaceship, only to find that the extra-terrestrials are the movie's comic relief, quoting incessantly from American television broadcasts. The mix of action and pop-culture insanity that worked so well in *Gremlins* fizzled here.

All three leads turned in good performances, though—and periodically, on the faces of both Hawke and River, you could see flashes of the adult actors they would become.

When Hawke left for home, River wept.

AS AN ADULT, HAWKE HAD nothing good to say about child acting: "I believe it is profoundly negative and hurtful. Sure, it's natural for kids to act in school plays, but to be adulated by fans is not natural. It's not natural for a fourteen-year-old to have adults fetch him coffee."

Hawke didn't appear in another movie for four years, although he did audition for *Stand by Me,* which would prove to be the movie that launched River to stardom. Hawke wasn't cast. He went home to New Jersey, and soon found that people wanted his autograph—because he knew River. "He would send me into fits of envy," he said. "Unadmirable fits of envy, because I respected him. He became wildly famous, and I was in French class."

It worked out in the long term for Hawke: he had a relatively normal high school life, and then left college after one semester to make *Dead Poets Society,* directed by Peter Weir. River very much wanted to be in *Dead Poets Society* and, having starred in Weir's *Mosquito Coast,* hoped he had the inside track. But even writing a song about the Dead Poets Society didn't get him the part—Weir wanted unfamiliar faces opposite Robin Williams. "The fact that I was unknown helped me get the part," Hawke said. "We were friendly competitors. He said he admired my work, but I didn't believe him. He liked to play head games."

Eating in a high school cafeteria instead of at the craft-services table gave Hawke perspective, and fostered ambitions beyond money and fame. He started a theater company and wrote novels—but after *Dead Poets Society,* he was so worried that he would become a cheesy sellout, he wrote himself letters reminding himself of his values, to be opened at age forty. "My biggest fear," he said, "was that you get a lot of success as a young person, you don't know who you are. I was just worried I would turn into somebody I hated. And that's what makes you come off as pretentious—but the one thing you

53

learn pretty quickly is that if you don't take yourself seriously, nobody else is going to." He smiled ruefully. "Ultimately, nobody else cares what you do."

Hawke never moved to Hollywood, which, ironically, may have helped with his longevity in the movie business: being three thousand miles away from the Viper Room proved to be a better way for him to become an artist.

In regard to River, Hawke said, "I would have really liked to work with him again. I had a really hard time with the idea that he wasn't going to give me the opportunity to be better than him. I'm a very competitive person. You remember the Daffy Duck cartoon, where Daffy's trying to do all this stuff in front of this audience and the cane keeps coming and dragging him off? And finally he does this big magic trick and kind of lights himself on fire and he gets a standing ovation, and as he floats up and away, he goes: 'It's a great trick, but you can only do it once.' I thought that about *My Own Private Idaho:* We got to watch River light himself on fire. And he did. And he was somebody really worthy of being competitive with."

54

17
IF THE SKY THAT WE LOOK UPON SHOULD TUMBLE AND FALL

"Chris Chambers was the leader of our gang, and my best friend. He came from a bad family, and everybody just knew he'd turn out bad—including Chris." That was how Richard Dreyfuss, narrating as the adult Gordie Lachance, described the character in *Stand by Me* that made River Phoenix a star.

River had been treating acting as a lark—he enjoyed doing it, but music remained his first love. After wrapping *Explorers,* however, he was fooling around on a motorcycle, racing it in a dirt field, and he took a spill, tearing up a tendon in his left knee. The injury gave him plenty of time to sit on the couch, thinking about life. River had an epiphany: acting in movies was not just a fluke detour in his life, it was important to him, and he wanted to do it well. Before he was fully healed, he went on an audition for *Stand by Me.* "I kind of limped in," River said, but he thought that the injury ultimately helped him land the part. "I had this tragic air to me 'cause I was bummed out by the accident."

River's character was tough, sensitive, and just a little goofy. In blue jeans and a white T-shirt, sporting a short fifties haircut, he looked like a screen star of the past—one in particular. Director Rob Reiner said, "He was a young James Dean and I had never seen anybody like that."

Wil Wheaton, who played the twelve-year-old Gordie, said that the movie worked, in large part, because the four young actors starring in it matched their characters so well: he was nerdy and uncomfortable in his own skin; Jerry O'Connell was funny and schlubby (looking nothing like the chiseled hunk he became as an adult); Corey Feldman was full of inchoate rage and had an awful relationship with his parents. "And River was cool and really smart and passionate," Wheaton said. "Kind of like a father figure to some of us."

55

At first, Wheaton was intimidated by River, who was fourteen to his twelve. He explained, "He was so professional and so intense, he just seemed a lot older than he was. He seemed to have this wisdom around him that was really difficult to quantify at that age." He was smart, he was musically talented, and he was one of the kindest people Wheaton had ever met. In other words: "He just seemed cool."

Stand by Me, based on the Stephen King novella *The Body,* is the story of four boys in small-town Oregon in 1959. Just before junior high school begins, they hike twenty miles down the train tracks to the spot where they have heard the corpse of a missing kid lies, and come home older and wiser.

Production began on *The Body* (as it was then known) in June 1984. Reiner, most famous for playing "Meathead" on *All in the Family,* had already directed *This Is Spinal Tap* and *The Sure Thing.* He didn't think a coming-of-age period piece had much commercial potential, but it was the sort of movie he wanted to make.

Reiner gave his stars tapes of late-fifties music and made sure they learned the slang of the era. More importantly, he summoned his four young leads one week early to Brownsville, Oregon (about a hundred miles west of where River was born, on the other side of the Cascade Mountains). Reiner led them in games drawn from Viola Spolin's book *Improvisations for the Theater:* River and the other boys mimed each other's gestures as if they were mirror images, told collaborative stories, and took turns guiding each other blindfolded through their hotel lobby. "Theater games develop trust among people," declared Reiner, who needed his four actors to become friends—quickly.

Feldman had known River a long time—they had become friendly on the L.A. audition circuit. "Whenever we saw each other on auditions," Feldman remembered, "we would hang out or play outside while everyone else was sitting in the room waiting for their shot."

The quartet soon bonded. When *The Goonies,* starring Feldman, was released that summer, they went to see it together; a few weeks later, they all went to *Explorers.* Wheaton's family organized weekend white-water rafting trips for the cast and crew. At the end of one outing, they found themselves at a clothing-optional hot springs that was hosting a hippie fair; some of the cast got to juggle with the Flying Karamazov Brothers.

At the hotel, the actors were testing their limits. When River found out Wheaton was adept with electronics, he encouraged him to monkey with a video-game machine so they could play for free, promising that he'd take the blame if they got caught. They soaked Feldman's wardrobe in beer; after his clothes dried, he smelled like a wino. And they threw the poolside chairs into the hotel pool—the closest four well-meaning young adolescents could get to acting like the Who.

Kiefer Sutherland had a supporting role as the quartet's nemesis, a juvenile delinquent named Ace Merrill. Sutherland was almost four years older than River, and spent most of his time on set in character, so the two actors didn't get to know each other very well. Nevertheless, on a day when River was in a destructive mood, he bombarded Sutherland's car with large dirt clods until it was covered in muck. "The other guys dared me to do it,"

River explained. "They knew it was Kiefer's car—I didn't. When I found out, I was scared for my life."

Soon after, Sutherland spotted River at a local restaurant and called him over to his table.

Terrified, River blurted out, "Kiefer, I'm really sorry."

Sutherland was confused; he was just saying hello. When River explained he was the culprit behind the dirt-clod fusillade, Sutherland laughed and said, "Don't worry about it. It's a rental car—they washed it off."

River was relieved, having conflated Sutherland with his character: "I didn't know if he was going to pull out the switchblade and slit my throat."

Feldman and River checked out a local underage nightclub. Feldman said, "There was no alcohol served there or anything, but of course, all the kids were drinking anyway." The locals offered booze to the visiting Hollywood actors and, with the lightest touches of peer pressure, got them to take their first drinks.

"Kids never got along with me," River said. The experiences that had made his life extraordinary had also made it impossible to find common ground with regular teenagers. "These kids, because this was Oregon and not L.A., and because we were actors and they admired us or whatever, they'd do anything to appease us. So they got me a forty-ouncer of beer, which I drank straight down just to show them. The only other thing I remember about that night was laying on the railroad tracks with everything spinning all around me."

Feldman said that he and River also had their first significant marijuana experience together. They were hanging out in another hotel room, this one occupied by one of the movie's technicians. When the two kids spotted a bong in his closet and asked what it was, he not only explained its purpose and workings to them, he (with what seems an astonishing lack of adult responsibility) let them try it out. Feldman recalled, "We both coughed a lot and had sore throats—but even though we were kind of bouncing off the walls of the hotel, neither of us seemed to be affected by it. It didn't change our state of mind in any way."

The coda: Some months later, when the *Stand by Me* cast stayed in a New

57

York City hotel for the movie's press junket, a distinctive aroma was wafting from River's room. "I could smell the pot coming all the way down the hallway," Feldman said. River laughed it off, saying it was somebody else's.

River turned fifteen while shooting *Stand by Me,* and seemed determined to grow up just as decisively as the movie's characters. The four young actors talked about sex all the time, despite (or because of) their lack of experience. "Sex was nearly all that River could think about," Feldman said.

River had a major crush on a friend of the family, an older teenager; the feeling was apparently mutual, since she propositioned him. "He decided it was time to end his self-imposed 'second virginity' and get on with his first teen sexual encounter," Feldman said. River and his friend went to his parents to get their blessing—Arlyn and John not only consented, they pitched a tent in the backyard of their rented house and decorated it to enhance the mood.

"It was a beautiful experience," Arlyn said later.

"A very strange experience," River said. "I got through that, thank God." He wasn't just relieving his teenage hormones: he was attempting to have a mature sex life uncolored by his experiences with the Children of God. His emotions may have been mixed, but he was outwardly overjoyed: the next day on the set, he was telling the news to anybody who would listen. He even wrote a letter to *Explorers* director Joe Dante, who knew about River's unslaked teenage lust, with the caps-lock on his handwriting: "WELL IT HAPPENED. IT FINALLY HAPPENED."

Although the cast and crew remember the idyllic shoot of *Stand by Me* as the best summer ever, they were also making a quiet little movie that would turn out to be a masterpiece. The movie is saturated with issues of mortality—even if the boys treat their journey like an impromptu camping jamboree, they are looking for a dead body—but the flip side is that it has an unusually warm, generous sense of what it means to be alive. *Stand by Me* is full of quotable lines ("Mickey Mouse is a cartoon. Superman's a real guy. There's no way a cartoon could beat up a real guy"), but the foundation of the movie is the friendship between Wheaton's Gordie and River's Chris.

The defining scene for Chris comes when, late at night by a campfire, he confesses his fear that no matter what he does, the town will always think of him as "one of those low-life Chambers kids." On the night the scene was shot, River delivered the monologue, telling the story of how he stole milk money from his school and then had moral qualms and returned the cash to a teacher—only to have her keep the money for herself, letting him take the blame and a three-day suspension.

Reiner wasn't satisfied with River's performance—it seemed emotionally flat. Sometimes he would act out dialogue himself so his young performers could hear what he was looking for, but this time Reiner had a quiet word with River, asking him, "Is there a moment in your life where you can recall an adult letting you down, and betraying you in some way? You don't have to tell me who it is. I just want you to think about it."

River walked away from the camera, replaying memories in his mind. A few minutes later, he returned and told Reiner he was ready to try again. This time his performance felt like an open wound: River wept while anger and pain roiled him. After the scene, Reiner went to River, who was still crying, gave him a big hug, and told him he loved him.

59

"It took him a while to get over it," Reiner said. "Obviously, there was something very hurtful to him in his life that he connected with to make that scene work. You just saw that raw naturalism. I've seen the movie a thousand times—and every time I see that scene, I cry."

Although River always praised the finished film (which changed titles from *The Body* to *Stand by Me* when marketers at Columbia Pictures worried that audiences would think it was a bodybuilding movie or a horror flick), he wasn't so happy with his own performance. "Personally, I didn't think my work was up to my own standards," he said. Perhaps he felt that by drawing on his wellspring of pain and betrayal, he had exposed his secrets to the world. "I was going through puberty and I was hurting real bad," he said of his emotional nakedness. "It's not easy watching yourself so vulnerable."

18

ECHO #2: *STAND BY ME*

At the end of the movie, when the boys return from their odyssey on the train tracks, Chris waves good-bye to Gordie and walks away from the camera. In voiceover, the adult Gordie (Richard Dreyfuss) tells how Chris took college-prep classes with him, worked hard, and ultimately became a lawyer—until one day, he tried to break up a fight in a fast-food restaurant and got stabbed in the throat for his trouble, dying immediately.

As he tells this story, the image of River fades from the screen, dead too soon. Reiner described this disappearance as "sad and weird and eerie"—just eight years later, the real-life River would be gone, too.

19

YOUNG HOLLYWOOD 1985

In 1985, Leonardo DiCaprio was dazzling the other kids at his elementary school with his Michael Jackson impression. Martha Plimpton was enjoying the success of *The Goonies,* in which she costarred with Corey Feldman—she played "Stef," the tough girl of the gang. Keanu Reeves made the movie that would be his Hollywood debut: *Youngblood,* the hockey drama starring Rob Lowe. Brad Pitt was attending the University of Missouri, where he was a member of the Sigma Chi fraternity, majoring in journalism with a focus on advertising. The following year, he would leave college only two credits shy of his degree and move to Hollywood to try to be in the movies.

Also in 1985, Red Hot Chili Peppers went to Detroit to record their album *Freaky Styley* with producer (and funk legend) George Clinton. The band and Clinton did copious amounts of drugs together; the song "Yertle the Turtle" featured a cameo spoken-word appearance from Clinton's Middle Eastern drug dealer. Clinton was in debt to him, but letting the dealer be on the record ensured that the supply of cocaine wouldn't get cut off. That year, Michael Stipe was touring with R.E.M. behind *Fables of the Reconstruction;* when he was off the road, he found himself being stalked by the members of the Texas punk band the Butthole Surfers, including lead singer Gibby Haynes. They had relocated to Stipe's hometown of Athens, Georgia, and declared their intention to park a van outside his house inscribed with the message "Michael Stipe / Despite the hype / I still wanna suck / Your big long pipe."

FAMILY AFFAIR

River's life-changing summer in Oregon came with a paycheck: $50,000 for ten weeks of work. Agent Iris Burton got a $5,000 commission, while the government withheld about $14,000 for taxes. John and Arlyn got a $7,500 commission as managers; after a few other minor deductions, River Phoenix was paid just over $20,000. He was Team Phoenix's breadwinner and he needed more work.

As soon as River returned to L.A., Burton booked him his highest-profile job yet: a guest appearance on TV's second-most-popular show, *Family Ties*. In its fourth season, the show was powered by the charisma of Michael J. Fox as Alex Keaton and by the best time slot in television (NBC, Thursdays at 8:30 P.M., right after the number one *Cosby Show*).

River played Eugene Forbes, a genius math student who tutors Alex—despite being, to Alex's chagrin, much younger than him. "Alex, you're still clinging to Euclidean geometry," River tells Keaton. "Embrace the abstract. Let go of rational thought!" Wearing a bow tie and a plaid sleeveless sweater, River was playing a variation on his *Explorers* character. While that movie got him this part, he had become a much better actor since making it, either because he had a year's more experience or because he had started taking the job seriously. His comic timing had hugely improved and his growing confidence let him command the screen. If he identified with Eugene not fitting in with kids his age, at least here he could play that for laughs.

It turns out that Eugene Forbes is pining for a girlfriend: "A companion, a confidante, a friend. A chick in hot pants." He becomes smitten with Alex's sister Jennifer (played by Tina Yothers), and awkwardly woos her, giving her an X-ray of his brain. He brings her to a university faculty party—which, as a date, proves to be a debacle. The episode ends with him asking her out for a soda instead.

62

21

TILT-A-WHIRL

Arlyn hired a family tutor, Ed Squires, who observed River's difficulty reading and concluded that he suffered from dyslexia. While it might seem astonishing that nobody in the family had ever considered this possibility—River, after all, *had starred in a TV movie about dyslexia*—John and Arlyn resisted the notion of seeing a doctor and obtaining a formal diagnosis.

Arlyn also hired a housekeeper, a young bearded man named Larry McHale, who would not only do laundry, but serve as River's personal assistant and companion. His job title was NANNY: "New Age Non-Nuclear Youth." McHale drove River around L.A., introducing him to his own friends—adults, some of whom liked to take drugs.

On one outing, McHale joined a group of pals on an all-day trip to the Magic Mountain amusement park. One of them, Pat Brewer—then a twenty-five-year-old acting student—didn't recognize the kid who seemed to be tagging along with McHale for no reason. Only fifteen at the time, River looked even younger. "We partied all day," Brewer said, "with River becoming the butt of a lot of jokes because he was so young."

At the end of the day, the group left the park, ending up at a Santa Monica home, near the Pacific Ocean. Somebody brought out a stash of cocaine and started cutting up lines. "River looked very unsure," Brewer said. "It was something new to him. I remember saying, 'I wouldn't give any of that to the kid.' But then River insisted on having his share. I think he was trying to prove himself in the group and felt peer pressure."

After snorting up the coke, River felt unwell and short of breath; he went outside to clear his head. Brewer ended up taking him on a walk down to the Santa Monica Pier. "I didn't even realize he was River Phoenix until some little girls came up and asked him for his autograph," said Brewer, who remembered River as not enjoying even his low level of stardom. "He just wanted to be John Doe and anonymous."

McHale and River hung out more with Brewer in the following weeks. It was mostly low-key: River would play guitar and talk about music. "At first he was very self-conscious about drugs and didn't really know what to do," Brewer said. "He soon picked it up, though." River's family didn't know that in just a few months, he had experimented with alcohol, marijuana, and cocaine. The Children of God had taught River that cocaine was "the devil's dandruff." It had also taught him to keep secrets.

PART THREE

"AN EXCUSE TO GET THAT FAR OUT OF YOUR HEAD"

SMALL-TOWN HOLLYWOOD

Ione Skye had just turned fifteen when her big brother, Donovan Leitch, brought home River Phoenix. She didn't know who River was and wasn't clear on how he had ended up in her house—she thought maybe he was shooting a TV movie down the street. "Our neighborhood kind of looked like Anywhere, U.S.A., even though it was right in the middle of Hollywood," she said.

Skye and River immediately hit it off. "His mother and my mother are similar," she said. "They're New York Jewish women who became hippies." (Skye's mother is model Enid Karl; her father is British singer/songwriter Donovan, who unlike his son, generally goes by a single name.) A couple of weeks later, River called Skye up and asked her on a date, inviting her to come along while the Phoenix family went busking in Westwood. She happily consented, but before it happened, he called back and canceled. "I can't, I'm gonna do a movie," River told her—and then he left town.

23 WELCOME TO THE JUNGLE

Youth evaporates in Hollywood like rain on hot California pavement—but it's unusual to find yourself too old for a part at age fifteen. For the plum role of the son in *The Mosquito Coast,* about a father (Harrison Ford) who uproots his family and moves them to the South American jungle, River was disqualified from the start: director Peter Weir was set on an actor not older than twelve, thirteen at the outside. Burton got River an audition anyway, but his tape was shelved, while Weir looked at dozens of younger actors.

Rewatching some of the audition tapes, casting director Diane Crittenden stumbled on River's and was astonished. She immediately took the videocassette to Weir and pressed it on him. "There's a boy on this tape named River Phoenix," she told him. "He's terrific, only he's fifteen." Weir watched the tape, and was duly impressed—but was leaning toward Wil Wheaton, River's younger *Stand by Me* costar. Then he read River's résumé, and was astonished to discover that he had spent years living in Latin America. The parallels between the actor and the role seemed too strong to ignore. Weir remembered, "I finally said to myself, 'What does it matter how old he is? He looks like Harrison's son!' And I cast him."

In his native Australia, Peter Weir had become an acclaimed director of moody art-house films (such as the brilliant *Picnic at Hanging Rock*); *The Mosquito Coast* (an adaptation of a Paul Theroux novel) was his second Hollywood film after *Witness,* which also starred Harrison Ford. Helen Mirren, not yet a grande dame of cinema, played Ford's wife. The cast also included the unlikely combination of Jason Alexander (with hair, not yet famous for *Seinfeld*) and Butterfly McQueen (best known for her role as a maid in *Gone with the Wind*).

68

Filming took place in the small Central American country of Belize, chosen for its variety of terrain (especially jungle), its English-speaking population, and its stable government. In late 1986, River flew down, with his father accompanying him as chaperon. Over a decade earlier, John had brought River along on his South American journey; now the roles were reversed.

ECHO #3: *THE MOSQUITO COAST*

Harrison Ford's character, Allie Fox, becomes disgusted with the United States and its disposable consumer culture. A genius inventor working as a handyman in Massachusetts, he packs up his wife and four children and books passage on a freighter bound for the "Mosquito Coast," the jungle stretching from Guatemala to Panama. From the boat, Fox shouts, "Good-bye, America, and have a nice day!"

This was not the exact trajectory of the Phoenix family, but their south-of-the-border odysseys was also rooted in contempt for the excesses of American materialism. Utopia collapses for the Foxes, just as it did for the Phoenixes. Allie Fox buys an abandoned town named Jeronimo and tries to turn it into a thriving jungle village, with an ice-making business at its center. The town is fueled by his hubris; when hoods with guns find it and try to take over, he blows the whole thing up.

The family ends up floating down the river on a boat, with Charlie (River's character) exiled to a smaller trailing boat for the sin of insufficient belief in his father. When they try to make shelter on a beach, a storm blows everything away. The beliefs of the patriarch have proved to be no more reliable than a makeshift tent.

"The Mosquito Coast tells you to be true to someone you love," River opined. (Not necessarily the most obvious moral—one could say it tells you to beware of how a loved one can take you to places you shouldn't go, but that wasn't something

69

River wanted to say out loud, or maybe even think.) "I knew that character so well because I was that character. I knew his whole path," River said.

"Paul Theroux didn't steal my life story," River declared. "I just misplaced it."

JUNGLE BOY

To make filming more efficient, the *Mosquito Coast* production team built Jeronimo in three stages. Reminding everyone that this was a real jungle, big snakes such as boa constrictors frequently visited the set. Harrison Ford stayed at a nearby hotel, but most of the film's cast and crew found accommodations in the jungle. "It was very hot," River said, "and there were a lot of mosquitoes, but I got used to it. We ate a lot of rice, mangoes, and coconuts, which is what I eat anyway." For variety, sometimes the production would fly in bagels from Miami.

Stand by Me hadn't been released yet, so many of the *Mosquito* filmmakers were agog at River's transformation from the pudgy nerd of *Explorers* into a lean young man with the face of an archangel. "In a matter of months, he seemed to have gone from Spanky McFarland to James Dean," unit publicist Reid Rosefelt remembered.

In order for the cast and crew to see dailies (the raw footage filmed on a given day), the film had to be flown to the United States for processing and then back to Belize. As they watched the dailies, it quickly became clear to everyone that River was turning into a movie star, more than capable of holding his own opposite Ford and Mirren. Sometimes he would back away from the camera, trying to let other actors be front and center. "But the more he stepped out of frame," Rosefelt remembered, "the more your eyes were drawn to him."

"River Phoenix was born to movies," Weir said. "He has the look of someone who has secrets. The last time I remember seeing it in someone unknown was with Mel Gibson." (Weir directed Gibson in *Gallipoli* [1981] and *The Year of Living Dangerously* [1982]; he proved to be perceptive about how both River and Gibson were concealing certain parts of their lives.) "It's something apart from the acting ability," Weir added. "Laurence-Olivier never had what River had."

River grew close to the sometimes-cantankerous Ford, and was smart enough not to pepper him with questions about Han Solo or Indiana Jones. "In his position, you have so many phony people trying to dig at you that you've got to have a shield up," River said. "The biggest thing about Harrison is that he makes acting look so easy; he's so casual and so sturdy."

Ford, for his part, lauded River's natural talent. "There are a lot of people who have that, but River is also very serious about his work, very workmanlike and professional, far beyond what you'd expect from a fifteen-year-old boy. I don't like to talk to other actors about acting. I think it's a real mistake. But River asks a lot of questions that require answers, none of which I can really supply—but they're interesting questions."

The movie shot six days a week. On his days off, River explored the nearby jungle. He would talk with the natives, snorkel with his dad in the barrier reef, or look for jaguars. Sometimes, he and Rosefelt played music together: Rosefelt had brought a small synth to Belize, and River arrived with his guitar. "I wondered if there was something strange about my hanging out with someone so much younger than myself," Rosefelt said. "But I found him much more stimulating company than most of the other people on the set." River didn't just talk shop: he could be alternately cosmic and introspective.

"I was a curious kid when I was younger," he told Rosefelt. He wanted to experience everything possible—so at age eleven, when he wondered how it would feel to cut himself with a razor blade, he tried it out. He confided, "I quickly realized that this pain thing wasn't the way to go."

John Phoenix kept encouraging his son to play hooky with him: to go off and jam on guitar together, or to take a trip to Guatemala on his day off. River

71

had to play the mature professional, explaining to his dad that he needed to be respectful of the film and the people making it, which meant being rested and ready when he got in front of the camera.

Weir could see the growing tension between father and son, although he didn't attempt to mediate. "With a young person who suddenly becomes the key breadwinner of the family, there's an incredible amount of rearranging things in the family hierarchy," he commented. "Sometimes a tension develops, particularly with the father."

Weir did see River indulging in small acts of open rebellion: when John wasn't around, he would eat foods never allowed in the Phoenix house. Not meat—his vegan beliefs were far too strong for that—but processed foods instead of all-natural snacks. "He'd stuff himself with a Mars Bar and a Coke," Weir said. "It seemed a healthy steam valve."

There was harder stuff than chocolate bars available on the set; nobody working on *The Mosquito Coast* who wanted alcohol or cocaine went unsatisfied. "It was like living in the drug capital of the Northern Hemisphere," River allowed a couple of years later. "I've been so much more *exposed* than my folks think," he said, with naked pain in his voice—regret that they had isolated him? Remorse for partying on the sly?

Also in the *Mosquito Coast* cast was the fifteen-year-old Martha Plimpton, the daughter of Keith Carradine and Shelley Plimpton (her parents met when they were both performing in the original Broadway run of the rock musical *Hair*). She played Emily Spellgood, the daughter of the Reverend Spellgood, a missionary who battles Allie Fox for influence over the natives. Emily has a crush on Charlie, as she lets him know in one of the most awkward come-ons in cinematic history: "I could be your girlfriend, if you want. I think about you when I go to the bathroom."

"The character's just so weird," Plimpton later said of Emily. "She's this missionary's daughter who's all sort of decked out in eighties new-wave teeny-bopper garb in the middle of the jungle, with her Walkman and her Lolita sunglasses."

River and Plimpton had met a year earlier. "But we couldn't stand each other," River said. Isolated in the jungle, however, romance bloomed. "We're just cooler, I guess," he quipped.

Plimpton said the relationship was founded on professional respect: "I knew what it was like to work with adults who took their job seriously, but most of the time, if I was working with people my own age, they weren't particularly interested in authenticity or studying what they were doing. So I think I had a kindred spirit there. And it was really great."

"Martha Plimpton was his first real girlfriend," Ethan Hawke observed. "Martha's wonderful and extremely smart, but it wouldn't be easy to have her as your first girlfriend. She doesn't buy any bullshit."

In his four months in the jungle, River grew three inches and lost the last remnants of his baby fat, dropping twenty pounds. Of his time in Belize, he said, "I learned that even among the chaos and discomfort you need to have the freedom of standing back and laughing, and not to take it all too seriously. Yet it is a serious job."

When *The Mosquito Coast* was finally released, its reviews were middling; many critics found the monomania of Allie Fox (Ford's character) as off-putting as his family ultimately did. Sheila Benson wrote in the *Los Angeles Times,* "Half the conflict of the film lies in the horrified awakening of Charlie (played with exquisite gradation by River Phoenix) to the fallibility and growing madness of his father, whose image in the boy's eyes once blotted out the sun. The film's focus should eventually shift from father to son. But Allie Fox is too indelible a character for the reasonable transfer of power." The movie wasn't a hit; Ford cited it as the only movie he had ever made (at the time) that hadn't earned its money back.

The Mosquito Coast is the movie where River discovered that he could immerse himself in a role so deeply that it would temporarily blot out his own personality and memories. He quickly decided that this was an excellent form of escapism. "It just feels so good," he said. "It has nothing to do with the idea of movies, it's just getting lost. Having an excuse to get that far out of your head is just a really good feeling." In River's telling, the pleasures of Method acting and large quantities of drugs sounded indistinguishable.

26

LAST YEAR AT THE VIPER ROOM

When Adam Duritz wrote "Mr. Jones," he thought of it as a playful little tune about the fairy tale of rock stardom. Then it became a jet engine that propelled his band, Counting Crows, to stardom, and their debut album, August and Everything After, *to sales of over seven million copies in the United States.*

After a year on the road, Duritz returned home to Berkeley, California, and discovered that he had transformed from an underdog musician who loved Van Morrison into a figure of contempt. "I was having a really rough time—I was too famous that week," Duritz said. "It just seemed like everywhere I went, for about six straight days, somebody came up to me and said something terrible—just something fucking nasty. And it was really all new to me then, so I was having a little trouble dealing with it."

At home, Duritz got a call from Sal Jenco, Viper Room general manager, who had recently become a friend. Duritz unburdened himself, talking about how unhappy he was with this sort of homecoming. Jenco put him on hold—which didn't seem like the most considerate response, except he returned a minute later to say that he had just reserved Duritz a plane ticket to L.A. at seven, and booked him a room at the Bel Age Hotel. "We're having this party tonight and Johnny wanted me to invite you anyway, so why don't you just come down?" Jenco asked.

Fuck it, Duritz thought. He threw a few things into a bag, headed to the airport, and never lived in Berkeley again. He went to the party and became a Viper Room regular.

"Adam was embraced by the Viper contingent," said another Viper habitué, singer Morty Coyle. "The Vipers always had a soft spot in their hearts for the glitterati."

Sometimes Duritz would even go behind the bar and pour drinks for a while.

"I did make great tips," he conceded. "I've never had a problem there. That's one of the reasons I moved [to Los Angeles]," he said. "With everybody else running around, who cares about me? At the Viper Room, it was like I was a totally normal guy."

HIS NAME IS RIO AND HE DANCES ON THE SAND

River was feeling vaguely uncertain about life, and considered his family's usual solution: changing his name. He started introducing himself to people as "Rio"—Spanish for "river"—and wondered whether Rio Phoenix, or maybe just the single name Rio, sounded more viable as a name for a rock star. Although he had resolved to make a real effort when he acted, he hadn't given up his first dream: having a musical career and changing the world through his songs.

While he dithered, fame overtook him: *Stand by Me* was released in August 1986 and became the sleeper hit of the summer. Within a few weeks, positive word of mouth had made it the number one movie in the United States, edging out *The Fly* and *Top Gun*. Reviews singled out River; *People* said he was being acclaimed as "one of the most exciting young actors on the screen."

"Because he made such an impact on that film, he was not just another kid actor," said preeminent film critic Roger Ebert. "He had a special quality, and it was a quality that he had all through his career. A certain cleanness or transparency, so it seemed that he was very natural and unaffected on the screen and not acting."

As the breakout star of a surprise hit movie, River found his life changing quickly. His quote went up to $350,000 per movie, giving his family a financial cushion for the first time in his life and making him the most important client of Iris Burton's agency. River attempted to block out the sensation that the world was now spinning on its axis five times faster than previously. "After *Stand by Me* came out, people were telling me 'You're so good,' 'You're going to be a star,' and things like that," he said. "You can't think about it. If you take the wrong way, you can get really high on yourself. People get so lost when that happens to them. They may think they have everything under control, but everything is really out of control. Their lives are totally in pieces." As River spoke, he seemed to shift gradually from describing people he had observed to describing the pitfalls and hazards of his own life.

River tried to find ways to undermine his new, exalted movie-star status. Burton accompanied him to Tokyo for the Japanese premiere of the movie; they stayed at the lavish Imperial Hotel. When River found that the park next to the hotel had groups of kids hanging out and playing guitar, he invited them up to his room. "That room was filled with kids from the park," Burton said. "He would play guitar for them and give them fruit and juice."

An undeniable indicator of River's new stardom: his appearance in the pages of celebrity pinup magazines like *Bop!* and *Tiger Beat*. (The class of publications is best typified by Lisa Simpson's favorite, *Non-Threatening Boys Magazine*.) Cooperating with the publicity departments of movie studios, River found himself the subject of photo sessions that turned him into a pinup alongside Rob Lowe, Kirk Cameron, and the members of Duran Duran.

Only a few years later, he shuddered at the memory: "They teach you how to pose, you know, they say, 'You *have* to do it like this!' And you tilt your *head* and they show you how to push your *lips* out and suck in your *cheek*." River groaned. "And then *all* the *outtakes* that you *never* want to see again in your *life* go through the teen magazines *forever*."

The peg for just about every mini-profile accompanying a pinup: River's taste in girls. One magazine quoted him thus: "I like girls who are so natural because I'm natural in everything I do." Another: "It's a great feeling to think that I can be a friend to so many people through my movies."

The notion that these magazines made him fodder for romantic fantasies disconcerted River, reasonably enough. "It's like there's a grandstand full of girls who think I'm the greatest without knowing anything about me personally. It makes me very nervous. It's as if everybody's getting all worked up over an image they don't know anything about. And if *you* are that image . . . I mean, don't they know I'm an actor?"

While it's disconcerting for any teenager to find himself an international sex object, River's situation was even more fraught. As a child, under the aegis of the Children of God, he had been drawn into sexual activity before he could understand it or consent to it. Although he was still a minor—just sixteen years old—he once more found his own personality submerged in the deep waters of other people's lust. He wasn't comfortable with it, but again, he went along with it.

Now legitimately famous, even appearing on *The Tonight Show* (with guest host Joan Rivers), River spent a lot of time worrying that he would lose himself in a whirlwind of celebrity and hollow praise. He struggled for ways to maintain his integrity—the same impulse that drove Ethan Hawke to write letters to himself. Reid Rosefelt said of River, "He told me that he had to get up every morning and fight to remain himself."

While a professional name change to Rio no longer made any sense, River kept using the name privately. Over the years, introducing himself to strangers as Rio proved to be a useful way to sidestep fame-addled encounters. Calling himself Rio became a symbol of integrity—a way to assert that he had an identity that was distinct from the "River Phoenix" that could be found on newsstands and billboards.

River wouldn't have necessarily put it that way at age sixteen. Not that he was inarticulate, just that he was more prone to sentences like this: "Yo, Mama-jama, can we have some OJ, pleeze!"

JOHN PHOENIX WAS LOOKING FOR more stability in his family's living situation—they had moved over forty times during River's life—and wanted to take a step away from what he saw as the iniquity of Hollywood.

The solution to both problems, financed by River's newfound success: renting a twenty-acre ranch just outside San Diego.

Burton started to find work for the other Phoenix children. Leaf was part of an ensemble of kids in *SpaceCamp*—which flopped when audiences didn't want to see a comic adventure about kids going into outer space only five months after the shuttle *Challenger* exploded and killed seven astronauts.

Leaf was also cast in *Russkies,* in the starring role of a Key West teen who captures a Soviet sailor. Summer played his little sister, edging out Liberty for the role. Meanwhile, Rainbow booked a small part in the Ally Sheedy comedy *Maid to Order.*

River took a paternal attitude toward his younger siblings, playing with them on the backyard trampoline and guiding them through Hollywood. He called them "my kids," speaking of his time with the family as if he were returning from a war zone rather than a movie set: "That's been a lot of fun, getting to know my kids."

"His parents saw him as their savior," Martha Plimpton observed. "And treated him like the father."

River filmed one last TV movie, *Circle of Violence: A Family Drama,* about elder abuse. River played unruly teen Chris Benfield, whose mother (Tuesday Weld), unbeknownst to him, is mentally and physically torturing her own mother (Geraldine Fitzgerald). The project was unnotable except for a line of dialogue that River later nominated, tellingly, as the worst he ever had to say on camera: "It was something like, 'Mom, why can't we be like most families and get along?' Like most families get along!"

28
MARTHA MY DEAR

"River went off to do *The Mosquito Coast,* and he came back with a girlfriend, Martha Plimpton," Ione Skye remembered. "So I was kind of bummed."

It wasn't just jungle love—once River and Plimpton were back on American soil, the relationship only got more serious. One night, when they were fifteen, they were both in New York City, and they went out for a fancy dinner. (Foraging for mangoes on the beaches of Venezuela was only seven years in the past, but it must have seemed like another life to River.) Plimpton ordered soft-shell crabs.

A horrified River abruptly left the restaurant. When Plimpton followed him, she found him walking down Park Avenue, crying. "I love you so much—why?" he wept. He was devastated that she was eating animals, but even more, he was deeply wounded that he hadn't been able to convince her that veganism was the better, more moral path.

"I loved him for that," Plimpton said. "For his dramatic desire that we share every belief, that I be with him all the way."

Plimpton stayed with the Phoenixes for a while. She said, "I love River's family; they brought him up to believe he was a pure soul who had a message to deliver to the world. But in moving around all the time, changing schools, keeping to themselves, and distrusting America, they created this utopian bubble so that River was never socialized—he was never prepared for dealing with crowds and with Hollywood, for the world in which he'd have to deliver that message. And furthermore, when you're fifteen, to have to think of yourself as a prophet is unfair."

29

COMING-OF-AGE STORY

Every day, all over Hollywood, thousands of people have meetings where they hash out the details of movies, most of which will never get made. One afternoon in 1986, writer/director William Richert returned from yet another Hollywood lunch to his office on Sunset Boulevard. His secretary told him that River Phoenix was waiting to audition for him, for a project of Richert's called *Jimmy Reardon*. There was industry buzz that River was excellent in *Stand by Me,* which hadn't been released yet, but nobody in Richert's office even knew how old he was: one person said twenty-five, while another said thirteen.

Richert went to his waiting room, where River was sitting in the shadows next to a potted plant. Then River stood up, "and he was completely surrounded by light," Richert said. He knew it was because of the way the California sun was streaming through the window, but he couldn't shake the feeling that River was glowing from within.

Richert said, "You know, you're a movie star."

River demurred; only one of his movies had even been released, and that was *Explorers.*

"And you're going to be incredible in my movie," said Richert, overcome by River's luminous beauty.

"But you haven't auditioned me—I haven't read anything."

"You don't need to."

"Oh, I should read it," River said. "Don't you want to hear me read it?"

"Do you *want* to read it?"

"Yeah."

Richert consented; they went into his office and River gave a fine reading.

When he was done, Richert instructed him, "Take the script and go home and call your agent. Tell them you've just been offered the lead in this movie."

Richert was a garrulous, strong-willed operator. Then forty-four, he had made a series of documentaries—one about the daughters of Richard Nixon and Lyndon Johnson, another about roller derby. When his political satire *Winter Kills* (with a cast including Jeff Bridges, John Huston, and Elizabeth Taylor) was shut down mid-shoot—the producers got busted for smuggling pot—he made another movie (*The American Success Story*) with much of the same cast in Europe to finance completion of the first one.

Jimmy Reardon, based on Richert's own semi-autobiographical novel, *Aren't You Even Going to Kiss Me Goodbye?,* was the story, set in 1962, of a high school senior from a middle-class family in Evanston, the upper-class Chicago suburb. Jimmy Reardon, a Casanova with women, is nevertheless out of place with his rich friends—who are heading off to Ivy League colleges and other exotic locales, while his father is steering him toward an uninspiring local business school. As Jimmy frantically tries to scrounge up enough money for a plane ticket to follow his girlfriend to Hawaii, all his schemes gradually come undone. If he doesn't arrive at an adult acceptance of his situation, he at least ends the movie with a greater understanding of the world he lives in.

River hoped it would be an "intelligent teenage comedy," a coming-of-age story that crossed *Risky Business* and *The Catcher in the Rye*. John was against River taking the role, feeling that it was too licentious, but Arlyn and Iris Burton both thought it was a good career move—a transition into adult parts—and their view prevailed. River signed the contract and started to prepare.

"In three months, he made himself look seventeen years old," Richert said. "He wasn't eating, and he was doing push-ups day-in and day-out, because he had a kid's body and he wanted to get some abs."

River went to Illinois for the shoot, joined by a cast that included Ione Skye, performance artist Ann Magnuson, future *Big Bang Theory* star Johnny Galecki (then just eleven years old), and in his first movie ever, future Friend Matthew Perry (Richert discovered him while eating breakfast in the San

Fernando Valley). Not there: John and Arlyn Phoenix, who opted to go to Key West to supervise Leaf on the set of *Russkies*.

River was chaperoned by his maternal grandfather, Meyer Dunetz—but the supervision proved to be nominal. "I could get away with a lot," River said, "because he didn't know me, so he didn't know how I acted. So I could not be River, and there wasn't my mom around to say, 'Hey, come on, what's going on, you're losing yourself.'"

Richert fondly remembered the time River stepped out of his trailer, still wearing a bib to protect his clothes from makeup. There were dozens of teenage girls sitting on a nearby lawn, a crowd waiting to catch a glimpse of River Phoenix, the latest teen idol. "He looked at me and said, 'How many blow jobs do you think are lying out there?'" Richert recalled, roaring with laughter. But the quip was much more like Jimmy Reardon than River Phoenix; it was mostly a sign that River was experimenting with staying in character.

According to Skye, the shoot had a "very party atmosphere," with the teens and the adults socializing together, and Richert leading the way. "It wasn't creepy," she said—it was exhilarating for the kids to be taken seriously by their adult coworkers.

If River was misbehaving, he did so discreetly. Cast member Louanne Sirota said, "The most out-of-control thing we ever did was order beer through room service when we were underage, and that was cool." Although River was in a movie full of attractive women ready to "rehearse" their sex scenes together, he seems to have resisted temptation. Mostly, anyway—actress Jane Hallaren, who played his mother, once found him entangled with a girl in a hallway.

"Don't tell anybody, okay?" River asked.

Like, yeah, I'm going to call his girlfriend, Hallaren thought. "But that was River," she said. "Whenever you thought you had him pigeonholed, he was someone else."

"I'm the monogamous type," River said. "I believe romance is important in sex. Doing it just for sensation and immediate gratification is selfish." And then, without missing a beat, he argued the other side of the equation: "We all have these kinds of urges and feelings inside us and we can't always suppress them."

Martha Plimpton visited the set the day after River had spent a late evening in his hotel room with one of the actresses, hanging out and listening to Roxy Music. Plimpton, apparently unthreatened, teased him: "You were listening to the ultimate makeout record, Roxy Music!"

"I remember thinking that was such a grown-up thing to say," Skye recalled. "I looked up to her—she was this New Yorker who was very intelligent and sophisticated."

While Richert likened the blond couple of River and Plimpton to a pair of Tinker Bells, his son Nick (who had a small part in the film), thought that Martha had River perpetually apologizing to her. "She seemed to be in charge," he said. "She was upset with him a lot of the time. I was never sure exactly what he'd done, but she probably had good reason."

Working on movies, River often sought out older men and adopted them as mentors and father figures (Rob Reiner or Harrison Ford, for example). *Jimmy Reardon* was no exception, as he and Richert bonded—their friendship would last for the rest of River's life.

Speaking of the novel that inspired *Jimmy Reardon,* Richert said, "I wrote that back when I was nineteen, and I shot it word for word. So the movie was written by a nineteen-year-old, directed by a forty-year-old, making a movie about himself with a kid who is acting out him, coming from a similar background. Because I came out of a Catholic cult and he came out of a Children of God cult."

After River got a haircut, Richert was astonished at how much he looked like James Dean. He showed River a photo of Dean, and even staged one shot specifically to evoke the teen idol of the fifties, who died at age twenty-four. River shrugged off the resemblance, indifferent.

One day, he asked Richert, "Where do I cry in this movie?" Asked what he meant, he replied, "I've cried in all my movies."

"Not in this one," Richert told him.

"I'm not going to cry?"

"No."

Realization dawned on River. "Because you want other people to cry."

River had never done a love scene on camera before; now he was starring in a film full of them, and Richert had to walk him through the mechanics. "He was very powerful and confident as a performer. And with grown-ups," Skye said. "But he was uncomfortable playing a ladies' man." River also worried about dialogue in which Jimmy encouraged his friends to get drunk, not wanting his fans to emulate that behavior.

There was only one line River wanted to add, Richert said, and it came in the scene where the older woman played by Ann Magnuson seduces him. River showed him what he had written in the script—"and his handwriting was like hieroglyphics, because River never really went to school," Richert said.

The new line: "Well, I really do want to say that I'm a firm believer that everything happens for a reason."

Richert was flabbergasted; not only did the idea seem precocious for a sixteen-year-old, "there aren't a lot of actors who change dialogue with a philosophical context, or even think that way. It didn't quite fit the scene, but I thought it was great. River was not one of us, not a person that would just go along with everything the way it was."

30 RATTLESNAKE SPEEDWAY

When the movie finished shooting, River drove two thousand miles back to Los Angeles, traveling in a motor home that he had bought, accompanied by housekeeper/aide-de-camp Larry McHale. Around 2 A.M. on a New Mexico highway, River got pulled over for speeding; McHale was sleeping in the back.

Still channeling Jimmy Reardon, River sassed the cop, calling him "ossifer" instead of "officer."

"Yeah, very funny, kid," said the patrolman, who proved to be a hard-ass. He didn't believe a sixteen-year-old would actually own a motor home, figuring it was more likely he'd stolen it for a joyride.

While the cop went back to his car to check it out, River started doing push-ups on the floor of the motor home. When the cop came back, River didn't stop.

Irate, the policeman thoroughly searched the vehicle for narcotics. Finding nothing, he finally sent River on his way, with a speeding ticket as a souvenir.

The ticket had a stern warning that you had to pay it or go jail—so River didn't mail it in for three months.

31
I AM AN ISLAND

In 1986, the major American film studios had not yet become subsidiaries of Japanese electronics manufacturers. The movie business was still run by misfits, eccentric geniuses, and runaway aristocrats: Chris Blackwell fit right in. Born to a rich white family in Jamaica, he grew up to found Island Records, home to Jimmy Cliff, Bob Marley, Roxy Music, and U2. "The bigger labels are supermarkets," he once said. "I like to think of Island as a very classy delicatessen." His offshoot company Island Pictures was financing *Jimmy Reardon,* so during the shoot, Blackwell visited the set in Evanston to check on its progress.

River made a point of meeting Blackwell, and of letting him know that he also played music. Blackwell called Kim Buie, who was Island's head of A&R on the West Coast, and asked her to meet with River, saying, "He seems like a really cool kid." (A&R stands for "artists and repertoire"—it's the department at the record label that signs and handles musicians.)

Buie knew who River was—when she saw *Stand by Me* in the theater, she had made a point of staying for the credits so she could learn his name. "My God, he just stood out," she said. "He was the James Dean of that movie—he had a commanding presence and a real vulnerability. A lot of emotion, coming through in such a mature way."

When the Phoenix family was all back in Los Angeles, River came to visit Buie at Island's offices, accompanied by John and Arlyn. River played her a few rough demos of his songs. She heard potential and, even more importantly, learned that music was his passion and his first love. "I just felt that there was a light there," she said. "A real desire was being conveyed to me through River and Arlyn. The father didn't say a whole lot—he just had this blank stare."

After the meeting, Buie told Blackwell that River wasn't ready to release a record, but they should try working with him. Island signed River to a development deal—"that was at a time when labels were still doing such a thing," Buie later said with a mordant laugh. "A development deal was a step past a demo deal. You help somebody, and give them some time and resources to be able to put a little more time into their music and figure out what they want to do." The money wasn't extravagant—about $20,000—but River was ecstatic that his musical career was finally starting, and that soon the world would hear his music, which he called "progressive ethereal folk-rock."

86

YOUNG HOLLYWOOD 1987

In 1987, the Fox network, cobbled together from previously independent stations, launched with the programs *Married . . . with Children* and *The Tracey Ullman Show.* The latter program, a sketch-comedy anthology, would ultimately launch *The Simpsons,* while the former, an unusually crass sitcom, would keep Christina Applegate employed for the next eleven years. Another Fox program, *21 Jump Street,* about the adventures of a group of police officers youthful enough to go undercover at high schools, cast Johnny Depp—and made him a teen idol.

That year, fourteen-year-old Leonardo DiCaprio was struggling to find an agent. His closest brush with show-biz glory: On a family trip to Germany, he entered a break-dancing contest and almost won. Brad Pitt had uncredited work on a variety of films with nihilistic titles—*No Way Out, No Man's Land,* and *Less Than Zero*—before booking a two-episode role on the NBC daytime soap *Another World.* Samantha Mathis was also filming an NBC program: *Aaron's Way* was a high-concept spin on *The Beverly Hillbillies,* starring former NFL star Merlin Olsen as the patriarch of an Amish family that relocates to California when his estranged son dies in a surfing accident. Mathis played one of Olsen's daughters, but the program lasted only fourteen episodes.

Gibby Haynes and the Butthole Surfers recorded and released their third album, *Locust Abortion Technician.* Working in the basement of Capitol Records, the Red Hot Chili Peppers recorded *The Uplift Mofo Party Plan,* the last album guitarist Hillel Slovak made with the band before dying of a heroin overdose. Singer Anthony Kiedis was dating Ione Skye and struggling with his own heroin addiction—when staying at his manager's place, he would use a fishing rod to retrieve the manager's car keys from his bedroom dresser without waking him up, so he could go score.

Kiefer Sutherland and Corey Feldman starred in the modern vampire movie *The Lost Boys.* The project marked Feldman's first time working with Corey Haim; the duo became an on-screen team, known to teenage audiences as "the Two Coreys." Ethan Hawke was attending high school in New Jersey. Wil Wheaton, having been cast as Ensign Wesley Crusher on *Star Trek: The Next Generation,* was traveling through the galaxy at warp speed nine.

I HOPE THE RUSSIANS LOVE THEIR CHILDREN TOO

Another story of parents in a foreign land, and a child who doesn't have any choice in the matter: Two Soviet agents live as sleepers in a wholesome American suburb, running a garden store and raising a teenage boy who has no inkling he's actually Russian-born until he applies for the Air Force Academy. This was the ludicrous premise of *The Sleepers,* later renamed *Little Nikita*— and the story didn't get any better, with a rogue Soviet agent named "Scuba" hunting down sleeper agents in the USA.

River's willingness to subject himself to such material at a point when he needed to elevate his career above teen tripe suggests that his judgment was clouded, either by money or by the emotional pull of yet another story where a son feels betrayed by his parents.

Little Nikita started filming in January 1987, in locations near the Phoenix family's San Diego ranch. The director was Richard Benjamin, who had made the transition from acting (*Goodbye, Columbus; Westworld*) to directing (*My Favorite Year; The Money Pit*). River, who had grown accustomed to being taken seriously by directors such as Weir and Richert, soon discovered that Benjamin was going to treat him like a kid: he wasn't allowed to see the daily rushes, and so couldn't assess how his performance was working on-screen. If the decision was meant to make River less self-conscious, it backfired, having the opposite effect.

"I felt so out of place with my acting," River said. "I just felt off. And maybe it's good, because the guy's *supposed* to be insecure and confused," he rationalized. ("The guy" being all-American Jeff Grant, who discovers his real identity as Nikita.) River delivered a withering but accurate self-review: "I feel like I gave a television performance, a combination of *Leave It to Beaver* and Kirk Cameron and Michael J. Fox."

"Is River Phoenix a star?" wrote critic Hal Hinson in the *Washington Post.* "Perhaps not. But his hair is. 'Little Nikita' would be nothing without River Phoenix's hair. It's the most engaging, the most watchable thing in the film. It has body. It has character. It even has drama. In other words, it has everything that's missing from the rest of the picture."

The good news, other than River being self-aware enough to point out his own failings: He found another father figure on the set, in the person of his costar, the legendary Sidney Poitier, then sixty-four years old. Poitier played the FBI agent trying to uncover the truth about the Grant family. Their scenes together were a contrast in styles, River jabbering away at the speed of sound, Poitier working at a deliberate pace, letting audiences see the thoughts on his face.

When they played basketball together, with River's bouffant haircut bouncing on his scalp, it felt like beefcake pitted against gravitas. River wanted the gravitas: he studied Poitier, trying to learn everything he could. Poitier, in turn, took a shine to River and made a point of praising him in public: "I feel River Phoenix is one of our finest young actors and destined to leave an indelible imprint on American films." If he sounded like the Lincoln Memorial coming to life to deliver film reviews, River still appreciated it.

"He gave me tips about life," River said of Poitier. "I learned not to take everything personally. Not to take the negative things about your acting personally and not to take this fame personally. It's just a job and I'm trying to do it well."

89

34

DINNERTIME FOR THE PHOENIX FAMILY, SPRING 1987

Arlyn pages through The Cookbook for People Who Love Animals, *surrounded by all five of her children. "Tofu cheesecake, please!" begs Liberty, eleven years old.*

"I get to lick the bowl," insists Summer, nine years old.

While Rainbow and Leaf do Julia Child impressions, River converts wheatgrass into juice. At their feet are the family dogs, Justice and Sundance, looking hopefully for scraps.

The location: an industrial kitchen in a deserted school. With the lease expiring on the San Diego ranch, the family has relocated back to the Los Angeles area, renting the school for $1,500 per month, putting six water beds in the classrooms and installing Havahart traps to catch the mice, which they then set free in the desert.

When dinner is served (whole-wheat spaghetti and salad), John says grace: "We are very thankful."

"Bless the cook!" River chimes in.

35

PARTY AT THE ZAPPA HOUSE

Ione Skye was dating Red Hot Chili Peppers lead singer Anthony Kiedis, but she still had a "big crush" on River. "He was very real and very fun. He had a wildness, in a way—he was a free spirit."

One day, Skye was supposed to pick up River at the Chateau Marmont, the exclusive Hollywood hotel. When she came to get him, he wasn't at the designated meeting spot: "He was walking on Sunset Boulevard without his shoes," Skye said. "He wasn't a buttoned-up kind of person."

Skye and River hung out; they improvised a free-form song about Judaism, in tribute to their Jewish mothers. They went shopping for vintage eyeglasses together; he confided that he was virtually blind in his right eye.

Periodically, they would spend time at Frank Zappa's house, which had become a salon for young Hollywood: they were both friendly with the Zappa kids, Dweezil and Moon Unit. "It was a really wild, eclectic mix of actors that would hang out at the Zappa family house," said musician and TV journalist Frank Meyer, who spent many evenings there as a teenage pal of Dweezil's. "Some famous TV star would walk in and go off with Moon. Dweezil would be waiting for Warren DeMartini of Ratt to waltz in so they could go jam. And then Frank would just wander in, in his robe, and he'd make peanut butter toast, smoke cigarettes, and chit chat with the kids. He was actually very friendly, in his own mysterious rock-star kind of way."

At age sixteen, River had finally found a peer group: artsy show-biz kids, some of them with weirder names than his. Happy not to be the center of attention for once, he was soft-spoken and unassuming.

Around the same time, Meyer met Matthew and Gunnar Nelson, the twin sons of Ricky Nelson, later famous as a pop-metal duo creatively named Nelson. Meyer said with a laugh, "I remember the Nelsons showing me how to apply eyeliner and coverup so that when you went out on the town, you had the proper amount of makeup on. This was not done ironically in any way, shape, or form. It was, 'Dude, you gotta fuckin' know how to use your makeup. We'll show you.'"

Meyer also spent time with the two Coreys: "Corey Feldman and Corey Haim were absolutely full of themselves and as obnoxious as you would think based on their movie personas. It was always me, me, me, me, me. So having met some of those teen heartthrobs, I assumed that all of them were kind of douchey."

And River? "He wasn't like those other guys at all. He was a normal dude.

Very charming. Quiet. Kind of in his own world. Really good-looking, but not rubbing it in your face, like Mr. Hollywood Guy." Meyer paused. "We were all teenagers, so who knows? He might still have thought of himself as a dopey kid."

To entertain themselves, Dweezil and Meyer formed a band called Grüen (named in tribute to rock photographer Bob Gruen), with over-the-top comedy songs like "Porno Queen," "We're Studs," and "Too Young to Fuck but Not Too Young to Suck." They recorded many of the songs, with musical contributions from Donovan Leitch, Scott Thunes (the bassist in Frank Zappa's band), a drum machine, and River Phoenix.

The music was raunchy, goofy, and sloppy. Listening to the demos in his car, over two decades later, Meyer commented, "You have to start together so you can fall apart." River mostly contributed backing vocals and handclaps, although he may have played some guitar on "Rock Out with Your Cock Out." He's definitely audible on that song doing high-pitched "whoo-ooh-hooh-hooh" backing vocals. "You can tell there's a guest vocalist—we actually sound remotely in key," Meyer said.

"There was a no-holds-barred vibe at the Zappa compound, but it was weird, because Dweezil's parents were around constantly," Meyer said. "They just chose to give a shit about different things than your parents did." Gail Zappa didn't mind if you said "fuck"—but she'd hammer you for having an uninformed opinion. "It was a very creative and intellectual place to be, especially for a young person when a lot of adults didn't take you seriously. River stumbled into this alternative universe for a few months—and then he got a movie, went on location, and disappeared."

ECHO #4: *RUNNING ON EMPTY*

Running on Empty *is the story of two sixties radicals (Judd Hirsch and Christine Lahti) who have been on the lam from the FBI since 1971, when they blew up a napalm laboratory (and accidentally blinded a janitor). Whenever the law gets close, they uproot themselves and their two sons, including seventeen-year-old Danny (played by River). But now Danny, an extremely gifted pianist, wants to go to Juilliard—which would mean declaring his true identity and not being able to see his family anymore, lest he lead the feds to them.*

River bristled when people compared Running on Empty *and his own life: "People think the Popes are like my family, but they aren't. My parents were never on the run . . . My parents would sympathize with the Popes, but they are pacifists." But the parallels extended beyond two families that kept changing their names: both the Popes and the Phoenixes were insular families, extremely devoted to each other and mistrustful of outsiders. While the Popes had battled the military-industrial complex, the Phoenixes were skeptical of American society in general. Both families had moved constantly: the Popes driven by the need to stay ahead of the law, the Phoenixes by the urge to change the world. At age seventeen, Danny Pope was finally asserting that he needed to live his own life away from the family; at age seventeen, River wasn't sure.*

"There's a connection there," River admitted when he was less defensive. "I think that's maybe why the Running *script appealed to me from the start."*

93

RUNNING INTO THE SUN
BUT I'M RUNNING BEHIND

The director of *Running on Empty* was the legendary Sidney Lumet, famous for *Dog Day Afternoon* and *Network,* among many other classics; he had the cast learn the script as if it were a play, and led rehearsals for two weeks before he started shooting. Lumet compared River to Henry Fonda, whom he directed in 1957's *12 Angry Men,* for the honesty of their performances. "He's never studied formally, but boy, does he know how to reach inside himself," Lumet said of his young star. "So long as River follows his instincts, takes stuff he believes in, there'll be no stopping him. I first saw him in *Stand by Me* and there was such an extraordinary purity about him. Then he did *Mosquito Coast* and you could feel the growth of his understated power. There were a couple of films he could have done without: *Little Nikita* and *Jimmy Reardon.* Terrible scripts. But he didn't have the choice then that he has now. He still has a long way to go. He has to make the transition from kid actor to grownup, but he has such intelligence and such a good heart, I don't have any doubt he'll do it."

Playing a musical prodigy, River practiced on the piano for six months before shooting. While he wasn't able to get up to concert-pianist proficiency, his "pianomanship" (as Lumet put it) got good enough that he could synchronize his fingers with the music on the soundtrack (actually played by Gar Berke).

In the middle of shooting one scene, River stopped and complained, "This feels fake to me." From another actor, it might have been a prima donna move, but coming from River, it was a genuine concern. Lumet, who didn't coddle actors, agreed with River that his character's motivations were sketchy

and cut the scene. "River doesn't have a false bone in his body," Lumet testi-
fied. "He can't utter a false line."

The script by Naomi Foner explored the emotional territory that *Little
Nikita* gestured in the direction of: a son's conflicted response to his parents'
legacy. At the time of the movie, Foner had two grade-school children, who
grew up to be the well-known actors Maggie and Jake Gyllenhaal. She was
fond of River, but astonished by the gaps in his knowledge. When his character railed against his father for becoming the authoritarian figure he claimed
to despise, he asked, "Who do you think you are, General Patton?" River,
who had never heard of the famous World War II commander, had to stop
the scene to ask, "Who's General Patton?"

Foner concluded that education had not been a priority for the Phoenixes.
"He could read and write, and he had an appetite for it," Foner said, "but he
had no deep roots into any kind of sense of history or literature." For River's
birthday, Foner gave him an assortment of classic novels.

On the set, River was an advocate for veganism and healthful eating,
even lecturing Christine Lahti, who played his mother, for drinking a Diet
Coke. Lahti (then thirty-six, and most famous for her Oscar-nominated performance in *Swing Shift*) found herself wrestling with competing biological
urges toward River, a beautiful creature with one foot in boyhood and the
other in manhood—did she want to mother him or seduce him?

The latter option was a passing fancy for a variety of reasons—to start,
River didn't need another Jocasta figure in his life. Also, Martha Plimpton
was on the set, playing River's love interest for the second time in three years.
The intensity of their relationship only grew: one day, during a shoot at a
high school, producer Griffin Dunne went looking for the couple and spotted
them by an athletic field. "As I got closer," he said, "I could see by their silhou-
ettes that they were having a really heated conversation. And I just watched in
the distance for a moment. They were both gesturing really strongly at each
other. And all of a sudden, they embraced with such passion, such love like
they were never going to see each other again." Dunne couldn't tell if they
were rehearsing a scene or really arguing.

95

Foner witnessed a happier scene between the couple, when River couldn't physically contain his joy as they walked down a New York City sidewalk. "He was leaping and jumping, sort of like a young deer," Foner said, recalling how River would twist his body in midair. "He would hail taxis, leaping like Baryshnikov, and Martha would say, 'That taxi's taken, River. See, the light's off.' He didn't care. He danced down the street."

38

EXT. PHILLIPS HOUSE

Danny Pope has been falling for Lorna Phillips, the daughter of the music teacher at his latest high school, but he keeps dodging her questions about his past and his future. The emotional turning point of Running on Empty *comes when he climbs into her bedroom late at night and leads her outside.*

She sits on the ground, wearing a blue nightgown and his sneakers, as he tells the truth to somebody outside his family for the first time in his life. At first, he speaks haltingly, unable to look her in the eye, and then the words come tumbling out of him, his face showing fear and relief. "I don't know what I'm doing and I love you," he concludes.

Both of them burst into tears and he buries his head on her chest. It's an astonishingly intimate moment, both between Danny and Lorna, and between River and Martha.

In the following scene, wrapped in each other's arms in a postcoital embrace, she says to him, "You have a lot of secrets? Now you have one more." A light sparks in his eyes, as if it's the truest thing anybody has ever said to him.

PART FOUR

"WE'RE ALL WORTH MILLIONS OF PLANETS AND STARS AND GALAXIES AND UNIVERSES"

MAKING PLANS FOR RIVER

John Phoenix wanted his family to quit Hollywood—both the town and the business. To his thinking, the family had some money in the bank, but they had lost sight of their original intentions: not just to pursue fame, but to bend Hollywood toward their belief system, rather than getting sucked into a vortex of commercial values.

"My father is worried that we could be ruined by this business," River said. "It's got a lot of pitfalls and temptations, and he doesn't want us to become materialistic and lose all the values we were brought up believing in . . . he's pleased we're doing well, but in a way he's almost reached a point where he could just drop out again like he did in the sixties and move to a farm and get close to the earth."

After some heated family discussions, Team Phoenix arrived at a decision. River would not quit acting—he loved it too much—but the family would leave California, and rely on Iris Burton to handle day-to-day contact with producers and studios. Hollywood stars have often left town in favor of a ranch (Harrison Ford relocating to Wyoming, for example)—River was younger and not as well established as other performers who chose that path, but he could always get on a plane to take care of (show) business.

Although John would have preferred that the family return to Mexico or Venezuela, they looked for a warm-weather American college town with a thriving music scene. They considered Austin, Texas, but settled on Gainesville, Florida, once home to Tom Petty and the Heartbreakers and still the host city of the University of Florida.

They also decided that it was time for River to put forward his beliefs more forcefully, using interviews as opportunities to change the world. Soon he was holding forth to journalists: "I'm against the nuclear arms race and apartheid in South Africa and cruelty to animals, which means that I'm a vegetarian. Diet is a good place to start making a change, because it's something I can do. I can't on my own change the regime in South Africa or teach the Palestinians to live with the Israelis, but I can start with me. I have strong opinions and people disagree with me, but there are those who agree, too."

Sometimes simplistic but always sincere, River quickly became a poster boy for environmentalism and animal rights, the sort of person prone to describing dolphins as "the gods of the oceans."

100

FOOD FOR LIFE

River Phoenix walks through the Gainesville campus of the University of Florida, carrying a blank check in his pocket. Seventeen years old, he's the right age to be a freshman here. "I like to pretend," he confesses. He is actually a movie star looking for a musician: surely, in a student population of thirty thousand, there must be a bassist who will jam with him in his garage.

Then, amid an ocean of southern preppies, he spots a candidate: a skinny white kid with his hair in dreadlocks. He's not carrying an instrument, or wearing a shirt that says BASS PLAYERS DO IT DEEPER. But River thinks he might be a fellow traveler. He can't quite work up his nerve to talk to him. Maybe tomorrow.

The blank check in River's pocket was signed by his mother—although the *bank account it draws on is filled with money he earned. River wants to spend $650 on a twelve-string guitar, but now that he has the ability to buy it, he's having second thoughts. Maybe, he thinks, he doesn't deserve it until he's completely proficient with the guitar he already has.*

In the center of the campus, two Hare Krishnas have set up a folding table, which is laden with large containers of vegan food. The pair—a man and a woman—are wearing bright orange robes, and have daubed their faces with white clay. River politely accepts a plate of free food and chats with the Hare Krishnas about veganism. When they ask his name, he just says, "River."

The man with the shaved head is startled. "River Phoenix?*" he exclaims.*

Later, his love of music triumphing over his self-doubt, River returns home without a blank check and with a twelve-string guitar.

CAMP PHOENIX

The Phoenix family moved to Gainesville in August 1987, and soon found a home in nearby Micanopy, a sleepy town (population six hundred) that had become a hippie encampment. They bought a seventeen-acre ranch, which the locals nicknamed "Camp Phoenix," and decorated the three-story house in the style of a sixties commune: hanging tapestries, environmental posters, and clotheslines instead of a dryer. There was a large deck, a swimming pool, and a second building, called either a guesthouse or a service shop, that River earmarked as a place where he could play music.

Arlyn hired another family tutor: Dirk Drake, a sharp guy in his twenties with long blond hair that was congealing into dreadlocks. As classwork, the Phoenix children started writing letters to world leaders about the environment and human rights. Drake assigned River *The Catcher in the Rye* and, seeing how he was struggling to read it, suspected (like Ed Squires before him) that River might be dyslexic.

Drake said, "River had his own way of writing and structuring paragraphs. He could understand the rules of grammar, but when he wrote things down, it was all very free form, like e. e. cummings."

Camp Phoenix had plenty of trees, especially oaks, which were covered with Spanish moss and lichen. A nearby lake was really more of a swamp, home to gators and countless frogs. To buy the property, River (or more precisely, his company, Phoenix in Flight Productions), took a mortgage of $123,950—which got paid off within a year.

SONGS IN THE ATTIC

"Gainesville is your basic college town," journalist Michael Angeli wrote. "Some disenchanted conquistador tossed his copy of *Summa Theologica* into a swamp and the University of Florida bubbled up from the cattails, Burt Reynolds and all."

For the first time in his life, River felt at home. He wandered around Gainesville, happy to be part of the crowd. He reveled in his anonymity, growing his hair long and letting it fall over his face whenever he went out. He explored the town, meeting people, skateboarding in parking lots, and checking out the bars and record stores.

"He came in one day and started talking about XTC," said Hyde & Zeke Records proprietor Charlie Scales. XTC, the British new-wave and psychedelic-pop band led by Andy Partridge, was never a force on the American charts, but had recently gotten a lot of attention for their angrily atheistic single "Dear God"; they had become River's favorite band. (River's family had become less devout and his faith had become less dogmatic since the days when he memorized the Bible in Spanish. He still prayed regularly, but conceded, "I don't know if the superior being is in the form of a man, woman, or jellyfish.")

Scales didn't recognize River, but he liked his passion for XTC, and even let him borrow a rare XTC bootleg. "I'm usually wary of lending people albums," he said, "but he loved the band so much, I let him have it. A week later, he came back with the album and thanked me."

River had been writing songs with titles like "Aleka Doozy Encircles" and "Dublin in Mardi Gras." One composition, "Mother Earth," conflated his love of Arlyn and Gaia, with lyrics like "Don't bite the hand that heals your wounds and keeps you fed / Mother dear was always there to tuck us into bed . . . / Still betraying Mother Earth." When he played it for visiting journalist Blanche McCrary Boyd, she nominated it as River's "worst song, but perhaps his most touching."

River needed a band. He put up signs around campus: NEEDED: BASS GUITARIST WITH YOUNG BLOOD WHO'S INTO PROGRESSIVE ROCK 'N' ROLL, JAZZ. FOR A DEMO.

The first musician to join him was actually a friend of the family: his aunt Merle introduced him to a drummer named Josh Greenbaum, whose father, Kenny, had grown up in the Bronx with Arlyn. Greenbaum was living in Fort Lauderdale, delivering pizzas and playing with a band called Toy Soldier. (They would evolve into Saigon Kick, and in 1992 score a number twelve single with "Love Is on the Way" and a gold record for their album *The Lizard*.) Greenbaum visited River for a couple of weeks and ended up moving in with the Phoenix family. "It wasn't just the music, it was the whole thing," Greenbaum said. "I met the whole family and I loved them from the start. They were like the family I'd never had. I'd never known such warmth and love."

Greenbaum and River spent hours sitting on the trampoline in the backyard, figuring out songs. They ate at the Falafel King and worked out together at the Gainesville Health and Fitness Club. Going to the gym was novel for River. "I've got more of a musician's build than a gymnast's," he said. "I've got really skinny arms." He reveled in the results of his workouts, feeling muscles develop in his body that he'd never had before. "Then there was this flu virus going around town and I got it!" he said. "That was the end of the health kick."

At night, the duo went to parties, sussing out Gainesville's music scene together. "We were like soul brothers," Greenbaum said.

After a few months, Greenbaum's dad, Kenny, called to check on him. Arlyn chatted with Kenny on the phone, catching up on life after the Bronx, and then suggested that he come live with them as well. "I've been doing that all my life," Kenny said. "Just give me five minutes to throw everything in my van and I'm off." The Phoenix family was on its way to building another commune.

Kim Buie, back in Los Angeles, suggested a musician she thought might be simpatico with River: Josh McKay, a twenty-two-year-old Texas guitarist with his own band, Joshimisho. River sent him a cassette of some of the songs he had been working out with Greenbaum, and McKay was pleasantly surprised. "I thought these tight jam-box garage tapes were really nice," McKay said. "This was about music and not just some movie star's hobby trip." He started figuring out bass parts for the songs—and when he and River spoke on the phone, they discovered they were both vegetarians and believers in animal rights. McKay's friends advised him not to join a band with a movie star, but he decided to take a chance, reasoning, "This is a very unusual thing to fall down from nowhere." He took his final exams in anthropology, flew to Gainesville, and moved in with the Phoenix family.

The next recruit: Tim Hankins, a classically trained viola player and a member of the Gainesville Chamber Orchestra. Seventeen years old, he had never played rock 'n' roll before (not that violas were in heavy demand from rock bands). Rounding out the group on harmony vocals: River's sister and longtime musical partner Rain, who had recently reverted from Rainbow to her birth name.

The band practiced for hours in the loft of the guesthouse, a space that River dubbed "Aleka's Attic"; soon that also became the name of the band.

River eventually developed a mythology around the name for anybody who asked: "Aleka is a poet-philosopher. The Attic is a meeting place where he lives and he has a secret society. They come and visit him and read his works. He then dies and they meet irregularly and continue the readings of his works, and from that learn their own, and become filled with this new passion for life. And they express it through music and form a band. We've put it in a fairy-tale setting."

Aleka was an obvious stand-in for River, who yearned to inspire the world. But disturbingly, even in this pastel-colored idyll, he could only achieve that dream by dying.

ORANGES AND LEMONS

Arlyn Phoenix changed her name for the last time, dubbing herself Heart Phoenix. John, meanwhile, worked on his organic garden and grew ever more fearful of the outside world. When a journalist visited the Phoenixes, she noticed that on the back of a happy family picture, John had written this list:

> *airplane crash*
> *radon leak—gas*
> *whites hacked to death*
> *garbage leak*

Those were the stories that had grabbed his attention in the morning paper.

When John got drunk—on port, vodka, or beer—he would rant against Hollywood, calling it "the great Babylon." He lectured, "They care for money and nothing else. It's an evil, bad place." He felt betrayed by how River had sided with his mother and stayed in show business.

John explained, "Heart thought she could look after River, protect all his interests within the system. But our original idea was for him to make enough movies to be financially secure—milk the system, if you want—then stop. We had made enough money to keep all those closest to us, in-laws, outlaws, friends, environment groups, whatever, and I wanted us all to get out. Still, the pressure was there to keep going."

River struggled to make peace between his mother and father, to reconcile his show-business desires with his religious upbringing—or as he put it, "The Devil is so pretty and tempting." River confessed, "I go back and forth about success and wealth."

When Martha Plimpton came to visit River, she found a household filled with tension and her boyfriend at the conflicted center. "We had five million talks about his compulsive personality and his guilt and fear over not being able to save his father," Plimpton said. "River and his father were *always* having breakthrough conversations where River would tell his father his feelings about alcohol, about their roles. But the next day, nothing would change. River would then say to me, 'Well, it's not *that* serious, it's not *that* bad.'"

River was drinking more himself—he favored pints of Guinness at a local bar, but sometimes would imbibe with John, finding a tenuous bond. Tutor Dirk Drake said, "You have to remember that River had never seen alcohol when he was growing up. When he finally started, he'd drink all-out. It wasn't like you or I would drink. He often became a fall-down drunk." On one of their nights out, River was arrested for public drinking.

River was also partial to cocaine and hallucinogenic mushrooms—and there was always plenty of "Gainesville Green" marijuana in the house. "He really liked getting drunk and high," Plimpton said. "But he didn't have a gauge for when to stop."

44

A NIGHT IN THE LIFE

Meanwhile, Island Pictures was having financial difficulties; Chris Blackwell shut down his film division. Fox bought the distribution rights to *Jimmy Reardon,* wanting to capitalize on River's growing fame—and then tried to recut it into a teen-exploitation comedy. The score by Elmer Bernstein was ditched in favor of one by Bill Conti, bolstered by period rock 'n' roll. Richert's narration was rerecorded by River. Some crucial cuts were made, including a closing-credits song by River, "Heart to Get."

Arlyn and John were worried about the line where Ann Magnuson tells River, "Jimmy, I want to fuck you," and how it would play with River's young fans. They threatened to have River not promote the film. Richert wouldn't remove the line entirely—it had too much personal import from the parallel incident in his own life—but agreed to silence the offending "fuck."

The original cut of *Jimmy Reardon* wasn't flawless, but the movie hit its target: a rueful story about a teen who discovers that his hustles have limits and that he's more like his father than he knew. The melancholy tone that made it work is exactly what Fox tried to stamp out with its changes—but the result was neither chalk nor vegan cheese.

A furious Richert railed against the studio execs, calling the president of Island Pictures a traitor and the Fox marketing department knaves. Somehow, this did not persuade them to change their minds: the recut, retitled *A Night in the Life of Jimmy Reardon* was dumped into the marketplace with little fanfare in March 1988. River had three movies released in 1988: *A Night in the Life of Jimmy Reardon* was followed by *Little Nikita* and *Running on Empty*. While none of them were hits, *Running on Empty* was well reviewed: Roger Ebert called it "a painful, enormously moving drama," while

107

Janet Maslin in the *New York Times* said River played the role of Danny "outstandingly well."

Of the three films, *A Night in the Life of Jimmy Reardon,* surprisingly, did the most box office. *Time Out* magazine captured the mixed critical opinion on the movie: "While the film has the charm of a rose-tinted retrospect and is often very funny, the pacing is wrong (it seems much longer than it is) and the sex scenes fail to convince."

River had always been nervous about the character of Jimmy Reardon and his caddish ways; the final cut of the movie had the glib tone he had feared. "I'm not sure I was even the right person for the role," he mused. "The whole plot revolves around the guy's sexual exploits that one night, and for it to work properly, I think you want to see somebody a little more masculine, like Tom Cruise. He'd have done it much better than me."

River's public comments on the movie progressed from "I chose the role because I wanted to play a complex character" to "It didn't turn out the way I thought it would" to "Let's not even think about that anymore, all right?"

WHY DID IT HAVE TO BE SNAKES?

River wandered through the house of his friend Anthony Campanaro, high on mushrooms, looking for the room with the best acoustics. For the first time, Aleka's Attic was going to play for an audience, and even for a small group of friends, River wanted everything to be perfect. He chose the open-air veranda, and the band set up for a late-night session, fortified with beer and cigarettes. Pleasantly buzzed, the band worked their way through River's catalog of songs, and improvised around loose grooves. Their music swirled into the humid Florida night.

After the performance, River was eager to start playing in front of larger crowds. But first he had to go make a major motion picture.

Indiana Jones and the Last Crusade was the third film starring Harrison Ford as a swashbuckling archaeologist, in a series that was responsible for the Tomb Raider video games, the advent of the PG-13 rating, and the mainstreaming of whips. With producer George Lucas and director Steven Spielberg returning to the franchise, it was also as close as one could come to a guaranteed hit—no small thing, given the tepid box office of River's recent films.

Although it was River's second movie with Harrison Ford, after *The Mosquito Coast*, they wouldn't be on-screen together: in an eleven-minute prologue to the movie, River played the teenage Indiana Jones in a Boy Scout uniform. In the hills of 1912 Utah, on an expedition with his Scout troop, Indy comes upon a gang of looters who have discovered an artifact called the Cross of Coronado—he grabs it and runs, hoping to put it in a museum. In a chase that goes from horseback to a circus train, we learn how Indiana Jones acquired his hat, his whip, his fear of snakes, and even the scar on his chin. (The only thing it doesn't seem to explain is River's anachronistic haircut flopping into his eyes.) It was a charming sequence, if a bit formulaic, and River acquitted himself well—although he wasn't a brawny guy, he seemed to be establishing his action-hero bona fides for some future franchise.

Although Ford didn't appear with River, he nevertheless spent a week on the set in Colorado, to give highly individualized instruction on how to play Indiana Jones. "Harrison came out and he helped me a lot with motivation," River said. "You know, where does all this come from, and what propels him, and what makes him really cool when he has to jump off a horse onto a train?" Like Ford, River did most of his own action sequences. "It would have been lying to have someone else do the stunts," he said.

River attempted to interpret Ford rather than mimic him, and was careful to say he wasn't interested in taking over the role of Indiana Jones. While this may have been politic, it had the advantage of being true. River's prologue ultimately inspired the big-budget Lucasfilm TV show *The Young Indi-*

109

ana Jones Chronicles, but when approached about appearing on the program, River declined.

As expected, *The Last Crusade* ended up being a big hit (the second-most-popular film of 1989, behind Tim Burton's *Batman*), receiving generally positive notices as well-made escapism. River wasn't hyped in the trailers or the publicity. Many reviews, focusing on the dynamic between Ford and Sean Connery (who played Indiana Jones's father), didn't even mention River.

46 DOWN WITH THE IONE

When River came to Hollywood on business, he would often stay with Ione Skye and her family. "It was a comfortable atmosphere for him," she said. "My mom had that hippie quality and was very welcoming." Sometimes River and Skye would share a bed, talking late into the night. "He was so kind and loving," she remembered. "He was almost like a saint—people really felt he was this golden person, but he had this anger inside him. There was a wild aspect to him."

One night, River did something unsaintly but totally human: he came on to Skye, even though she was in a long-term relationship with Anthony Kiedis. "I was kind of depressed," Skye said, "because Anthony was a terrible drug addict, and at the time, River and I both weren't doing hard drugs like that. I stopped it, which is not like me. I was very precocious and very free. Any other night, I would have, but I was just in a weird mood." Kiedis wasn't around, probably because he was out scoring drugs, Skye said.

And River? "I felt maybe we were too similar," Skye said. "We were both Virgos. He was a very free person."

OUR BAND COULD BE YOUR LIFE

Rock Promotion 101: Try to break even. For their debut nonveranda show, in December 1988, Aleka's Attic rented a Gainesville theater for sixty-five dollars and charged the first sixty-five members of the audience one dollar each; everyone else got in free. The audience, mostly friends and family, gave them a standing ovation, although there were some mixed reviews. "I thought they were a little amateurish," remembered Charlie Scales of Hyde & Zeke Records. "The songwriting had not yet developed, and after the first couple of songs, which were pretty new and novel, it kind of stalled."

Nevertheless, after the new year, the band piled into River's motor home for a short East Coast tour. Although River didn't want his name used to promote the band, word got out, and at some shows, the audience consisted of hundreds of young female fans, screaming at the top of their lungs and flinging underwear at the stage. While many of the twentieth century's greatest musical acts (Frank Sinatra, Elvis Presley, the Beatles) started by inspiring teenage girls to creative heights of hysteria, River was embarrassed and started performing with his back to the audience. In New York, when the band played CBGB's, mecca of punk bands and unhygienic bathrooms, River had to hire security guards to keep the situation under control.

In New York, Aleka's Attic also played a "Rock Against Fur" benefit for the animal-rights group PETA, on a bill with the B–52's, the Indigo Girls, Lene Lovich, and Jane Wiedlin of the Go-Go's. For this cause, River allowed his name to be on the poster. Martha Plimpton introduced the band, proclaiming, "Three years ago, a friend said to me, 'You can change the world.'"

River hit the stage wearing eyeglasses, blue jeans, an unbuttoned plaid shirt over a T-shirt, and a forest-toned plaid jacket. The shirts looked unwashed—

life on the road—and his face had some spots and some wispy stubble, but the overall image was a hunky TA leading a discussion of literary theory. The band played half a dozen songs, with River fervently singing of a "mythical place where there's no worrying."

At their shows, Aleka's Attic sold a four-song cassette sampler of their music. "Goldmine," which began with the lyrics "Working the goldmine / Pushing a pencil around," was the most blatantly XTC-influenced, with River even imitating the vocal mannerisms of Andy Partridge. "Too Many Colors" had some twitchy guitar work and the lyric "Somehow we get strapped into unlikely straitjackets," but mostly just chugged along pleasantly. "Blue Period" was slower and more soulful, while "Across the Way" was the best track on the tape. Not only did it have some clever turns of phrase ("this myth won't wash away" and "no rocks, no tools, no stepping stones"—a nice twist on the old Monkees lyric "I'm not your steppin' stone"), it showed off the band's strengths, especially the viola of Tim Hankins and the harmonies of Rain. When PETA released a compilation album two years later, with tracks from k.d. lang, Howard Jones, and the Pretenders, River wisely picked "Across the Way" to represent Aleka's Attic. On the whole, the music was a credible effort by an eighteen-year-old leading a band for the first time—but River's fame meant that, for good or ill, that wasn't how Aleka's Attic would be judged.

The band traveled in the motor home and slept in cheap motels. After-show parties attracted a crowd that enjoyed cocaine and weed—to the consternation of violist Tim Hankins, who abstained. Early one morning, after a late night of festivities, the phone rang in River's room: it was Iris Burton, informing him that he had just received an Academy Award nomination, as best supporting actor, for his *Running on Empty* performance.

"Oh, my baby!" Burton exclaimed.

River grunted his agreement, rolled over, and went back to sleep. That night, Aleka's Attic played a show at the Philadelphia club JC Dobbs. Killing time between sound check and the show, River watched some TV—and a story came on about the Oscar nominations, featuring him. "Holy shit!" he said. "Did Iris call me this morning?"

ROLLING ON THE RIVER

River attended the Oscars with his girlfriend, Plimpton, and his mother, Heart. Plimpton sported a blond crew cut on the red carpet, having shaved her head for her role as a cancer patient in *Silence Like Glass*. Uncomfortable with the spotlight, River spoke modestly of his nomination: "It's an official bonus to the satisfaction that I had already felt after seeing the movie."

The other nominees were Alec Guinness as an imprisoned debtor in the Dickens adaptation *Little Dorrit*, Kevin Kline as a deranged hit man in the farce *A Fish Called Wanda*, Martin Landau as an auto-company financier in *Tucker: The Man and His Dream*, and Dean Stockwell as a Mafia boss in the comedy *Married to the Mob*. It was an experienced group—on average, fully thirty-nine years older than River. At the lunch for Oscar nominees a week before the awards ceremony, River made a point of meeting Kline: they were slated to work together later that year, in a film called *I Love You to Death*.

Infamously, the 1989 Oscars had no host—but began with a production number that included Rob Lowe and an actress dressed as Snow White duetting on Creedence Clearwater Revival's "Proud Mary." When the time came for the best-supporting-actor category, Sean Connery and Michael Caine (the winners the previous two years) clowned around with Roger Moore before reading the nominees. While they did, River awkwardly posed for the camera with one finger resting on his cheek—but when Kline was named the winner, he cheered with wild enthusiasm for his new costar, even pumping his fist.

River wanted to run over and hug Kline, but his mother stopped him.

113

WE ARE ALL MADE OF STARS

River was relieved to return to Florida, and Aleka's Attic; the band got a regular gig at a small punk club called the Hardback. But his Gainesville anonymity was slipping away, due to the Oscars and an article in the local paper. Another Gainesville band, called the Smegmas, decided to torment River by posting copies of one of his early pinups all over town. River was wounded and confused, but instinctively tried to play peacemaker: Aleka's Attic opened a gig for the Smegmas, and although the show was attended by hundreds of teen fans of River, he made sure the Smegmas got all the money.

He tried to brush off people who spotted him, insisting that his name was actually Rio. That wasn't sufficient at one party, when a gang of racist skinheads tried to pick a fight with him.

River smiled sweetly at his tormentors and told them, "If you want to kick my ass, go ahead. Just explain to me why you're doing it."

After a confused pause, one of the skinheads said, "Ah, you wouldn't be worth it."

"We're all worth it, man," River said with a beatific smile. "We're all worth millions of planets and stars and galaxies and universes."

114

Previous page:
River Phoenix in 1987,
at age sixteen.

The Phoenix children
in a backyard pyramid
in 1985, with River
and Rain serving as the
foundation.

The Phoenix family in 1986
(from left): Summer, River,
Rain (aka Rainbow), John,
Liberty, Joaquin (aka Leaf),
and Arlyn (aka Heart).

The young stars of *Stand by Me* in 1985 (from left):
Jerry O'Connell, River, Wil Wheaton, and Corey Feldman.

Martha Plimpton with River in 1987: "He was just a boy, a very good-hearted boy who was very fucked up and had no idea how to implement his good intentions."

Making *Running on Empty* in 1987 with director Sidney Lumet.

Left: River in 1986, in Belize, on the set of *The Mosquito Coast.*

Walking the red carpet at the 1989 Academy Awards with Martha Plimpton (who had recently shaved her head for a role).

On the set of *Dogfight* with Lili Taylor in 1990. "He was such a hippie, and here he was playing this marine," Taylor said of River. "It actually caused him a lot of discomfort."

River in the arms of Keanu Reeves in *My Own Private Idaho*
(filmed in 1990), simulating a narcoleptic episode and reenacting the Pietà.

River in 1991: onstage at Wetlands in New York City,
playing guitar with Aleka's Attic.

River in *The Thing Called Love* with Samantha Mathis. They met during the 1992 shoot;
a year later, she was with him at the Viper Room when he died.

Following page: River in 1991.

50 ALONE WE ELOPE

There were rumors that River and Martha Plimpton had gotten secretly married before the Oscars—Plimpton batted them away, saying that she and River had engaged in a spiritual ceremony that celebrated their love, but were not wed. "It was kind of a private thing," she declared.

In fact, their relationship was crumbling, mostly because of River's determination to get drunk and high. Plimpton implored him to get clean, to no effect. Exhausted from the emotional turmoil after three years together, she broke up with him shortly after the Oscars. "When we split up, a lot of it was that I had learned that screaming, fighting, and begging wasn't going to change him," she said. "He had to change himself, and he didn't want to yet."

115

51 YOUNG HOLLYWOOD 1989

After some commercial work, Leonardo DiCaprio got his first real acting job in 1989: a guest appearance on the syndicated TV series *The New Lassie* (starring a fifth-generation Lassie as the lead collie). The same year, Ethan Hawke had his breakthrough role in *Dead Poets Society,* the movie starring Robin Williams as an inspirational English teacher. Before getting cast in the movie, Hawke had enrolled in the theater program at Carnegie Mellon, but lasted only one semester. He got thrown out of his voice class on the first day after arguing with his teacher. Hawke also balked at wearing tights, reasoning that Jack Nicholson wouldn't do it.

Wil Wheaton was still working on *Star Trek: The Next Generation,* but unhappily—his character (Ensign Wesley Crusher) had become unpopular among *Trek* fans, with some of them sporting buttons at conventions reading "Put Wesley in the Airlock." Corey Feldman starred in his third movie with Corey Haim, a body-switch comedy that also starred Meredith Salenger (River's love interest in *Jimmy Reardon*). Feldman was also developing some serious drug habits; the following year, he was arrested for heroin possession. ("It makes you realize drugs aren't just done by bad guys and sleazebags," River said sympathetically. "It's a universal disease.")

Brad Pitt was starting to get work in movies, albeit not good ones. He appeared in the Patrick Dempsey/Helen Slater rom-com turkey *Happy Together,* about a guy and a girl who are accidentally assigned to each other as college roommates and find true love. He also had a starring role as a high school basketball star in the low-rent slasher film *Cutting Class* (alongside Donovan Leitch, Martin Mull, and Roddy McDowall.)

Ron Howard directed the ensemble comedy-drama *Parenthood,* with an ensemble cast that included Steve Martin, Martha Plimpton, Leaf Phoenix, and Keanu Reeves. Also released that year was the time-travel comedy that fixed Reeves's public image for many years as a dim-witted stoner savant: *Bill & Ted's Excellent Adventure.*

Ione Skye starred in *Say Anything . . . ,* the first movie directed by Cameron Crowe. America collectively developed a crush on her as huge as that of John Cusack's character, who stood outside her house with a boom box playing Peter Gabriel's "In Your Eyes." She almost ended up as the topless cover model for the Red Hot Chili Peppers album *Mother's Milk;* even without her, it became the band's first gold record. It was also their first album with nineteen-year-old guitarist John Frusciante. He replaced his hero, founding member Hillel Slovak, who had died of an overdose.

At the end of the year, Skye and Kiedis broke up. He had gotten sober, but they hadn't found a new dynamic for their relationship, he said: "I was still the jealous, raging, controlling, selfish, bratty kid that I had been, only drug-free." They fought a lot, until just before Christmas, Kiedis told Skye, "Take your stuff and get the hell out of here." She did—and then a few days later, Kiedis found himself wondering why she hadn't come back.

The cult movie of 1989 was *Heathers,* the dark comedy in which the heroes kill popular classmates at their high school and stage the deaths as suicides. It was a star-making film for actors Christian Slater and Winona Ryder. Johnny Depp started dating Ryder, and soon sported a "Winona Forever" tattoo (which he redacted to "Wino Forever" when they broke up).

At age twenty-six, Depp had become a major teen idol. When director John Waters, famous for *Hairspray* and beloved fringe films such as *Pink Flamingos,* was looking for an actor to star in his new musical, *Cry-Baby,* "I went out and bought about twenty teen magazines, which was really mortifying," the not-easily-embarrassed Waters said. "I found myself hiding them under my jacket. When I got home and started looking through them, Johnny Depp was on the cover of almost every one of them."

Sending up his own stardom, Depp played a fifties teen-idol rocker, in a cast that also included Ricki Lake, Traci Lords (in one of her first non-pornographic roles), and as a crossing guard, famous heiress and kidnapping victim Patty Hearst.

Depp was still under contract to *21 Jump Street,* although he chafed at the series and its authoritarian premise of undercover cops in high school. Flying back to Vancouver, where it filmed, he was unhappy to be leaving Ryder, unhappy to be taping more episodes of "that show." Sitting in the comfort of the first-class cabin, he wanted to turn everything upside down, and he had a thought in his head he couldn't get rid of, something he felt he needed to say.

"I fuck animals!" he announced to his fellow first-class passengers.

Heads jerked in his direction. The Vancouver-bound travelers took in the source of this provocation and then coolly swiveled forward again, trying to ignore him. Except for the man at Depp's elbow, an accountant. He considered Depp, and then broke the silence with a question.

"What kind?"

WHIP IT

Not long after the Oscars, River had to leave Florida again for another movie. His departures were beginning to rankle the other members of Aleka's Attic. "We'd practice for six or eight months, and we'd kind of reach this apex, and then he would go off for three months and do a film," violist Tim Hankins said later. "It was like *coitus interruptus,* you know?"

While River's stardom brought the group a lot of attention, his absences had a way of killing the band's momentum—and underscored that no matter what he said, his real first priority was movies. Greenbaum said, "We were all kind of at the mercy of his career."

I Love You to Death was directed by Lawrence Kasdan, famous for directing *Body Heat* and *The Big Chill* (and writing *Raiders of the Lost Ark* and *The Empire Strikes Back*). He hired River after a phone call, never having met him, and added him to an impressive ensemble cast, including Kevin Kline, Tracey Ullman, Joan Plowright, William Hurt, and Keanu Reeves. The plot, loosely based on a true story, is that Rosalie Boca (Ullman) finds out her husband, Joey (Kline), is cheating on her. She resolves to kill him, but he seems impervious to her efforts, surviving poison, bullets, and a car rigged to explode. It's the only out-and-out comedy River made in his career.

River played Devo Nod, a chef with New Age beliefs working at Joey's pizza parlor. Infatuated with Rosalie, he helps her in her efforts to knock off her husband, even hiring a pair of inept, stoned hit men (Hurt and Reeves). The film doesn't really work, partially because Kline gives one of his broadest, hammiest performances. But it's fun to see so many fine actors goofing around, and River serves ably in a middleman role. As usual, River absorbed all the knowledge he could from the older performers, particularly the British chameleon Ullman. "Tracey and I clicked especially well," he said. "We'd just mouth off, get clever on each other, and play word games."

He formed an even closer bond with Reeves; they knew each other through the movie *Parenthood,* in which Reeves had appeared opposite Martha Plimpton and River's brother, Leaf. Reeves—who despite his Hawaiian name had grown up in Toronto, aspiring to be a hockey goalie—was River's elder by six years. River joked, "He's like my older brother, but shorter."

The production filmed exterior shots in Tacoma, Washington; River and Reeves did their best to locate the local nightlife. One evening, the daughter of a local coffee-shop owner was watching as a drunk River stumbled across the coffee shop's parking lot and then pissed on the back of her father's old Ford. Soon after, her father sold the vehicle, for $200. She let him know that he had made a big mistake: "You could have gotten ten times that much! All you had to do was write on that quarter panel, 'River Phoenix peed here.'"

The movie got worse reviews than River's late-night urination, and flopped at the box office. In the *Chicago Tribune,* Dave Kehr dismissed River's performance as "strangely timid."

Around this time, River explained his mature acting process, which required lengthy preparation: "You can't just wake up the next morning and *be* the character," he said. "I start off by stripping myself of who I am, by thinking more neutral. You *have* to neutralize yourself before you can become another character. I become nonopinionated, refusing to think from River's perspective, and then, slowly, I add characteristics and start thinking the way the character would. I fantasize about being the character, and I play mind games with myself until the transition takes place."

Stripping away his own identity meant that once River was deep inside a character, be it Jimmy Reardon or Devo Nod, he would often act like him offscreen and find it hard to switch back to being River Phoenix once the movie was over. After *I Love You to Death* wrapped, River confessed, "Devo is bouncing off the walls wherever I go and it's very hard to let myself out and open my eyes."

Not that he wanted to learn how—on the contrary. He cited Kasdan as

119

having given him the best acting advice he ever received. "He said that the best actors and actresses have at least half of themselves in the role," River said. "I'm still the type to have only one-eighth of myself in the role." He wanted to give more of himself, but he recognized the danger: "The point is to not lose yourself *completely*."

Veteran British actress Miriam Margolyes, who played Joey's mother, praised River. "He is a wonderful actor," she said. But she cautioned, "At the moment, he has no way of distancing himself from a part."

HOW DO YOU SAY GOOD NIGHT TO AN ANSWERING MACHINE?

120

On the last day of filming *I Love You to Death,* River left a rambling message on William Richert's answering machine, providing a glimpse at a teenager trying to find himself and lose himself simultaneously:

Hello, Bill. If you're sleeping, please, by all means, ignore this message. But in fact, if you are awake, then you'd better not ignore me . . . I had the most amazing day. It was just beautiful, the things I learned, through the pain and misunderstanding, and through being displaced, discombobulated. I come out on my last day of work as a triumphant failure. I stand here; need not I die nor I need drink, for I know that my soul will keep. And who's to say he or she is the one, for I to know from where it has begun? Doctor Bill . . . where am I coming from? Who cares? Do I need to know where they're coming from to get along with them? No, I accept them. But I come from a place that is so foreign, a place where no other eyes see . . . the stuff is so vague . . . in case. And did you know that? There is? And wait. Not. No. Sure. But maybe. That doesn't matter. All those words. All those broken phrases. They don't mean anything. But where was

the point? You have missed the point. But don't take it upon yourself. Don't carry
that weight. It's not your fault . . . I would say that it's safe to guess that people
simply don't understand.

SENSES WORKING OVERTIME

Back in Florida, River happily expunged Devo Nod from his system, cleared
his lungs of Hollywood smog, and resumed his bohemian life as an aspiring
musician. He had become a fixture on the Gainesville scene; when he walked
around town, approximately once per block a local hipster would greet him
with "Hey, Riv!"

When he went out for Mexican food, he would down the salsa straight
from the bowl. He also liked to eat at the vegan Bahn Thai restaurant; his
favorite menu selections, owner Pam Maneeratana said, were "number 89,
Tofu Yum-Woon-Sen, served at room temperature, and number 92, Gang-
Ped-Tofu, a Thai curry dish, and he loved the garlic tofu spread." River would
sit in a booth with his back to the entrance so nobody could spot him. He
continued to hang at the Hardback Café, drinking his Guinness. Soon Aleka's Attic had resumed their weekly gig there; River worked on drumming
up other gigs.

Over in Pensacola, Florida, Gus Brandt was working at a club called the
Nite Owl when the phone rang. It was River Phoenix, whom he had never
met, asking if he ever booked shows. Brandt allowed that he did, and Phoenix
explained that his band was called Aleka's Attic. "The nicest, most unassuming guy," Brandt said. "He sent me his tape himself."

Brandt listened to the tape and deemed it up to the standards of the Nite
Owl, so soon after, "The whole band rolled up in a yellow school bus." Brandt

remembered the show as a success, although the crowd didn't much look like River's scruffy band: "It was mostly teen girls, along with some music lovers and curious people."

Wanting to stay in Gainesville and play music, River started turning down movie work. He dropped out of *Coupe de Ville,* a period comedy about three sons driving a Cadillac convertible from Detroit to Florida for their father (Alan Arkin); Patrick Dempsey took his place as the youngest son. He was repeatedly approached to star in *A Kiss Before Dying,* a remake of the 1956 film noir. "They came back eight times to try to get me to do it," River said. "They kept coming back, I kept saying no, no, no, and they went up, up, up with the money." Ultimately Matt Dillon took the part.

Another regular act at the Hardback was the Mutley Chix, an all-girl band who had been playing in Gainesville (with personnel changes) since 1984, their music evolving from three-chord "humorous noise" into proggish modern rock on self-released albums like *Burn Your Bra.* On Halloween 1989, they debuted two new members, one of whom was saxophonist Suzanne "Suzy Q" Solgot. She had graduated from the University of Florida that spring with a B.A. in fine arts (photography) and a pawnshop saxophone, and decided to stay in town for a while. "When you're a Mutley Chick, Gainesville rolls out the red carpet for you," Solgot sarcastically told a local reporter. "People stop me on the street all the time and say, 'Aren't you in the Mutley Chix?'"

River met Solgot at a party and introduced himself as "Rio." Another woman challenged him, saying that he looked a lot like River Phoenix. "I'm not that guy," River told her. "I'm nothing like him." On that night, it may have even felt like the truth.

"He was very private and mysterious," Solgot said. "We never talked much about our past or who we were, though I was always curious." Solgot, five years older than River, was a beautiful blonde with a countercultural bent. They started seeing each other, and soon became serious enough that they decided to move in together. Nineteen years old, River moved out of the Micanopy family ranch and rented a large apartment in Gainesville.

He wasn't accustomed to paying bills; most months, the landlady would have to call to remind her tenants that the rent was late. Solgot would say, "Mrs. Phoenix, she'll take care of it," and the landlady would call Micanopy. Heart would drive up to the property in a battered truck, send in one of the Phoenix children with a check, and then drive off. River was asserting his identity as an adult, even if his mother still controlled his bank account. Heart gave him some space, at least nominally.

With no job or movie set requiring his presence in the morning, River routinely stayed out half the night, bringing a crowd of friends home after the bars closed. "River had a little too much time on his hands and I don't think he knew how to handle it," his friend Anthony Campanaro said. "I would look at him and say, 'If you can just survive these next three or four years, you're going to be one hell of a star.' He was going to be a great actor, if he could just hold on."

Publicly, River was vehemently antidrug, and said he couldn't stand the cocaine culture of Hollywood. "People look at you if you have a *cold*. You feel you can't blow your nose," he complained. "It depresses me. The biggest thing that gets me are the girls, because of . . . the way men use women. It really upsets me—the wonderful extra-virgin olive oil young ladies, who are so wholesome and so together and their heads are on tight and you see them a year later and"—River affected a blank expression—"all they've got left is just a recorded message in their heads."

By this time, the Micanopy property had over a dozen extra people living on it, in trailers, the old motor home, and the vacant space in River's re-cording studio. They served as gardeners and gofers, but River's friends with actual jobs just called them "Klingons" (as in "cling-ons") or "the tofu mafia"; ultimately, River paid all the bills.

One person who was no longer living in Micanopy was John, River's fa-ther. Having lost the battle for the soul of the Phoenix family, he checked out of the United States altogether. River bought him property in Costa Rica—seven hours away from the airport by bus and ferry—and he ran a (low-capacity) bed-and-breakfast.

River also bought a Florida home for his grandparents, and gave $10,000

123

to a *Jimmy Reardon* cast member so he could afford to go to school. He quietly bought hundreds of acres of rain forest in Latin America to stop it from being turned into beachfront hotels.

When he saw a journalist from *Vogue* use only half a sheet of paper in her notebook, he lectured her on her wastefulness. "We cut down an area the size of Connecticut *every year*. The Forest Service plant trees, sure, but for wood pulp. I think wood pulp should only be used for writing materials. People *waste* so much paper. In every hardware store, you get acres of paper for every receipt. Three copies of all this crap—surely our technology is more advanced than this! I mean, if they can make a plutonium generator that will orbit Jupiter and stay out there for *forty-three years,* surely they can make a receipt that will save paper."

55

SEMPER FI

And then River Phoenix joined the marines. Admittedly, he was only a movie leatherneck, but it still seemed like a stretch for a crunchy rain forest-saving vegan. The movie was *Dogfight,* set in 1963. The story: Some marines have the night off in San Francisco before they ship out to Vietnam, which they've barely heard of. For their evening's entertainment, they organize a "dogfight," a contest where each marine brings the least attractive girl he can find to a party. Whoever brings the ugliest date wins.

River plays Eddie Birdlace, who invites Rose Fenny, a plain coffee-shop waitress and aspiring folk singer played by Lili Taylor. He has misgivings about taking her to the dogfight—and rightly so, because she's hurt and livid when she finds out the nature of the party. After he attempts to apologize, they spend the rest of the night walking around the city, making an unlikely but real human connection.

The director was Nancy Savoca, who had made an impressive debut with *True Love,* an independent film starring Annabella Sciorra as a young Italian-American bride overwhelmed by her own wedding (to Ron Eldard)—it won the Grand Jury Prize at the Sundance Festival in 1989. That year turned out to be a turning point for Sundance: the Audience Award went to *sex, lies, and videotape,* directed by Steven Soderbergh, who just the year before had been driving a shuttle bus at the festival. A bidding war broke out for Soderbergh's film; it went on to make over $25 million and he went on to a career as a great American director. Sundance became the launching pad for a new generation of auteurs: Richard Linklater (*Slacker,* 1991), Todd Haynes (*Poison,* 1991), Quentin Tarantino (*Reservoir Dogs,* 1992), Robert Rodriguez (*El Mariachi,* 1992), Kevin Smith (*Clerks,* 1994), and David O. Russell (*Spanking the Monkey,* 1994).

Sundance regulars grew accustomed to movie stars trudging through the snow and agents sitting in the back row of screenings, talking on cellular phones (they weren't just "phones" yet) about deals until the moment the lights went down. American indie films pushed aside Europe fare on the art-house circuit, and the distributor Miramax grew into a powerhouse.

If the Hollywood studios didn't completely understand this new generation of low-budget filmmakers, they could at least throw money at them: Savoca found herself directing *Dogfight* with a mind-boggling (for her) $8 million budget. During the negotiations with Warner Bros., Savoca and her husband, producer Richard Guay, were leery of the studio executives in Burbank. Savoca said, "I had one foot out the back door the whole time we were talking to them."

Savoca insisted on directing a tough-minded version of the story: Rose might grow into herself in the course of her night with Eddie, but she wouldn't, as the studio had once wanted, turn into a beautiful talk-show host in the coda. Savoca also insisted that although ninety-nine percent of the movie took place off duty, the actors playing marines needed to feel like soldiers. So two former drill instructors trained and berated the cast for five days on Vashon Island, near Seattle.

Actor Anthony Clark said, "When we first got to Seattle, we were all these meek and mild actors ready to work together and give each other back rubs. Then they put us through marine boot camp."

River was a particular focus of the instructors, both for his name and for his vegan diet, which they referred to as "twigs and bark and foo-foo shit." They asked him how he planned "to kick ass on that kind of hippie fruitcake diet."

As usual, River stripped away River Jude Phoenix to immerse himself in the mind-set of his role. But this time he got deeper, even before filming started. After boot camp, some of the cast went to a party at a club, and got so rowdy—making rude gestures, projectile-vomiting, being generally belligerent—that somebody called the police. "River was the head of that whole thing," Clark said. "I hate to talk bad about him, but he had a mean streak. He wanted to get into a fight. That night, he was a marine."

To play Birdlace, River cut off his hair in favor of a high-and-tight military style. The studio worried that, like Samson, River drew his strength from his follicles, and asked that he at least get blond highlights. River complied, although the results weren't really visible. Off camera, he would fold his arms or hold them in parade-rest position, having learned that a marine never puts his hands in his pockets, even in civilian clothes.

During the shoot, River said, "I like the character of Birdlace because he's a simpleton. An average boring guy with a boring life, like so many who joined the marines. Birdlace is your average goon-squad leader. He's an easy read. He just wants to go out and have a good time. And one day his conscience catches up with him."

All well and good—River knew there was some daylight between himself and Birdlace—except that manifestly isn't how he played the role. Birdlace has confusion and rage coming out of every orifice, but he's clearly not stupid, and River didn't portray him with the contempt that his words suggest. River sounded defensive—he'd found the Birdlace within himself, and didn't want to acknowledge that any part of his soul could be a jarhead.

On a day off from shooting, Clark joined River and Heart on a trip to visit a nearby redwood forest, where he found that the Phoenixes were literally tree huggers. "Hug a tree, Tony," Heart urged him. Clark resisted, but left impressed by the impossibly tall trees swaying in the wind, and by just how important the planet was to the Phoenix family.

Back on the set, they usually worked at night: most of the film takes place after dark, but because they were shooting in Seattle during the summer, the production had only seven hours until sunrise each day. On a street corner outside the Rose's Coffee Shop set, Savoca—unruly red hair, blue jeans, pink Converse All Stars—conferred with her crew while River and Taylor sat down in the fake coffee shop, reconstructing the emotional state of their characters before they played their next scene.

"Okay," Taylor said. "It's 2 A.M. and we've had two hours of frolicking and talking."

"Yeah," River agreed. "We felt good, and we kissed."

"And now what? What about you?"

River looked nervous, tapping into Birdlace's discomfort at having gone behind enemy lines at the dogfight. "Well," he said, and paused to think. "I guess I'm curious to see how far it'll go."

Dogfight wasn't seen by many people beyond the immediate families of the filmmakers: Warner Bros. never released it in more than twenty-four theaters, and it grossed less than $400,000. On its opening weekend, it sold not even one percent of the tickets bought for *Freddy's Dead: The Final Nightmare*. But it's a beautiful film: Rose and Eddie fumble their way toward each other, trying to transcend the cruelty of the dogfight, their ignorance of the world, and the fleeting nature of their encounter. River gave the performance of his life, showing the vulnerability behind Birdlace's bluster without ever falling into sentimentality.

Savoca was concerned that River was playing the character with insufficient warmth—but her fears were allayed by the end of the shoot: "I realized, the way he's playing that character—and it was revealing itself to me every day—it was actually much more complicated than what I had imagined [the role] to be."

"By trying to be about so little, telling a simple fragile romantic story," Louis Black wrote in the *Austin Chronicle*, "*Dogfight* is about so much—war

127

and peace, love and romance, sex roles and cultural myths." The movie generally received warm reviews, although some writers had reservations: Peter Travers in *Rolling Stone,* for example, opined that "what could have been an incisive movie about alienation deteriorates into a conventional romance." But he did praise the male lead: "River Phoenix busts out of his usual sensitive mode . . . to deliver a performance of blunt intensity."

Also in *Dogfight,* making his film debut, was Brendan Fraser, playing a drunk sailor who gets into a brawl with Birdlace's marine pals. The following year, Fraser would rocket to stardom in *Encino Man* and *School Ties,* becoming a very different type of leading man from River: a broad-shouldered hunk with comedic timing who felt like a throwback to the studio system. One could imagine Fraser as a contract player at MGM in the forties, something that seemed much more improbable for River. In *Dogfight,* Fraser had but a single line. Let history record that the foundation of his film career was his convincing delivery of "How'd you like to eat my shit?"

Although Fraser didn't act opposite River, he did meet him on the set. "I anticipated River having a lot of hostility," he said. "I think I wanted him to be standoffish and cold—but he was really gentle and sweet." Fraser had been telling himself that Hollywood actors were phony sellouts, which gave him an excuse to stay in Seattle. Meeting River and discovering an example to the contrary changed his life: he packed up his mountain bike and drove south, to the film career that awaited him in Los Angeles.

INT. STILL LIFE CAFÉ

Rose and Eddie, played by Lili Taylor and River Phoenix, step through a red velvet curtain. The scene is a folk club, closing down for the night. Rose has brought Eddie here to show him the contours of her dreams. "I'm waiting for my hair to get a little longer and write my own stuff," she says shyly. "Then I'll be ready to hoot."

Eddie tells her to sing a song—almost orders her, in fact. She sits down at a piano and performs "What Have They Done to the Rain?" by Malvina Reynolds (most famous for "Little Boxes"). Taylor plays the scene with a mixture of fear and pride as Rose sings in a thin, shaky voice.

Eddie, the only person in the audience, sits at a table, listening and blowing cigarette smoke through his nostrils. River makes his face into a concerto of mixed emotions: he's uncertain about where he is and what he's doing, and trying to keep control. When Rose finishes her song, he claps loudly, enthusiastic and relieved.

57

THE FIRST CUT IS THE DEEPEST

129

Tim Burton, with carte blanche to make just about any movie he wanted after his humongous success directing *Batman* in 1989, opted for a gothic fable he had been contemplating called *Edward Scissorhands*. The title character was not only unused to human society, he had large shears instead of fingers, making him the ultimate Burton misfit in suburbia.

Burton met with Tom Cruise for several hours to discuss the part before the actor bowed out, concerned with Edward's general lack of virility. Michael Jackson wanted to play the role but was rebuffed. Tom Hanks opted for *Bonfire of the Vanities* instead. William Hurt and Robert Downey Jr. were both interested, but Burton opted for Johnny Depp.

Depp, eager to shatter his hipster teenage cop image, threw himself into the part. Although he was clad in black leather and had a huge mop of jet-black hair for the role, he said that he based his performance on "a combination of a dog that I had when I was growing up and my experience hanging around with newborn babies. When we made it, my sisters had brand-new little babies—I watched how they could be utterly fascinated by the remote control or any piece of string."

Edward Scissorhands is the movie where Johnny Depp figured out his way forward: he wanted to work with great directors (John Waters approvingly called him an "auteur hag") and get as weird as possible on film. His career decisions were based on instinct and his internal compass of what was cool, rather than a methodical Hollywood playbook or a calculating effort to burnish his image as a tough young hipster dude.

"If it's something that I do," he said of his film choices, "I do it because I want to do it and I love it—because I see an opportunity to try something that could be fun, a little bit different."

Although Depp committed to his roles, and enjoyed the pleasures of stardom, he never lost himself in either. "I'm a dumbass and I poisoned myself for years," he acknowledged many years later, looking undamaged from his chemical adventures. Protected by a strong sense of his own self and a healthy appreciation for the absurdity of his chosen career, Depp spent years of his life walking up to the edge, but never falling off.

130

THE GOLDEN AGE

An actor and a role exist in symbiosis, finding a way to live together that benefits both. But if an actor gives enough blood to a part, it can become a parasite, not letting go and fundamentally changing its host.

River had wanted to put more of himself into his roles—with Birdlace, he had succeeded, to stunning effect on the screen. But now Birdlace didn't want to be cut loose. Bobby Bukowski, the cinematographer for *Dogfight*, became close friends with River and saw the aftermath of the film. "After *Dogfight*, I remember thinking he was being a real jarhead asshole," Bukowski said. "It took a month for him to become sweet again."

This was the golden age of River Phoenix, when every aspect of his life seemed blessed. He had come into his own as an actor, and seemed to have found a way to pick roles outside the Hollywood studio factory. Aleka's Attic kept getting better, and Island remained encouraging. He and Solgot were blissfully happy together. When he drank or used drugs, it seemed like an indulgence rather than an addiction. The years he spent in the Children of God had not defined his life as an adult. If he hadn't saved the planet yet? Well, he had time.

"One day, you just wake up and you feel your age," River said of his new balance and maturity. "I woke up and it was like, 'Wow, I feel twenty.' What a fucking relief."

PART FIVE

"BARRELING THROUGH SOMEONE'S PSYCHOSIS"

THE BOTTOM OF THE BOTTOMLESS BLUE BLUE BLUE POOL

Over a thousand miles on a motorcycle. Just before Christmas 1989, that was how Keanu Reeves went to see his friend River Phoenix, riding his motorcycle from Canada all the way down the eastern United States, until he reached Gainesville, Florida. His cargo: the treatment for a movie called *My Own Private Idaho,* by director Gus Van Sant. The project upped the perspiration rates of both actors' agents, managers, and other handlers—Iris Burton had refused to pass it on to the Phoenix family. The lead characters were street hustlers who sexually service male customers—subject matter that was not just outré, but taboo in mainstream moviemaking.

Gus Van Sant grew up in Darien, Connecticut, and attended the Rhode Island School of Design. After he saw Stanley Kubrick's *A Clockwork Orange* his freshman year, he abandoned painting in favor of film. "The camera was this little machine that could make images, like paintings, twenty-four times a second," he said. After graduating in 1975, he failed to make it in Hollywood, and ended up in Portland, Oregon. His experimental movies eventually blossomed into 1989's *Drugstore Cowboy,* starring Matt Dillon as the leader of a gang of drug addicts knocking over pharmacies; it was named the year's best film by the National Society of Film Critics.

On New Year's Day 1990, River and some friends watched *Drugstore Cow-*

boy and were duly impressed. Not long after, he and Reeves were both in L.A.; heading out to a club, they drove down Santa Monica Boulevard and discussed the movie, words spilling out of them at maximum speed.

"We were excited," River said. They were also both nervous about the project, and especially scared of committing to it and then discovering that the other one had backed out: "We just forced ourselves into it." They agreed to do it together, shaking hands on the deal.

"They probably felt the risk," Van Sant opined later. "If there's no risk at all, it's not that much fun."

A few weeks later, Van Sant flew to Florida to meet his young star; River and Solgot picked him up at the Gainesville airport. River quizzed Van Sant about every aspect of the movie, and hit it off with the quiet, amiable director—although he told friends afterward that he thought Van Sant had a crush on him and was chasing him. Nevertheless, he was in, predicting, "This will get me off the cover of *Tiger Beat*."

While Van Sant assembled financing, River made *Dogfight* and Reeves starred with Patrick Swayze in *Point Break,* Kathryn Bigelow's loopy action movie about surfers who rob banks while wearing masks of U.S. presidents. River prepared for his role as a street kid, reading John Rechy's novel *City of Night* and meeting Mike Parker, the hustler friend of Van Sant whom his character was based on. (Parker had been slated to star in the movie; when River took his part, Parker ended up with a smaller part in the ensemble.)

According to Parker, River's preparations included dabbling with queer sex, including a dalliance with a male cast member in *Dogfight*. "I think maybe he had feelings that way," Parker said. "Everybody has a level of curiosity. River struck me as real curious. Maybe not because he was gay but because he wanted to understand."

"If he loved somebody, male or female," Suzanne Solgot said, "he felt he should check it out."

MY OWN PRIVATE IDAHO FUSES two plot lines. Mike Waters (River) is a narcoleptic hustler searching for his mother, while Scott Favor (Reeves) is an updated version of Prince Hal in Shakespeare's *Henry IV* plays: the wayward son of the mayor of Portland, slumming on the streets to amuse himself before he comes into his inheritance. The movie has an abundance of Shakespearean dialogue, rendered in modern language, and a Falstaff character: Bob Pigeon, the charismatic king of the street hustlers.

Daniel Day-Lewis was rumored to be playing Bob Pigeon, but he never committed to the role. River wanted the part to be played by his friend William Richert, who had directed him in *Jimmy Reardon,* but when Richert read the screenplay, he balked, saying, "It's a big fat pederast." Richert called up River and asked, "Is this what you think of me? Is this what you think I should be playing? Because I haven't been an actor before, so this is how people are going to see me."

"No no no, Bill, it's the energy," River assured him. "It doesn't matter how big you are." Richert turned down the part, his vanity wounded—he was dating a much younger woman and didn't want her to think of him as even vaguely resembling Bob Pigeon.

River, however, kept wooing Richert for the role and, while visiting his house one day, invited Van Sant over to join them. When Van Sant arrived, he and River started reading the script out loud on Richert's porch. Feeling coerced and insulted, Richert stayed inside and smoked a joint instead. But after sulking for a while, he joined them.

"Do you want me to read it, River?" he asked.

"Oh, would you, Bill? That would be so cool. Right, Gus?"

Richert read the part, and noticed that River had memorized the entire script. Afterward, he reiterated that he still didn't want to play the role—but privately, he had a grudging respect for River's relentlessness. "It was a total operator move," he said. The Bob Pigeon role was filled by eighty-two-year-old character actor Lionel Stander, best known for his work as Max the chauffeur on the TV show *Hart to Hart.*

River flew up to Portland, Oregon, for filming, but then one night he called up Richert. "Hey, Bill, I'm here with Keanu. We're shooting scenes with Bob Pigeon tomorrow and we want you to come, because we fired the actor."

"You fired the actor? You and Keanu?" asked an astonished Richert.

"No no no no no—Gus. But we all agreed that he just doesn't have the energy. Maybe you can come up on Thursday?"

River put Reeves on the line to persuade Richert.

"Where are you?" Richert asked.

"We're in the hall at Gus's house," Reeves told him.

"Why are you in the hall?"

"He doesn't have any furniture yet."

After receiving assurances that the move had Van Sant's blessing, a worn-down Richert succumbed. Van Sant picked him up at the Portland airport in his Volvo.

"I met the costume designer and she put me in a fat suit and put enormous red things all over me. I started getting into the character because I could feel my roly-poly, Falstaffian, larcenist nature," Richert said. "River would visit me every night—he became my second director."

138   **RATHER THAN CHECK INTO A** hotel, River stayed at Van Sant's house during the shoot. Soon, much of the young male cast, including Reeves and Flea of the Red Hot Chili Peppers, had joined him, turning the house into a crash pad littered with futons and musical instruments. Overwhelmed by the number of guests, Van Sant moved out of his own home for the duration of the shoot.

Late-night parties and jam sessions became the rule. Reeves and Flea had brought their basses; River bought a handmade Irish guitar from a Portland music store. They were joined by Mike Parker, actor Scott Green (formerly a Portland street kid), editor Wade Evans, and sometimes Van Sant himself. They would get drunk and stoned in Van Sant's garage, next to his BMWs, and then play what River called "sort of a fusion-funk Latin-jazz thing."

Parker, who typically manned a drum machine in the garage band, said, "River would just start playing these tribal rhythms on guitar and he'd go into a trance. We'd play these amazing jams that would last for three hours without stopping." River and Flea were the stalwarts, and their love of music became the cornerstone of their friendship.

Blissed out, River would close his eyes while he played, and block out the rest of the world. He delighted in playing to the point of exhaustion, when he would fall asleep holding his guitar.

As it happened, River had learned about inappropriate slumber for the movie: his character suffered from narcolepsy, meaning that he would fall asleep abruptly, especially in stressful situations. River spent some time with a narcoleptic friend of Van Sant's, discussing how and why his "fits" happened, and the lucid-dreaming hyperreal quality of the ensuing sleep. River never saw an actual fit, but Van Sant declared his simulations of them to be just like the genuine article.

River also spent a lot of time on the Portland streets to prepare for the role, learning tricks of the trade: for example, giggling nervously can entice older guys on a power trip. According to Parker, there were two basic types of hustler: the glamorous ones and the unbathed grunge boys. River opted for the latter: "a definite pickup on the street," opined Parker.

Green served as tour guide to River and Reeves in the "Vaseline Alley" district, where they watched boys as young as twelve get into cars for forty-dollar "dates." Green would even get into johns' cars to haggle out a deal, with River following him to see how it was done. Sometimes, River would enter the negotiation himself, Green said. "But after we agreed to the deal, I'd say, 'I'm sorry. We can't do this.' And we'd jump out of the car leaving these guys wondering what the hell was going on."

One potential customer didn't take the rejection well. He kept circling the block, yelling at them, "But I'm so lonely!"

To immerse himself further in the role, River started experimenting with hard drugs. He was friendly with Matt Ebert, a former street kid who acted as a production assistant on both *Dogfight* and *My Own Private Idaho*. Before they did heroin together for the first time, River assured Ebert that he had done it before. "I remember thinking, 'He's lying,'" Ebert said. According to Ebert, there was "rampant heroin use" going on among the cast and crew of *Idaho*. "He would come up to visit me, and we would do drugs together," Ebert said of River. "Let me tell you, it did not take him long to go from, you know, a casual user to having an intense drug problem."

Early in the shoot, River got busted for drunk driving. The film company confiscated his car so it wouldn't happen again, and kept the incident under wraps. Word got to River's agent, Iris Burton, who exploded, more out of embarrassment than concern for River. "Imagine, I had to find out from the movie's fucking accountant," she complained. "I never liked that fucking *My Own Private Idaho*. It should have stayed in the trash where it belonged."

Going deeper into his role than ever before, River was vanishing in plain sight. His hair was greasy; his skin was sallow; his body was clad in second-hand clothes. He looked like a mournful street kid, not a Hollywood star. When he went to do research at Portland's City Nightclub, the owner threw him out for looking like a bum.

"I'm River Phoenix," he objected, but when challenged, couldn't produce any ID. "Well, if you're River Phoenix, you can certainly afford to pay the six-dollar cover charge," club owner Lannie Swerdlow told him. But River didn't have any money either. "Stop putting me on," Swerdlow said, and had the bouncers escort him out the door.

140

While River wasn't doing so well at getting onto the dance floor, he delivered an astonishing performance on camera. In his hands, Mike Waters stumbles through his life half asleep, looking for a mother he can't really remember but who haunts his dreams. Dressed in shades of red, Mike looks like the salmon that Van Sant periodically cuts to: a creature fighting to return home, even if the effort will kill him. Mike Waters keeps up his guard so he can survive on the streets; River Phoenix let us see the character's tender heart.

The production rolled up I-5 for two weeks of shooting in Seattle. Journalist Dario Scardapane witnessed the filming of a scene on a ferry, where Mike Waters is in a narcoleptic trance while the hustler characters of Rodney Harvey and Keanu Reeves take in the view and suck on a pot pipe.

When River shambled onto the set, Scardapane wrote, "Quite honestly, he looks like crap: his hair's a mess, stubble flecks his face, his grungy red pants don't fit, and more than anything else, he appears in dire need of a good night's rest, which the actor seems intent on getting, promptly collapsing on a bench in the ferry's cabin."

When Van Sant started shooting, "almost unnoticed, River lies in a puddle near his costars' feet, a position he'll keep for most of the day. Frankly, there's not much difference in his performance when the camera is rolling and when it is not."

The scene was ultimately cut from the movie.

The filmmakers all insisted that the characters Reeves and River played weren't actually gay; they just made money by having sex with men. "It's as much about gays as *Five Easy Pieces* is about oil-well diggers," River insisted, a bit disingenuously.

Reeves put it less elegantly and more defensively when pressed by an interviewer about how he had prepared for his role: "I didn't have to suck dick, if that's what you mean!"

Nevertheless, they had a three-way sex scene with a German businessman played by Udo Kier, staged as a series of frozen tableaus, and they were both nervous about it. Just before shooting the scene, River tried to break the ice with a joke: "Just think, Keanu, five hundred million of your fans will be watching this one day." This backfired, making Reeves feel intensely self-conscious. They made it through the day's shoot, but afterward, River said, the usually gentle Van Sant severely chastised him for his ill-timed humor. "He scolded the shit out of me," River said. "I almost cried."

The centerpiece of River's performance, and the film, is a campfire scene with Reeves. Scott Favor takes Mike Waters on a road trip (on a stolen motorcycle) to visit Mike's brother. At night, sitting by a fire they've made, they discuss their respective childhoods: "If I had a normal family and a good upbringing, then I would have been a well-adjusted person," Mike insists. What's really on his mind: he's in love with Scott, and he's terrified of saying so.

"I only have sex with a guy for money," a reclining Scott tells him. "Two guys can't love each other."

A miserable Mike says haltingly, "I could love someone even if I, you know, wasn't paid for it. And I love you, and you don't pay me." Curling up in a ball, he tells Scott, "I really want to kiss you, man." The scene ends with Scott gently holding Mike, stroking his hair.

"This is the best part in the film," Van Sant said, "and was chosen by River to be his big scene." At River's request, Van Sant scheduled it for the last day of shooting. River rewrote it himself, making it more lyrical and making his love for Scott explicit (in Van Sant's original script, the relationship was more ambiguous).

" 'I love you, and you don't have to pay me'—I'm so glad I wrote that line," River said. "I think that in his private life, Mike was probably a virgin, so he only relates sex with work." River had spent some time thinking about situational virginity, and the emotional consequences of having sex when you didn't want to have it.

The final scene of the movie, however, is River Phoenix, all alone by the side of a lonely northwestern highway (filmed just fifteen miles away from Madras, where he was born). Mike Waters is stranded, without any obvious future and without Scott Favor, who has accepted the mantle of city scion, with a hot Italian girlfriend on his arm. Mike peers into the distance and staggers into sleep, escaping from the world.

Later, a truck pulls up; two guys steal Mike's shoes. Then, with a steel-guitar version of "America the Beautiful" quivering on the soundtrack, we see a long shot of a car stopping: the driver puts Mike into the car and speeds away. It could be his brother taking him home, a john with malicious intent, or maybe (if you're a romantic), Scott returning to rescue him.

In 1997, Van Sant was doing a reading at a bookstore from his novel *Pink*. (Dedicated to River, the book starred a thinly disguised version of him.) An audience member asked him who had hoisted River Phoenix's body into the car.

"I was hoping that viewers would project themselves into the film and decide for themselves who it was," he told her.

"Okay, then," she replied. "Who picked him up in *your* version?"

Van Sant paused. "In my version . . . in my version, I pick him up."

YOUNG HOLLYWOOD 1991

Brad Pitt became famous in 1991 as a vision of temptation. In *Thelma & Louise,* Ridley Scott's movie about two women on the run from the law, he played J.D., a hunky young hitchhiker who turns out to be a criminal himself. In fourteen minutes of screen time, Pitt looked good with his shirt off, spent the night with Geena Davis (playing Thelma), and drawled lines like, "Well, now, I've always believed that, if done properly, armed robbery doesn't have to be a totally unpleasant experience." The role instantly established him as a sex symbol and a movie star. J.D. steals $6,000 from Thelma and Louise; a popular conversational topic among women at the time was whether Thelma's night of passion was worth that much.

Ethan Hawke was getting lead roles in movies both solid (*White Fang,* a Disney adaptation of the Jack London novel about a wolf dog in the Yukon) and terrible (*Mystery Date,* a wacky teen comedy). Leonardo DiCaprio made his film debut in the otherwise unmemorable horror movie *Critters 3,* playing what he described as "your average, no-depth, standard kid with blond hair." It was straight-to-video, but at age seventeen, he was working as an actor. DiCaprio gloated, "All you math teachers who've been scolding me all my life, ha ha! I laugh."

Martha Plimpton appeared in *Stanley & Iris,* which starred Robert De Niro as an illiterate cafeteria worker and Jane Fonda as the woman who teaches him how to read. Samantha Mathis was cast by Nora Ephron in her directorial debut, *This Is My Life,* playing the disaffected teen daughter of Julie Kavner, who has made a career shift from selling cosmetics to stand-up comedy.

The Butthole Surfers crisscrossed the country as part of the first-ever Lollapalooza. The package tour, an invention from the fevered mind of Jane's

Addiction lead singer Perry Farrell, also included Nine Inch Nails, Living Colour, Ice-T, Siouxsie and the Banshees, and headlining, Jane's. (The following year, the Red Hot Chili Peppers filled the headlining slot.) Lollapalooza was a huge success, becoming a brand name for the nineties counterculture and demonstrating the commercial clout of "alternative" music. A few months after the tour ended, Nirvana released "Smells Like Teen Spirit" and turned popular music upside down; when the band's album *Nevermind* hit number one, that was generally regarded as the moment when "alternative" put a knee on the windpipe of mainstream rock 'n' roll.

R.E.M. also redefined the mainstream in 1991, hitting number one with *Out of Time,* powered by the omnipresent mandolin riff of "Losing My Religion." The Red Hot Chili Peppers' *Blood Sugar Sex Magik*—with photography and art direction by Gus Van Sant—made it to only number three on the *Billboard* charts, but it ultimately sold over seven million copies in the United States. The breakthrough hit was "Under the Bridge," a coded paean to Anthony Kiedis's misadventures with heroin. After the album was completed, Kiedis said, guitarist John Frusciante had a hard time emerging from the studio and readjusting to day-to-day Western civilization: "It got to the point where he wouldn't want to see a billboard for, say, *The Arsenio Hall Show,* or an advertisement for lipstick. He wanted to be in a world that was a beautiful manifestation of his own creation. You're not going to find that on a promo tour." One consequence: "John started to dabble in using heroin."

Christian Slater made a traditional Hollywood trade: he cashed in some buzz for a studio paycheck, with a supporting role as Will Scarlett in the dull but wildly popular *Robin Hood: Prince of Thieves,* starring Kevin Costner. He also got to live out a dream by putting on a Starfleet uniform for a cameo in *Star Trek VI: The Undiscovered Country.* Wil Wheaton, meanwhile, had quit *Star Trek: The Next Generation* in favor of a desk job with the computer company NewTek, doing testing and quality control on the Video Toaster 4000, a pioneering home video-editing system. The company was based in Topeka, Kansas: "I figured that was about as far from Hollywood as I could possibly get, both geographically and culturally," Wheaton said.

As 1991 began, Johnny Depp was basking in the success of *Edward Scissorhands*. It was not only his first film with Tim Burton, but also his first with Winona Ryder. Burton affectionately dubbed the couple "an evil version of Tracy and Hepburn." Depp and Ryder had the unpleasant experience of being the object of tabloid obsession, meaning that they had to fend off paparazzi and swat away constant rumors that they were sleeping with other people. But at home together, life was good.

Depp rented a house in the Hollywood Hills and stuffed it full of clown paintings, Jack Kerouac memorabilia, and a nine-foot fiberglass rooster. (He would cite it as evidence that he had the "biggest cock in Hollywood.") Now that he and Ryder were in the same place, he always made her breakfast in bed, she said: "Eggs, hash browns, bacon, toast, and coffee," she specified. "Lots of coffee."

61 PSIONIC PSUNSPOT

River was having difficulty shedding his Mike Waters skin. Tabloid photographers spotted him at New York nightclubs—the Limelight, Danceteria—wearing his thrift-store *Idaho* clothes, talking about how he was doing "research," stripping off his shirt, and hitting the dance floor bare-chested. Even if the reports were exaggerated, it was out of character for River. As time passed, his internal gyroscope righted itself and his natural personality returned—but the drug habit wasn't so easily disposed of.

River kept his life compartmentalized; he once told William Richert, "You're my best friend in your age group." This is an occupational hazard for many actors—for a few months, a team of people make a movie and feel like a family, and then they scatter, most of them never to be seen again—but

River reveled in the peripatetic life more than most. One result is that different people who knew him saw divergent aspects of his personality—and his consumption of various substances.

"The hardest drink I ever saw him drink was carrot juice," said Dan Mathews of PETA. "He liked red wine—that was his thing. I don't think drug use was a long period of his life," said Ione Skye. "We had the same heroin dealer. I used to see him there all the time," said a former Viper Club employee.

They could all be telling the truth as they knew it, of course. One way River avoided having people track on his drug use was his habit of hopscotching from one social group to another. He also liked to mention that he had heard rumors of his taking drugs, which let him preemptively dismiss them. And he was a binge user: he would indulge intensely for a while, and then get clean and wait before starting the cycle again. "Here's a kid that does not know how much to take," said Matt Ebert. "When I saw him do drugs, I was always scared for him."

146

YOU'RE WHERE YOU SHOULD BE ALL THE TIME

River returned to Gainesville and reconvened Aleka's Attic; their track "Across the Way" was included on the PETA compilation *Tame Yourself,* and they prepared to tour the East Coast. He had been gone from Gainesville for most of 1990, and some band members resented having their professional and artistic lives be contingent on his film career. Drummer Josh Greenbaum said, "Having a movie star as the front man for a band is a double-edged sword."

Aleka's Attic started a ten-week tour: the centerpiece was a week in New

York. They did three rain-forest benefits at Wetlands, opening up for the Spin Doctors, the jam band that was still a few months away from releasing their debut album and having the inescapable hit singles "Two Princes" and "Little Miss Can't Be Wrong." They also attended the release party for *Tame Yourself* at the Hard Rock Cafe; River met other contributors to the album, such as Canadian chanteuse k.d. lang and R.E.M. lead singer Michael Stipe.

Stipe and River were both vegetarians, both socially conscious, both considerate to the people around them. Each had moved repeatedly in their childhood (Stipe's father was in the army) and settled in the southern United States. They soon became fast friends.

Kim Buie, the A&R rep at Island working with River, remembered seeing an Aleka's Attic show in Athens, and afterward being told that Stipe wanted to talk to her. When he met her, he grabbed her hand and then said, looking intently into her eyes, "I just have to tell you that I think he is *really special* and *really good*. If there's anything I can do to help you, just let me know."

To promote *Tame Yourself,* PETA arranged for Aleka's Attic to do an interview with *Sassy*. Between 1988 and 1995, *Sassy* was an extremely cool magazine for American teenage girls, one that didn't condescend to its readers but did speak in their language. Although the magazine was alternative-rock friendly—editor in chief Jane Pratt was close friends with Stipe and appeared in R.E.M.'s "Shiny Happy People" video, while Sonic Youth contributed a flexi-disc to the magazine—sometimes hip celebrities would give them grumpy interviews, either because they associated the magazine with pinup magazines like *Tiger Beat* or because the very notion of having teenage girls as fans made them nervous. When that happened, the magazine bared its teeth, as it did in this article, written by Christina Kelly and slugged "River Phoenix's Little Hippie Band" on the cover. (Other cover lines in the June 1991 issue: "Black Kids Who Are Fed Up," "Eavesdrop on 3 Heavy-Duty Couples.")

Kelly captured the tenor of an excruciatingly uncomfortable group interview with Aleka's Attic, where River drank from a room-service bottle of Moët champagne and swatted away questions. River was wearing his olive-green army jacket from *Dogfight,* which he had rendered less militaristic by

147

putting an antifur pin on it. Violist Tim Hankins said that he had spotted *Tame Yourself* in a record store, but he didn't have any money, so he couldn't buy it. Rain talked about how she was studying opera at the University of Florida. "She has a very flat stomach, is short with dark skin and hair and features that are pretty and ugly at the same time," Kelly wrote. "Rain was very serene and quiet. She seemed like a nice person."

Although Kelly clearly was frustrated by the awkward hour she spent with the band, she seemed genuinely shocked by River's physical deterioration: "I was stunned at how different River's once shiny, silky blond hair looked. It was short, a dirty color, and kind of brittle. I don't know if the Riv was trying to dread or what, now that he is 21 and has left his teenage years behind him."

After the tour, the band went into River's home studio in Micanopy and recorded a bunch of songs, which they called the "Here's Where We're At" demos.

River felt sufficiently at home in Florida to tell a *Rolling Stone* reporter, "I'm kinda like Gainesville's godfather. Or dogfather, I should say—it's a backwards town." Although he was joking around, many locals were insulted when the article appeared. He also tried a new tactic for deflecting his own stardom: he talked about himself in the third person, but called himself "Rubber Penis." The explanation: "When you see the name 'River Phoenix' everywhere, you gotta, like, joke about it."

River and Solgot had two canaries, which they let fly around unfettered in their enclosed porch. The male canary was called Honeypie Ice Cream; the female canary had no name at all. The moral apparently was that if somebody in the Phoenix family couldn't come up with an elaborate, unconventional name, it wasn't worth having a name at all.

The Rubber Penis household was filled with plants and wall tapestries. A mattress on the floor was surrounded by piles of books and dirty dishes. In one corner was an empty suitcase, belonging to Solgot: a symbol that she was an independent woman who could leave whenever she wanted.

In the middle of the dining room was a massage table—Solgot had begun studying massage therapy. That gave her something to work on, but her course schedule meant that she usually couldn't travel with River when he went on tour or on location. "It sucks and it kinda doesn't suck," she said. "Because it gives us space."

River objected to being tagged as a "hippie"—especially on *Sassy*'s cover—but he and Solgot had a relaxed attitude toward personal hygiene. "River and Sue never took baths," Richert remembered. "And they let all their hair grow—River had incredibly hairy legs."

A visiting journalist, Michael Angeli, noticed that River had the same outfit on two days in a row: "the same threadbare print shirt hanging out of the same migrant work pants he wore the previous day."

"Jesus, River," Angeli exclaimed, "you slept in your goddamn clothes."

"No, man—I slept in a blanket of warm flesh."

When the Aleka's Attic demos were finished, River headed out to the West Coast, to do press and visit friends. Frustrated by the continued delays, and by years of working on a project "that never came to fruition," Hankins quit the band. The viola player also had personal issues with River, whom he described as a "serious drinker" and a "junkie."

149

River drove a white Mercedes from Los Angeles all the way to Portland to visit Van Sant. Back in L.A., he hung out with the Chili Peppers, who had finished recording *Blood Sugar Sex Magik* and had some downtime before its release. He was tight with Flea because of their time on *Idaho,* but now he was jamming and philosophizing with the whole band, becoming especially close with guitarist John Frusciante. "River loved nothing better than hanging around the Chili Peppers," said a friend of his. "I remember how happy River was when he was with the Peppers. His beaming face said to me, 'This is where I want to be.'"

River invited the band to join him on a trip down to Costa Rica to visit his father; they accepted. Down there, they explored the rain forest and saw a total eclipse of the sun. John was content to stay out of the United States, and had become more sociable; at the local bar, people called him "Don Juan." Father and son stayed up late talking, discussing their addictions. Scott Green said that River acknowledged he was an alcoholic: "During one of our conversations, he said he thought he might have inherited his dependence from his father but he didn't think it was in any way his father's fault."

On the plane back to the United States, the in-flight movie was *Awakenings,* starring Robert De Niro as a man who emerges from a yearslong coma and has to figure out the modern world he is suddenly, unwillingly a part of. River watched it and wept copiously.

THE REFRIGERATOR PARABLE

River's asking price for movies had reached a million dollars per picture. He told a friend, "I want to make $1 million on my next picture, $2 million on the one after that, and $3 million on the one after that." This wasn't just so he could afford room-service champagne: he was financing the family compound in Micanopy, and felt the weight of that responsibility—not to mention his desire to buy up more rain forest, although that proved to be a more complicated proposition than he had originally imagined.

"River realized that his family's ideas had been a little simplistic," a good friend said. "The idea that when he bought up rain forest in Costa Rica he was preventing Third World people from making a living there left him confused and unhappy."

River's long-standing dream was to use his money to buy land and set up a sanctuary for damaged children, "all sorts of homeless kids and kids from foster homes or kids who have been in and out of mental institutions." He envisioned a farm, so the children could help grow their own food, also populated by stray cats and dogs. "The kids would be assigned to an animal of their own and they would have this cycle of caring for something. The farm would have solar panels and be self-sufficient. It wouldn't be isolated because it would be a whole community in itself. There would be room for individual expression and creativity. It would be really wonderful."

Fairly transparently, River was describing his idealized version of childhood. If he felt that he hadn't been protected in his own youth, he didn't want to wallow in self-pity: he tried to convert that feeling into charity. (Often, his intentions were better than his follow-through.)

River invested in a business Richert was starting: manufacturing a coffee alternative from soybeans. Richert put up $300,000 of his own money and River had Heart cut a check for his $50,000 contribution to the Incognito Coffee Company. Richert opened up a storefront in Venice Beach, but when the business had cash-flow problems, he asked River to invest another $25,000.

River visited Richert's home, with a few friends in tow, including Joaquin and Chrissie Hynde of the Pretenders (another PETA supporter, who had once joked about fire-bombing McDonald's restaurants). He handed the check to Richert, who put it on the kitchen table. They all hung out for an hour or two, and then River left with his crew—at which point Richert realized he couldn't find the check. Thinking he had misplaced it—"I've lost a lot of checks in my time"—he searched every room. When he couldn't find it, he decided that River must have taken the check home, although he had no idea why.

Irate and worried about making payroll, Richert called up River: "Hey man, where's the twenty-five grand? You took it back, right?"

River just laughed. "No no no, it's right there. You're probably standing next to it. Are you in the kitchen? Just look in the refrigerator."

Richert found the check in his freezer. "You put it in the freezer?" he said. "Why would you do a thing like that?"

"Why would you lose twenty-five thousand dollars?"

River was acting out a real-life parable, one with the sensible message "be careful with your money, especially when it's actually my money."

River bleached his hair, looking to play the young Andy Warhol in a Gus Van Sant film about the artist; the movie never got off the ground. He was offered the male lead in *Sliver,* an erotic thriller starring Sharon Stone with a screenplay by Joe Eszterhas—their follow-up to the hugely successful (if slightly incoherent) erotic thriller *Basic Instinct*. He turned it down, and the role was taken by William Baldwin.

"I get offered a lot of stuff," River said. "And sure, you pause when they say on the phone, 'You won't do this for two [million], well, how about three?' But after the movie comes out, I think, 'Man, I'm glad I didn't do that. It's just not worth it. It's all in the script and whether I believe in it."

One script that River fervently believed in was Richard Friedenberg's screenplay for *A River Runs Through It,* based on Norman Maclean's semi-autobiographical book. River usually didn't need to audition for roles anymore, but he did for director Robert Redford—"me and about a thousand other guys," he said with a laugh. "I had a really good talk, good meeting with Redford, but I think he's gonna find *the* guy. The guy who just is that image—that Montana mountain boy, fly-fisherman image. That's what I think he should do. I believe so strongly in it, I just want the best guy for it. If I get it, great. If I don't, I wasn't right for it."

The movie is the story of two sons—one dutiful, one wayward—of a Presbyterian minister, growing up in Missoula, Montana, in the 1920s. The minister teaches them the art of writing and the art of fly-fishing. It's no wonder River was drawn to the project, since the story's underlying theme is an Americanized version of *Siddhartha,* the Hesse novel that gave him his name: the river will reveal its wisdom to you if you listen carefully enough. "Beneath the rocks are the words of God," the minister tells his children as they walk on the riverbank. Or as the narrator concludes, "Eventually, all things merge into one."

The part of Paul, the reckless brother who grows up to become a hard-drinking newspaper reporter with crippling gambling debts, went to Brad Pitt, transforming him from shirtless sex symbol to leading man. While River certainly could have played the role well, Pitt had a robust quality that the part needed, giving the audience the physical sense that nothing could ever kill this avatar of American manhood. Pitt considered it to be one of his weakest performances—that may be because it was a film where he didn't need to stretch. As River anticipated, Redford found somebody who embodied the golden-boy part just by showing up.

WHILE VISITING L.A., RIVER WOULD often end up at Richert's Malibu home—they'd talk until 2 A.M., at which point Richert would stagger off to bed and River would stay up playing guitar. Sometimes, River would just show up in the middle of the night. "He knew ways to get in," Richert said. "I'd wake up and there'd be River and some girl looking at me."

When River came during daylight hours, Richert would always get advance warning—not from River himself, but from the flurry of phone calls made by other people looking for him.

"Hey, can I talk to River?"

"No, he's not here."

"He's not? Do you know when he's coming?"

Soon River would arrive, often with a coterie of family and friends. He'd bring his own food—"he wanted to make sure that he had his diet right"—and his own cigarettes. (River had learned to smoke for his *Dogfight* role and never quit, although he tried to conceal his habit from the public.) Richert regarded his interactions with River as evidence that he couldn't possibly have had a secret life as an addict: "River was around people all the time."

153

MY OWN PRIVATE IDAHO **WAS** released in October 1992; the film and its two young leads mostly received raves. In *Entertainment Weekly,* Owen Glieberman singled out River: "Phoenix's slightly anonymous quality works for him here, and he gives an extraordinary performance. His Mike is dazed and weirdly becalmed, like a drugged-out animal living on his last shreds of instinct. When his pain comes to the fore, it's startlingly direct. Sitting around a campfire with Scott, who he knows sleeps with men only for money, Mike says, 'I really wanna kiss you, man,' and it's the saddest, loneliest declaration of love imaginable."

River missed *Idaho*'s Hollywood premiere. He said it was because he had driven all the way from Florida and misjudged how long it would take. He did make it to the New York premiere; Solgot stayed in Gainesville, so Martha Plimpton walked the red carpet with him.

In general, River dreaded doing interviews, and when he felt they weren't going well, he would undermine them, either by withdrawing or by making up answers to amuse himself. As he put it, "I have lied and changed stories and contradicted myself left and right, so that at the end of the year you could read five different articles and say, 'This guy is schizophrenic.'"

So it wasn't too surprising that when River had a press junket for *My Own Private Idaho,* he found a way to sabotage it. He had a full day of interviews scheduled at Hollywood's Chateau Marmont hotel, but he overslept, either because he had been up too late the night before or because he had learned the crucial lesson of narcolepsy: sleep can let you avoid unpleasant experiences. Mike Parker, who was also doing the junket, had to wake him up.

"River walked into the room, set up for the television interview with lights and everything, after just waking up," Parker said. "His hair was all matted and he looked a mess."

The interviewer said, "How are you today, Mr. Phoenix?"

River responded by scratching himself. "Not too bad," he said, "except for the crotch rot."

154

64
ACROSS THE WAY

> KEANU REEVES: *I'm not against gays or anything, but I won't have sex with guys. I would never do that on film. We did a little of that in* Idaho, *and it was really hard. Never again.*
> RIVER PHOENIX: *I thought you liked that. Was it something I did?*
> KEANU REEVES: *Shut up, dude!*

Since the beginning of Hollywood, its male actors have often strived to assert their heterosexuality, regardless of whether they actually like to go to bed with men or women. Acting is a feminizing job in many ways (judging by the general mores of Western civilization for the past century): when you go to work, you put on makeup and let yourself be ogled by the camera, even in action roles. Especially in action roles.

Panic about actors' sexuality has been around since Hollywood had groves of orange trees. Take Rudolph Valentino, the Italian actor who became the exotic sex symbol of silent movies, starring in such films as *The Sheik* and *The Four Horsemen of the Apocalypse* (both released in 1921). When a journalist compared him to a pink powder puff in 1926, Valentino felt compelled to prove his masculinity by challenging him to a boxing match. Valentino won the fight—just a few weeks before he died, at age thirty-one.

Classic Hollywood was full of sham marriages and fake romances, efforts to protect matinee idols like Tab Hunter and Rock Hudson from gossip and insinuations. Even the suave Cary Grant, married four times, spent twelve years living with his "housemate," western star Randolph Scott. Given that a gay public image was considered to be a career killer, it's perhaps not too surprising that most on-screen homosexuality was coded, as in the *Spartacus* scene where Laurence Olivier and Tony Curtis discuss the difference between "eating oysters" and "eating snails." (That one may not have been coded enough, actually—it got cut from the film.)

On the rare occasions when gay characters appeared in movies, they were usually presented to be as exotic or as depraved as possible—most famously in the 1980 film *Cruising,* where Al Pacino played a straight cop who dons leather and goes undercover in the gay S&M world to track down a serial killer. William Hurt won the Oscar for his portrayal of the homosexual Luis Molina in *Kiss of the Spider Woman* (1985)—the character was not only gay, but a pedophile, which is why he spends most of the movie in a Brazilian prison cell.

Street hustlers and underage prostitutes aren't the societal norm either. If you view *My Own Private Idaho* through the reductive lens of "does this movie present positive gay role models?" it is yet another entry in the "er, no" column of the Hollywood ledger. So how did River become a gay icon? (Beyond his ultrahandsomeness, of course.) He never condescended. Not just in his public statements while promoting the movie, where it became clear that he was relaxed about and around gay people, but in the movie itself, in which Mike Waters, while not without flaws, felt like a real human being.

It's no wonder that rumors flew about River actually being gay or bi; whether he experimented with homosexuality or not, he didn't have any protective distance between himself and his character. It's also not surprising that *Idaho* provided a catalyst for young gay men to come out of the closet.

Two years later, Tom Hanks won the Best Actor Oscar for playing an HIV-positive gay lawyer in *Philadelphia*. But while Hanks was earnest and well intentioned, his character felt like a noble cipher. The same year, Will Smith had his breakthrough role in *Six Degrees of Separation* as a young gay con man—but on the advice of Denzel Washington, he refused to kiss another man on-screen.

Twenty years after *My Own Private Idaho*, many gay actors have come out of the closet—at first loudly, and then matter-of-factly. Movies and TV shows are rife with homosexual characters; what remains taboo is the depiction of same-sex physical affection, even relatively chaste kisses. River shattered this unofficial prohibition in the opening minutes of *My Own Private Idaho;* when we first see Mike, he is in a hotel getting a blow job from a john. It's about as graphic as you can get without actually inspecting River for crotch rot—we know exactly what's happening by looking at his face.

As River said when discussing the scene, "God, the physical sensation of ejaculating can be *orgasmic*."

THAT NIGHT AT THE VIPER ROOM

Wednesday nights became theme nights at the Viper Room, called Mr. Moo's Adventure, named after Johnny Depp's dog. One Wednesday might be "Women in Prison" night, with the VIP booths turned into prison cells; another might find the club

converted into an airplane; another would have the black walls covered with alu-
minum foil. *These elaborate evenings were money losers, but fun for the club staff.*

The Viper Room hosted two episodes of their version of The Dating Game; *for
one of them, bar back Richmond Arquette recruited his younger brother, actor
David Arquette (*Scream*) to be the bachelor. Richmond wrote some questions for
his brother to read to his romantic prospects, but when David attempted the first
one, he laughed so hard, he couldn't get the words out. The question was "I like to
masturbate for hours on end until I'm in danger of dying from dehydration. What
do you like to do in your spare time?"*

Another night, the bachelor was actor Norman Reedus (now most famous for
The Walking Dead*). "They sort of set him up," Richmond Arquette remembered.
"One of the bachelorettes was this Mexican tranny. They gave her the best answers,
and he picked her.* When Reedus's choice was revealed, *"even though it was all
in jest, you could see her vulnerability. He did this beautiful thing: he kissed her,
said 'I'm so happy,' and was really gracious about it. I always liked him for that."*

157

SATIATE LACK

After the emotional wringer of *My Own Private Idaho,* "I just did not feel like
barreling through someone's psychosis," River said. He opted for a low-stress
money gig: *Sneakers.* As one actor in the film said of the title, "It sounded like
a bad teen comedy about a hapless junior-high basketball team that is saved
when they recruit a girl point guard who's a great shot."

The movie was actually a heist caper centered on a band of professional
computer hackers and security consultants; the NSA dragoons them into
stealing a black box that is the ultimate code-breaking tool. Director Phil
Alden Robinson (*Field of Dreams*) assembled an absurdly star-studded cast:
Robert Redford, Sidney Poitier, Dan Aykroyd, and Ben Kingsley, not to men-

tion Mary McDonnell, David Strathairn, and James Earl Jones. A hugely classy ensemble—but the studio wanted to make sure that there was also some youth appeal, and pushed for River.

On the set, River quickly bonded with Aykroyd (another actor who really just wanted to rock). The two of them would gaze awestruck at Redford and Poitier, River said. "We'd think, 'These guys are like national monuments, like the pyramids.' And that poses the question, 'But what are we?' Well, I guess we're sand crabs or scabs or something less dignified."

Aykroyd and River had a host of running jokes; they dubbed the catering truck the Roach Coach, which evolved into calling each other Mr. Woach and Mrs. Woach. River would pinch the fat on Aykroyd's waist, or blow on his bald spot. "Just complete, absolute, total irreverence," Aykroyd said. "And he could get away with it."

The first day of shooting, Robinson thought River was fine—but when he saw him in dailies, he was much more impressed. "He makes very quirky choices that really come alive on film," the director said.

The quirkiest choice of all comes during a montage at a party, where most of the cast takes turns dancing with Mary McDonnell while Aretha Franklin's "Chain of Fools" plays. Poitier is all stiff reserve, while Aykroyd proves to be a surprisingly accomplished swing dancer. And then River flails around like a punk moshing at a Germs concert, kneecaps bobbing and arms waving. It's the most visually arresting seven seconds in the movie.

The shoot stretched over five months, but River had plenty of downtime, both because he had a supporting role in a large ensemble and because breaks were built into the schedule; Redford insisted on ten days off at Christmastime so he could go on his annual skiing vacation. So River pushed forward with Aleka's Attic.

Drummer Josh Greenbaum came to California and spent hours jamming with River between scenes. The two-year development deal with Island had been going on for roughly four years; the label wanted to see if their investment had paid off. A&R rep Kim Buie engaged top-flight producer T-Bone Burnett (Elvis Costello, Los Lobos) and River went into the studio to record two songs with Greenbaum, Rain, and Flea.

When Chris Blackwell heard the tape, he decided not to pick up the option on the band—to River's dismay. "It turned out that my voice wasn't star-quality," River said sardonically. "I'm so glad that it didn't happen, because I don't want to make music for the masses. I just want to make it for my friends and the people I play with."

"In hindsight, I'm not sure that River having a band was necessarily the best decision," Buie said; she thought he might have done better as a solo acoustic performer. "A band takes time. And his acting career was always competing for his time. Finding the flow and the continuity within a band, it was a challenge. I think he just wasn't at a place where he could do it full-time, and figure out what River Phoenix—the musician, the artist, the songwriter—wanted to be."

While *Sneakers* shot in Los Angeles, River stayed at Flea's house. The bassist was out of town on tour, but plenty of his friends still came around, giving River easy access to whatever drug he wanted, including heroin. Not that it was all party time: one disagreement led to a drug buddy chasing River through the house with a butcher's knife.

Soon after that incident, River's former tutor Dirk Drake came to visit and was extremely concerned by the heroin situation. He told River that he was "furious about the glamour those friends attached to skag."

To which River replied, "Don't worry, I have the fear of God."

That infuriated Drake, who suggested that River should change careers from actor to Baptist preacher.

Jim Dobson, who had been the publicist on *Jimmy Reardon,* saw River for the first time in years, and was astonished by the transformation. "He was 100% different," Dobson said. "He'd gone from a cute, well-groomed kid to someone who wouldn't bathe, and his face was very gray. We all assumed he was on drugs."

Aykroyd, who had lost his close friend and performing partner John Belushi to a drug overdose, tried to steer River away from heroin. "I think Aykroyd was a very good influence on his life," Dobson said.

Drake said that there were multiple interventions by River's friends about his drinking and drug abuse, but none of them had any effect: "River had a strong passion and love of sensation, whether it was watching a full moon or tossing some pints."

Sneakers is not without charm—in a climactic scene, the principals are being held at gunpoint by the NSA, but then realize they have the black-box MacGuffin, and hence, the upper hand. They start making demands before they hand it over. Redford's character obtains a promise that the federal government will leave him alone, while Aykroyd's gets a fully kitted Winnebago. River's character, Carl Arbogast, just asks for the phone number of "the young lady with the Uzi." Moments like that are why the film was not only a solid box-office hit, but also has retained a small but devoted cult following across the decades.

The film received generally positive, if not effusive, reviews. Rita Kempley in the *Washington Post* called it an "entertaining time-waster," describing River's performance as "sweetly underwhelming."

Ultimately, for all its twists, turns, and reverses, the picture feels thin and formulaic. River didn't care for it, and told his friends not to see it. "I play this cyberpunk nerd, just full on," he said. "I've really degraded myself. He's very hyper, always twitching, the kind of guy you avoid playing if you want to walk with dignity and grace at the premiere."

In keeping with its code-breaking theme, the opening credits of *Sneakers* has the names of some of the film's major players presented as anagrams before they get unscrambled: "BLOND RHINO SPANIEL" becomes "PHIL ALDEN ROBINSON," while "FORT RED BORDER" turns into "ROBERT REDFORD" and "A TURNIP CURES ELVIS" reveals itself as "UNIVERSAL PICTURES." Not all cast members got their names shuffled—if they had, the world might have discovered that one anagram for "RIVER PHOENIX" is "VIPER HEROIN X."

THE MOVIES OF RIVER PHOENIX, RANKED BY AMERICAN BOX OFFICE

Indiana Jones and the Last Crusade ($197.1)

Stand by Me ($52.3)

Sneakers ($51.4)

I Love You to Death ($16.1)

The Mosquito Coast ($14.3)

Explorers ($9.8)

My Own Private Idaho ($6.4)

A Night in the Life of Jimmy Reardon ($6.2)

Running on Empty ($2.8)

Little Nikita ($1.7)

The Thing Called Love ($1.0)

Dogfight ($0.3)

Silent Tongue ($0.06)

All numbers are in millions of dollars and not adjusted for inflation or rounded up, meaning that *Sneakers* grossed $51,432,691, *Dogfight* $394,631 and *Silent Tongue* just $61,274.

68

COWBOY MOUTH

With *Sneakers* all laced up, River went straight to New Mexico to make *Silent Tongue*. The western ghost story was written and directed by Sam Shepard, the acclaimed playwright who had found primal poetry in surreal tales of family conflict such as *True West,* winning the Pulitzer for *Buried Child*. He was also famous for playing Chuck Yeager in *The Right Stuff*—he received an Oscar nomination for best supporting actor—and for his long-term relationship with Jessica Lange.

Another *Silent Tongue* actor was Dermot Mulroney, who became friendly with River and tried to bring him up to speed on their director's awe-inspiring CV. "Imagine me having to be the one to educate River on what Sam Shepard has written," he said. "He had no concept of Sam as a playwright or a screenwriter or a director, or anything other than a sort of actor or well-known something or other. I had to explain to him what a Pulitzer Prize was and what Sam won it for and why: 'Here's another play, River, I know you're not going to read the whole play, but please read these three pages before you have to jump up and do something else.' He was undereducated and overintelligent."

Aside from Mulroney, the cast included Bill Irwin, Alan Bates, and Richard Harris. River played Talbot Roe, a settler on the American frontier in 1873, driven mad with grief over the death of his wife, the half–Native American Awbonnie (Sheila Tousey). His father (Harris) visits Eamon McCree (Bates), who runs the traveling Kickapoo Indian Medicine Show, and offers him gold for his daughter—the sister of Talbot's wife. Meanwhile, Talbot sinks deeper into insanity, putting a shotgun to his chin, covering his face with white paint, and refusing to dispose of Awbonnie's corpse, declaring, "I

162

will not stop until your hair has blown away"—even after her ghost appears to him, demanding that he burn her body so she can move on to the spirit world.

The movie, stronger on mood than plot, isn't very good—*Silent Tongue* ended up being the second and final film directed by Shepard. But if its ambition exceeds its reach, at least it has ambition.

As was his habit, River found an older man working on the movie to be his role model and surrogate father for the duration of the shoot. In this case, it was the hard-living Richard Harris, an Oscar nominee in 1967 for *This Sporting Life* and in 1990 for *The Field,* and also a top-ten recording artist with his version of "MacArthur Park."

River was very protective of the sixty-year-old Harris, driving him to the set every day and making sure that he had company. "He looked upon me as a kind of father figure. He'd knock at my door and ask if he could come in and sleep," Harris said. "He'd sleep on the couch. I could hear him rehearsing his lines—at four in the morning. I said, 'Fuckin' go to sleep.' He'd be in the bathroom, taking a crap, doing his lines."

River's actual father, John Phoenix, was well aware that his son had filled his absence with a series of other men—which didn't stop him from abdicating to Costa Rica. When John met William Richert, the longest running of the substitute patriarchs, he looked him in the eye and said, "You know, I think you're his real father."

Richert replied, "No, I'm his real *friend.*"

John, who might have preferred to be friend rather than father, ended up not really being either.

River was booked to work only three weeks on *Silent Tongue,* but he ended up staying for the whole seven-week shoot. When he was playing Talbot, he did so with vigor, his voice cracking, his eyes wild, his face a rictus of grief and madness. River was so fully grunged up as an unwashed frontiersman, he was barely recognizable.

Mulroney said, "Sam was, in my opinion, completely and utterly perplexed by River. He was truly taken with him but couldn't figure him out.

Sam would always have that crooked smile, watching, trying to figure out how much of this was River preparing to play an uncultured mad dog, and how much of it was really River."

Some of the filmmakers wondered whether River was acting under the influence, but everyone was impressed by his spirit and his generosity. This was consistently true—even during his periods of heaviest drug use, River didn't succumb to the solipsistic worldview of the junkie, where humanity separates into people who can help you get your next fix and people who can't. The *Silent Tongue* production had only four trailers, which were assigned to the top talent. When River discovered that Sheila Tousey, who played his wife, required long hours for her revenant makeup and extensive vocal exercises, but had access only to the communal makeup trailer nicknamed the "honey wagon," he volunteered to swap spaces with her. Producer Carolyn Pfeiffer remembered, "I'd never had an actor say, 'May I give up my comfortable space for a smaller one because one of my fellow performers needs it more than I do?'"

164

BURN HOLLYWOOD BURN

While River Phoenix was in New Mexico, Los Angeles caught on fire. After four policemen brutally beat Rodney King at the end of a high-speed chase—an act caught on videotape—they went on trial for assault and excessive force. When they were acquitted, on April 29, 1992, the African American community of Los Angeles exploded, furious at the jury condoning the white-on-black police brutality. Thousands (of all ethnicities) rioted over the course of a week; there was almost a billion dollars in property damage and over fifty people died. The violence was quelled only by the arrival of the National Guard and federal troops.

The Cosby Show, which had presented a prosperous black family in Brooklyn Heights for eight seasons without dwelling on race relations, aired its final episode on April 30, with the riots in full swing and nobody in the United States thinking about anything but race relations.

With the LAPD unable to provide security, the studios shut down location shoots. A mob of one hundred attempted to storm the headquarters of the Directors Guild of America, where a screening of *Big Girls Don't Cry* was being held. The Lakers and Clippers both moved their playoff games out of town. David Bowie and Iman, intending to begin their married life together in Los Angeles, flew into LAX just as the riots began; they ended up living in New York. *Playboy* didn't cancel the Playmate of the Year lunch at the Playboy Mansion, crowning Corinna Harney as its youngest-ever holder of that title.

There were dead bodies in the streets.

By the time *Silent Tongue* wrapped, the riots were over, but L.A. was pockmarked with rubble—buildings and entire minimalls that just weren't there anymore, like a pearly-white smile that had a few teeth knocked out. Nevertheless, River flew west to L.A. rather than east to Gainesville. After he'd gotten dropped by Island, there didn't seem to be much point to revving up Aleka's Attic again. L.A. offered him the opportunity to figure out his next move, and to have a good time.

River visited Richert, with Joaquin tagging along—he had decided to drop "Leaf" and revert to his birth name. Richert's house had a two-story atrium with a glass dome on the top. The day was cold, so the glass had fogged up. Richert looked up to discover that "Joaquin had drawn Satan in every single window."

Worried that Joaquin might fall through the glass, killing himself and the people below, Richert yelled at him to come down. Joaquin, framed by the scrawls in the condensation so that he appeared to have horns himself, just laughed.

"Joaquin had a whole other kind of energy," Richert said. "He was not River. His mother was not River. None of those people were River, even if he took care of them and they all called themselves Phoenix."

"I'm a minor, stupid talent compared to my brother," River said.

River was fond of pranks himself, although without a diabolical edge—his taste lay more in the direction of tall tales. Nick Richert, son of the director, said, "River would just bullshit and say anything and you'd believe it. He was a mind-fucker. I always had to stay aloof from him because I didn't want to get drawn in and seem gullible."

River decided that he would surprise Solgot, who was in San Francisco on her birthday. He flew up to visit her, accompanied by Richert. They went to her birthday party—but just before they entered, River pulled out a paper bag and put it over his head. "Nobody knew it was him, even his girlfriend didn't," Richert said. This seems, frankly, implausible—even if somehow Solgot didn't recognize his voice or his body, surely the presence of River's close friend Richert was a dead giveaway.

Whether they were genuinely fooled or just humoring River, everyone at the party played along, interacting with Mr. Sack as an anonymous party guest. River didn't drop the gag, keeping the paper bag on for three hours; eventually everybody accepted that there was a guest with unusual headgear. "He was watching what everybody else was doing," Richert said. "I remember thinking how devoted he was to a trick that he wanted to pull off. He never took this bag off."

MANY RIVERS TO CROSS

River started meeting with John Boorman, the British director of *Point Blank, Deliverance,* and *Excalibur.* Back in 1979, Boorman and Irish director Neil Jordan had written a science-fiction script called *Broken Dream,* and had been trying to get it made ever since. River agreed to play Ben, a magician in a dystopic world—Ben's father teaches him to make things (and ultimately people) vanish. Winona Ryder signed on as well, and when Jordan had a big hit with *The Crying Game* in October 1992, it looked like the movie was finally happening. But then—in a common film-world setback—the funding collapsed and the project was shelved. (Two decades later, in 2012, Boorman announced the revival of the project with Ben Kingsley, John Hurt, and Caleb Landry Jones—although a year later, there appeared to be no forward motion, meaning the *Broken Dream* clock had been running for over thirty-four years.)

"I met with River a few times," Boorman said. "He was streetwise, but at the same time, there was this fragility about him. You felt that somehow he had to be protected."

German director Volker Schlöndorff (*The Tin Drum, The Handmaid's Tale*) wanted River to star in the film version of Christopher Hampton's play *Total Eclipse* as Arthur Rimbaud, the enfant terrible of nineteenth-century French poetry. As a teen, Rimbaud famously had a torrid affair with the older French poet Paul Verlaine, which ended when Verlaine shot him in the wrist. Rimbaud, ravenous for all forms of human experience, did his most famous work ("Le Bateau ivre" ("The Drunken Boat") and *Une Saison en Enfer* (*A Season in Hell*)) before the age of nineteen, when he renounced poetry.

One hundred and one years after Rimbaud's death, River felt so deeply connected to him that he started carrying around a copy of *Time of the Assassins,* Henry Miller's biography of the poet. He obsessively found connections between his own life and Rimbaud's and would quote key passages from Miller's book to friends.

Time of the Assassins portrayed the artist as the most exalted and the most wretched creature on earth: "Conditioned to ecstasy, the poet is like a gorgeous unknown bird mired in the ashes of thought. If he succeeds in freeing himself, it is to make a sacrificial flight to the sun. His dreams of a regenerate world are but the reverberations of his own fevered pulse beats. He imagines the world will follow him, but in the blue he finds himself alone."

For River to discover himself in Rimbaud's life and Miller's prose was simultaneously self-aggrandizing and self-pitying. Tellingly, he was more interested in Miller's book than in Rimbaud's actual writing: he responded to Rimbaud not as a poet, but as a symbol.

John Malkovich signed on as Verlaine. While River waited for the project to come together—for any project to come together—he stayed in L.A. and kept partying. Solgot thought of Los Angeles as the poisoned wellspring of River's drug problems; too many people there were eager to supply him with whatever substance he desired. The couple's relationship was undergoing tremors as two tectonic plates ground against each other: River's drug use and his denial of the idea that it was a problem. "He didn't want me nagging him," Solgot said. "Pointing out the contradictions between his public stands and what he was doing to his body."

"He was hanging around with people who didn't really care about him," said Louanne Sirota, who had acted with him in *Jimmy Reardon* and *Seven Brides*. "I know he was hanging around with a couple of English dudes that couldn't have given a shit about who he was, as far as a human being goes; they were about as shallow as a two-foot pool."

At a 1992 wedding, River's decline was obvious to everyone in attendance. "It was a formal affair," said one of the guests. "Even the Chili Peppers were wearing cheesy seventies tuxedos. But River arrived at 9:30 A.M., drinking a bottle of wine, dressed in sneakers, a pair of shaggy, ripped shorts, and a dirty T-shirt. People were angry with him."

Martha Plimpton would sometimes talk with River on the phone, but "his language had become at times totally incoherent," she said. "He'd often be high when he called, and I'd listen for twenty minutes to his jumbled, made-up words, his own logic, and not know what the fuck he was talking about. He'd say, 'You're just not listening carefully enough.'"

River was not blind to addiction—he personally drove a rock-star guitarist friend to rehab. Twice. And he knew that his consumption of hard drugs was not congruent with his tree-hugging image, even wondering aloud, "What would those twelve-year-old girls with a picture of me over their bed think if they knew?" But that didn't mean he would actually admit he had a problem.

"He fooled a lot of people and he fooled himself," Solgot said. "He was a great actor."

Paul Petersen, a former Mouseketeer and star of *The Donna Reed Show,* had started a support organization for former child stars, called A Minor Concern. In mid-1992, he got "a frantic phone call from a journalist pal who saw River and five other young actors shooting up in the bathroom of the Roxy," he said. The Roxy was a storied rock club on the Sunset Strip, a quarter mile from the Viper Room's future location.

Believing strongly in the power of intervention, Petersen gathered a medical doctor and another former child star, and went to visit River in his hotel room.

River opened the door a crack, but wouldn't let them in. He told them that the Roxy story was a lie, declaring, "I don't even eat meat." (True, but a non sequitur.)

"He was in heavy denial and obviously loaded," Petersen remembered.

"I don't need your help," River told them. And then he shut the door.

169

THE LAST PICTURE

In an effort to get her top-earning slice of filet mignon working again, Iris Burton sent River the screenplay for *The Thing Called Love,* a tale of romance among aspiring singer/songwriters in Nashville.

A few days later, River called her back. "This script really isn't ready at all," he chided her.

Burton agreed, but said that she was confident it would be whipped into shape, since the director was Peter Bogdanovich. River, however, had no idea who that was.

In the late sixties, Peter Bogdanovich had turned his autodidactic film obsession into a career as a movie director—much like Quentin Tarantino two decades later, except Bogdanovich's training ground was programming the film series at the Museum of Modern Art in Manhattan, not working behind the counter at the Video Archives video-rental store in Manhattan Beach. After filming two movies for low-budget schlockmeister Roger Corman, Bogdanovich made his masterpiece in 1971: *The Last Picture Show* was an elegiac black-and-white picture about coming of age in a dying Texas town. Bogdanovich was nominated for two Oscars, and left his wife (editor Polly Platt) for his star, Cybill Shepherd. His movies after that included *Paper Moon* and *Mask,* but he entered into a long, slow artistic decline. He became most famous for dating Playmate Dorothy Stratten—and then, after she was brutally murdered by her ex, marrying her younger sister, Louise.

Burton told River to go to the video store and rent *The Last Picture Show.* He did, and was blown away; he told Burton he wanted to make a movie with "the guy who directed that picture."

"Iris had called in every favor she had to secure River the lead," her assistant, Chris Snyder, said. The studio, Paramount, would have preferred meathead country singer Billy Ray Cyrus, who was enjoying blockbuster success with his debut album, *Some Gave All,* and the single "Achy Breaky Heart." (He would later be famous as the father of Disney starlet Miley Cyrus.) But Bogdanovich got on the phone with River and asked him how he would convey the dangerous qualities of the male lead, James.

River paused, and then said, "Silence."

Duly impressed, Bogdanovich hired River (who was paid $1.5 million), although he didn't meet him until filming started, a month later. Before he showed up, River offered his advice on casting, recommending Dermot Mulroney (whom he knew from *Silent Tongue*) for his romantic rival and Anthony Clark (a *Dogfight* costar) for the ensemble. Impressed by his instincts, and by how River was considering the big picture, Bogdanovich said he "increasingly wanted him involved in all script conferences, all writing sessions, all music discussions."

Clark noted, "It's one thing to be the star and carry a motion picture, but he wanted to write the music, perform the music, and be in on the decision making."

When Bogdanovich told River that he should be a director, River confided that he had been thinking about it. "Well, be sure and cast me, will ya?" Bogdanovich joked. Bogdanovich asked River how he became interested in show business; River told him a tale about how his mother had read stories to him as a kid. He had liked that, he said, so now he liked being part of a bigger story.

The bigger story in this movie was the young musician Miranda Presley (played by Samantha Mathis) moving to Nashville to make it as a singer/songwriter, and having two rival singers (River and Mulroney) compete for her heart. K. T. Oslin played the owner of the Bluebird Café, where Miranda gets a waitress job, and Sandra Bullock played her roommate, long on spunk and short on talent. (The energetic Bullock ended up stealing the movie.)

Shooting began, and things quickly went awry. Iris Burton got panicked phone calls from the film's producer, John Davis; Bogdanovich; and an array of Paramount execs. Davis sent her a VHS tape of River's dailies, and the problem became clear:

> The first take was River opening the door to a truck. Instead of walking to his mark, he stumbled and almost fell. His face was ghastly white and his blond hair, freshly dyed black, was slicked back. He looked awful . . .
>
> River did his scenes over and over. His eyes were unfocused. He mumbled his lines into the ground, not looking at the other actors or the camera. In an hour of dailies, there wasn't one good scene. Even after twenty takes he never managed to get it right.

According to Bogdanovich, on the night of the truck scene, "River was wandering around the parking lot, looking forlorn and agitated." The director asked his star if he had been using drugs; River said that he had taken a pain pill and drunk a beer, and the two weren't interacting well. Bogdanovich then asked him about his behavior; Mathis had complained that he was being rude

171

to her. A contrite River said that he was just trying to get into the head of James Wright, his hard-edged character. Bogdanovich quoted a maxim from legendary Method acting teacher Stella Adler: "To play dead, darling, you don't have to die!"

River told him that he thought that James had "been into drugs," which had made him "a bit of a bastard." When Bogdanovich encouraged him to downplay that aspect of the character, River blithely assured him that he didn't have "a problem with drugs"—he was just figuring out James.

Bogdanovich would later minimize River's troubles that night and insist that he "didn't cause me another problem on the entire picture." But the situation was deemed serious enough that Burton flew out to Nashville, to her great displeasure ("What am I supposed to do? Give him a spanking?"). Nobody else was willing to confront River, including Heart—who was not only his mother, but also still his manager.

In Nashville, Bogdanovich told Burton that the studio was freaking out because they didn't understand the role River was playing. When she spoke with River, he sobbed in her arms, swearing that he didn't do drugs and blaming the punishing production schedule. She stayed in Nashville to make sure there would be no more lapses on her client's part.

River confessed to Bogdanovich that Solgot had recently told him that she had cheated on him during his long absence from Florida. He acknowledged that he hadn't been faithful himself, and that his behavior might have prompted her dalliance—which didn't lessen its sting. He then proceeded to argue the case from her perspective, conceding that cheating might be a defense mechanism that let her feel in control of the situation.

At the same time, River was nursing a crush on Mathis, counting the days until their first kissing scene. The night they shot it, River told Bogdanovich to make sure the camera was fully loaded with film, because it was going to be a long kiss. He then proceeded to list the things he wanted to do with Mathis, itemizing the parts of her body he wanted to kiss.

They shot about seven takes, all of them steamy. "Samantha managed a pretty impassive, professional look between takes," Bogdanovich said, "while

River just loudly asked for 'another one—we need another one, don't you think, Peter?' Samantha laughed."

Mathis had been dating actor/comic John Leguizamo (they had been in the *Super Mario Bros.* movie together); he came to visit her in Nashville, but stayed only one day. Mathis broke up with him, and she and River became a couple.

Samantha Mathis grew up in Brooklyn, the daughter of actress Bibi Besch, who appeared in various soap operas but was perhaps best known for her role in *Star Trek II: The Wrath of Khan* as Carol Marcus, the mother of Captain Kirk's son. Besch discouraged her daughter from following in her footsteps, even bringing her to work for a 4:30 A.M. call time in the hope that the pre-dawn work hours would dissuade her, but Mathis persisted. At age twenty, she had a memorable role opposite Christian Slater in the pirate-radio movie *Pump Up the Volume* (she dated Slater, too); two years later, she was playing the central character in *The Thing Called Love.*

River wrestled over the script with Allan Moyle, the writer/director of *Pump Up the Volume,* who had been brought on the set to punch up the *Thing Called Love* screenplay. "River was determined to keep his character from being bubblegum and easily figured out," Moyle said. "Unfortunately, one of my jobs as a ghostwriter was to make him accessible." River was also campaigning to write his own songs for the movie, but the studio approved just one, "Lone Star State of Mine."

173

Moyle was planning a remake of the 1966 British film *Morgan—A Suitable Case for Treatment* (aka *Morgan!*), about a husband who responds to his divorce with ill-advised stunts such as crashing his ex-wife's wedding while wearing a gorilla suit. As Moyle got to know River better, he thought he might be perfect for the manic, unbalanced title role. River affected apathy when Moyle pitched him, but a few days later, when they were alone in his trailer, he gave a command performance as Morgan.

"River's face was contorted like a demented gorilla," recalled Moyle. "I was awed and shocked by his transformation. He was hooting and pogoing and swinging wildly and dangerously and trashing everything in sight." River was pure simian for thirty seconds—and then he stopped. He never repeated the performance, even when Moyle begged him.

River's best acting on *The Thing Called Love* may have been convincing his fellow filmmakers that he had everything under control. Clark said, "I knew maybe there were problems with . . . I didn't really know what . . . I was scared to even ask, because a few times I did talk to him about his intense situation with alcohol. I brought it up, but he was such a great actor that he would make you feel crazy for even asking him, 'Is everything all right?' And I wish to God that I could have stepped in and intervened, but he just seemed so incredibly together."

The shoot moved cross-country to finish at the Disney-owned Golden Oak Ranch, north of Los Angeles. River told Bogdanovich that he didn't care for L.A., confessing that it was a bad influence on him. Burton accompanied River back from Nashville, but he insisted on wearing a black ski mask the entire way. She was embarrassed, but pretended everything was normal.

Heart came to watch over River for the rest of the shoot; she was beginning to realize that her eldest child might have a problem. She didn't force the issue—either because she didn't believe the situation was that serious, or because she was avoiding conflict with her son (and management client). Burton's assistant, Chris Snyder, lamented, "No one wanted to confront him—not even his own mother."

The shoot concluded; River and Mathis paid for a wrap party at a Japanese karaoke club with a leaky roof. When the movie was cut together, the fact that everyone had attempted to ignore was on the screen, undeniable: River was in bad shape. He gave a sullen, distant performance, looking like a coke dealer and sulking his way through every scene.

The Thing Called Love received a minimal release; after River's death, critic Roger Ebert accurately described the movie as "a painful experience for anyone who remembers him in good health. He looks ill—thin, sallow, listless. His eyes are directed mostly at the ground. He cannot meet the camera, or the eyes of the other actors. It is sometimes difficult to understand his dialogue. Even worse, there is no energy in the dialogue, no conviction that he cares about what he is saying."

Ebert allowed that the filmmakers might have convinced themselves that River was giving a Brandoesque performance, one that would blossom on-screen. His final judgment, however, was that "the world was shocked when River Phoenix overdosed, but the people working on this film should not have been . . . this performance should have been seen by someone as a cry for help."

The rest of the film had virtues and flaws, but they hardly mattered when the male lead was wasting away before the audience's eyes, turning into a shadow of himself.

YOUNG HOLLYWOOD 1993

175

For his *Idaho* follow-up, Gus Van Sant was offered the job of directing a movie about famed gay politician Harvey Milk, with Oliver Stone producing and Robin Williams starring. He spent a year working on the project, but instead made *Even Cowgirls Get the Blues,* an adaptation of the cult Tom Robbins novel about a girl with abnormally large thumbs (played by Uma Thurman). Reeves played her husband, a repressed Mohawk named Julian Gitche; Rain Phoenix also appeared as the sexually liberated cowgirl Bonanza Jellybean. The film debuted to widespread critical derision. (It was rumored that River made a cameo, but Van Sant insisted not.) Later in the year, Reeves started filming *Speed,* everybody's favorite bus-that-can't-slow-down-because-there's-a-bomb-strapped-to-it movie, costarring with Sandra Bullock; it would prove to be an enormous, star-making hit for both of them.

Leonardo DiCaprio was handpicked by Robert De Niro and director Michael Caton-Jones to play De Niro's stepson in *This Boy's Life,* a drama about an abusive family. Critics raved that DiCaprio gave as good as he got from De Niro; the New York *Daily News* called it "the breakthrough performance of the decade." (And although the decade wasn't even half done, they were probably right.)

DiCaprio then teamed up with Johnny Depp: they played brothers in the moving, off-kilter Lasse Hallström drama *What's Eating Gilbert Grape?* Depp starred as Gilbert, stuck in a small town caring for his family, which includes his five-hundred-pound mother and his mentally impaired brother (DiCaprio, in a great performance). DiCaprio had been offered a part in *Hocus Pocus,* a forgettable comedy with Bette Midler, Rosie O'Donnell, and Sarah Jessica Parker as a family of witches. "I knew it was awful," DiCaprio said, "but it was just like, 'OK, they're offering me more and more money. Isn't that what you do? You do movies and you get more money.' But something inside me kept saying, 'Don't do this movie.'" All of his advisers were telling him to take the job, but he decided to audition for *Gilbert Grape* instead. Artistic virtue was rewarded when he received an Oscar nomination for his work on the movie.

Depp had largely put his career on hold the previous two years while Winona Ryder worked almost continuously, but he knew they were growing apart; they broke up in May, right after *Gilbert Grape* wrapped. "Johnny was pretty unhappy then," Depp said of the *Gilbert Grape* shoot. Mercifully switching to the first person, he continued, "I was poisoning myself beyond belief. There was a lot of liquor, a lot of liquor. I was in a pretty unhealthy state."

He did find solace during the shoot by attending a Neil Young show, where he met and befriended Gibby Haynes; the Butthole Surfers had recently released their sixth album, *Independent Worm Saloon.* For fun, Haynes and Depp started a new band together. Called P ("spelled u-r-i-n-e," Depp helpfully explained), the band also included songwriter Bill Carter and Depp's close friend Sal Jenco. They mostly played sloppy, squalling rock with a sense of humor, as in their cover of Daniel Johnston's "I Save Cigarette Butts."

Brad Pitt followed up on his success in *A River Runs Through It* (the *Los Angeles Times* called his performance "career-making") by scuffing up his wholesome blond image. He and his then-girlfriend Juliette Lewis starred in the serial-killer drama *Kalifornia* (she would make a more successful version of the same movie the following year with *Natural Born Killers*). He also had a small role in *True Romance* (directed by Tony Scott, written by Quentin Tarantino) as a metal-head couch potato, getting stoned from a honey-bear bong, unfazed by the appearance of gangsters with shotguns. Christian Slater starred as the comic-book clerk who marries a hooker named Alabama (Patricia Arquette), kills her pimp, and heads to California with a bag full of uncut cocaine.

R.E.M. was still releasing singles off the massively successful *Automatic for the People,* generally regarded as the best album the band ever made. Michael Stipe had stopped giving interviews (guitarist Peter Buck and bassist Mike Mills took care of that), but since he was interested in photography and film-making, he oversaw the band's videos.

Martha Plimpton was working steadily in little-seen projects: the improvised film *Chantilly Lace* (on Showtime), the dystopic movie *Daybreak* (on HBO), and the child-runaway movie *Josh and S.A.M.* (a theatrical flop). Jerry O'Connell had slimmed down dramatically since his *Stand by Me* days, and began an adult leading-man career playing a one-legged character opposite Jason Priestley in the period film *Calendar Girl,* about three friends on a mission to meet Marilyn Monroe.

Ethan Hawke followed up his appearance in *Alive* (plane crash! cannibalism! survival!) by making *Reality Bites,* a Generation-X romantic comedy, opposite Winona Ryder and director Ben Stiller, that captured both the exciting and annoying aspects of discovering you're part of a generation.

John Frusciante had abruptly quit the Red Hot Chili Peppers the year before—during a tour in Japan, he told them, "I can't do this anymore. I will die if I don't get out of this band right away." Before he left, he had been getting sloppy and erratic. Kiedis said: "I don't know if it was a combination of the wine and the pot, but it seemed like he was drinking psycho juice rather than just wine." Frusciante flew back to California, where he was free to play guitar and ingest whatever he liked without worrying about the rest of the world.

Depp and Haynes made a twelve-minute experimental film about Frusciante, called *Stuff.* In it, the camera pinwheels around Frusciante's home, showing guitars, sagging shelves of vinyl records, and debris on pretty much every flat surface. On the soundtrack, wheezing psychedelic music by Frusciante plays while the camera lingers on the walls of his home, covered with angry red scrawls of incoherent graffiti such as KILL PIGS BY LETTING THEM BECOME SHITS PEANUTS. The house is small enough that halfway through, the filmmakers just start repeating footage, which is perhaps more claustrophobic than intended. Somebody reads a poem on the soundtrack, and we finally see Frusciante—short hair, gray sweater, button-down shirt—and then LSD guru Timothy Leary, bald and in a psychedelic waistcoat. Surrounded by his clutter, Frusciante doesn't look like he has any intention of ever leaving his house again.

73 TONIGHT'S THE NIGHT

There's nothing in Hollywood so harrowing that it can't be presented with artifice. A West Hollywood chapter of Alcoholics Anonymous, for example, held its meetings in a fake log cabin. River went to a couple of meetings, but he didn't buy into the program, complaining, "I'm here because my manager and my publicist and my agent want me to be here. I drink and I do drugs, but I don't have a problem."

A British model/actor with the pseudonym of Cedric Niles had been holed up freebasing cocaine for two days straight—and then River showed up at his door, guided there by friends who knew they had shared interests. Niles didn't immediately recognize River, and not just because he had spent the previous forty-eight hours freebasing. River "was wearing those flared-out hippie pants and one of those hooded Mexican shirts" and no shoes. River had grown his hair long again; he kept it hanging over his face.

The two of them smoked their way through River's ample stash of co-caine, and then went wandering down Melrose Avenue, barefoot, looking for a guitar. Over the following two weeks, they kept getting high. River told Niles the password that would get phone calls put through to his room at the upscale St. James's Club & Hotel: "Earl Grey."

According to Niles, River lived in fear that his drug use would become general knowledge. River would call Niles when he got bored, but would never leave his name on the answering machine: "Hey, is anyone there? Is anyone there? It's . . . it's . . ." And then he'd hang up.

Another friend remembered River as always having top-notch pot, plus Valiums. His suspicions were aroused by River's tiny pupils—in his experi-ence, that meant heroin. "When you do blow, your eyes get huge," he said. But when he asked about heroin, River denied it emphatically. Apparently, some things were secret, even from drug buddies.

The first time the two of them freebased coke together, Niles recalled, River said, "Gee, I've never done this before." But when they prepped their works, River "knew exactly how to do it. We freebased all night at the St. James's Club in West Hollywood, staying up 'til 6 A.M., getting totally para-noid. It was a nightmare, really. When he was very high, he'd play and sing these songs with the most bizarre lyrics. Through it all, though, he was an absolute sweetheart."

It wasn't hard to find drugs in Hollywood. The Sunset Strip was practically a narcotics supermarket, where it was easy to get cocaine, Ecstasy, weed, and a potent dose of heroin branded "Body Bag." (Explained one dealer, "That's what they'll take you out in if you use it.") Heroin had recently acquired a hipster sheen; junkies could snort lines in clubs instead of shooting up in a filthy crash pad. "Heroin chic" and emaciated models became trendy—with Calvin Klein's 1993 ad campaign starring a skinny Kate Moss, the look and vibe of the drug went mainstream.

The intoxicant of the season in Los Angeles, however, was GHB, a chem-ical cocktail of gamma-Hydroxybutyric acid, nicknamed "Grievous Bodily Harm." "People say it's an amino acid, and it's all natural, but it's really a

179

drug, like liquid Ecstasy," said one Sunset regular, then in her twenties. The euphoric effects were similar to Ecstasy, which had fallen out of vogue, both because regular users found their bodies habituated to it and because a lot of dealers sold placebos. Bodybuilders started using GHB to take the edge off steroids, and the drug then crossed over to the club scene. Doses got passed around as a clear liquid.

Another Sunset regular said, "I tried it once, and I was never so high in my life. The guy who gave it to me said it was a ginseng drink, but it tasted like salt water. An hour later, I couldn't put one leg out in front of me to make it out of the building." Sneering rock star Billy Idol took too much GHB and went into convulsions outside the hip club Tatou; he was rushed to the hospital and survived to release the 1993 flop album *Cyberpunk*.

As one graffiti artist summed up the Los Angeles nightlife, "The real drug of choice in this city is 'more.'"

Pleasant Gehman, a former roommate of Belinda Carlisle (lead singer of the Go-Go's), was a writer who also performed in a band called the Ringling Sisters. She helped put together an annual orphanage benefit at the Roxy nightclub. While Gehman was running around, organizing audience raffles, she noticed "a really cute boy passed out backstage," looking sweaty and unhealthy. Time passed, and he didn't get up. Finally, Gehman demanded, "Who is that really cute and really fucked-up boy that's laying on the floor? We have to get him out of here."

Somebody informed her that it was River Phoenix.

"*That's* River Phoenix? Jesus."

Flea, formerly a heavy-duty drug user himself, saw the condition River was in and urged him to get help, to no avail. Early one morning, River stumbled into the house of his friend Bobby Bukowski, the *Dogfight* cinematographer, blotto on a speedball of heroin and cocaine, and crashed. When he finally woke up, he staggered to the kitchen and attempted to purge his system with his preferred cure: garlic, raw vegetables, and lots of water. Bukowski confronted him, saying, "I'd rather you just point a gun at your head and pull the trigger. I want to see you become an old man, so we can be old friends together."

River started crying, and promised to stop using. "That's the end of the drugs," he promised. "I don't want to go down to the place that's so dark it'll annihilate me."

Meanwhile, River needed to book his next job. With word out around town about his erratic behavior in Nashville, offers and scripts were no longer flowing into the office of Iris Burton. And the clock was ticking: the release of *Silent Tongue* and *The Thing Called Love* were going to make him even less employable. Or as he put it, "When my next two films are released, I'm only going to be doing B-movies." (*Silent Tongue* didn't hit theaters until after River died, but it had already played Sundance, and Todd McCarthy had slammed it in *Variety* as "a bizarre, meandering, and finally maddening mystical oater that will find few partisans.")

Burton's assistant Chris Snyder remembered one night at 3 A.M. when he got a drunken phone call from River, in a car with Samantha Mathis, wanting to know why the agency had been hiding scripts from him—specifically, the screenplay of *Reality Bites*.

"You've had that script for a month," a groggy Snyder told River. "I've asked you to read it *five* times. You told me to pass on it for you."

"Samantha said it was great. I trust her. I don't trust you!" River yelled. "I just want to do the fucking movie!"

"I think Samantha wants to do the fucking movie," Snyder snapped. "You want the script, you'll have it tomorrow, but tell Samantha, Winona Ryder already has the part she wants."

The next day, Snyder delivered the *Reality Bites* script to River at the St. James's Club. River came to the door, soaking wet in a towel, and hugged Snyder, soaking his shirt. Having finally read Mathis's copy of the script, he decided that the project wasn't actually right for him. He still hadn't read *Interview with the Vampire* or *Dark Blood,* projects that the agency was keen on him doing—to demonstrate his lack of interest in the *Vampire* script, he threw it across the room.

"Do you have any idea how hard Iris and I have worked to get you considered for these parts?" Snyder asked him.

"I don't want to work any more!" River replied. "You can tell Iris and my mother! My passion is my music." Moments later, reality set in: "I have to work," he conceded. "After all these years, I still don't have enough money to just say 'Fuck you' to this town. The band is expensive. So is Costa Rica."

River asked Snyder how he could get a bank account that was solely in his name; Snyder assured him that he probably had more money than he thought. "Not enough to never have to fucking bleed in front of the camera again," River said. "Maybe I should just disappear for a while." In one breath, he was wondering if he could stop acting and go to college; in another, he was thinking about picking films that his grandchildren could be proud of.

Around this time, River said to Snyder, "I don't even like this business any more. I don't know if I ever liked it. I wasn't exactly given a choice."

When he was thinking about future movies, River juggled projects like the Hollywood pro he had become. He talked to William Richert about doing *The Man in the Iron Mask,* a Dumas adaptation, but cautioned him, "You know, Bill, I'm working with a lot of directors right now."

182

Some of those projects were less fully formed than others: for example, Polish actress/director Agnieszka Holland had a meeting with River around 1 A.M. in his hotel room. She later wrote:

> *He was sweating, drunk, tired, very beautiful. I suspected he had just read* Jack and Jill, *a screenplay by Robbie Baitz which is supposed to be my next movie. He very much wants to play Adam. He played Adam for an hour. He achieved what he wanted; I escaped from his room, I was dying of fatigue, but I was sure that none of the other wonderful actors I had met for this role would have such truthfulness, would have such courage and self-awareness of auto-destruction as River does.*

Burton and Snyder were also leaning on River to do *Safe Passage,* a domestic drama about a mother who has psychic premonitions. Susan Sarandon and Sam Shepard were signed on as the parents, and there were opportunities for multiple Phoenix children to be in the cast.

John Boorman, undaunted by the failure of *Broken Dream* to move from screenplay to actual film, was pitching River another project, called *Noah*. In this update of the Bible story, River would have played the title character, a stuttering zookeeper at the Bronx Zoo. God visits him and instructs him to build another ark. Noah reluctantly builds a ship and leads his animal charges to the East River to get on it. At the movie's end, he looks over the rising waters and sees countless other boats bobbing in the water. This time, when the world floods, everybody gets a boat.

River was also talking about making his directorial debut with a movie called *By Way of Fontana*. It would have told the story of his father's tumultuous childhood; Joaquin would have played John. The real-life John implored River to take a break from Hollywood and come down to stay with him in Costa Rica for a while, to flush out his system and get healthy. River rebuffed him.

George Sluizer was a Dutch director, sixty-one years old in 1993, best known for the chilling abduction drama *The Vanishing* (he also helmed the inferior American remake of the same name, starring Kiefer Sutherland). He was putting together a movie called *Dark Blood,* about a Hollywood couple who get stranded in the southwestern desert and meet a mysterious figure called Boy. He wanted River to star as Boy.

Sluizer met River in a chic hotel restaurant; early in the meeting, he apologized for being vague, saying he was suffering from a terrible headache. "River didn't ask the waiter to get aspirin," Sluizer said. "He left the table and ran, more than walked, to the pharmacy to get me aspirin." Duly impressed with River's charity toward somebody he had just met, Sluizer officially offered River the part.

River related a more cynical version of the meeting: "I told the director I loved the movies he'd made. Blah, blah, blah. I've never seen one of his fucking movies. I told him I *loved* the script and that I *really really* wanted to do his movie. The usual." But he agreed to star in *Dark Blood,* and to appear in a small but prominent role in *Interview with the Vampire,* as the interviewer.

Even when River regarded Hollywood courtship rituals with a jaundiced eye, flashes of generosity—running for the aspirin—came through. He kept putting himself in situations almost guaranteed to bring out the worst in people (all-night freebasing sessions, for example), but once he was there, somehow the best aspects of River would still shine.

I'M IN A TRANSITIONAL PERIOD, SO I DON'T WANT TO KILL YOU

Three years later, Quentin Tarantino surveyed the state of the movie business in the nineties, when the realization sank in among studio executives that the rules for commercial success had been upended. "Basically, that whole Touchstone formula that was existing in the eighties, that couldn't miss, is missing now. It doesn't work," he said gleefully. "The movies that are, like, sequels to the real big ones work because the audience has an investment in the franchise. But either the movies that used to be making $100 million are barely making $20 million or they're not even making that. I think right now is the most exciting time in Hollywood since 1971. Because Hollywood is never more exciting than when you don't know."

Tarantino did as much as anyone to upend those expectations when his *Pulp Fiction* did over $100 million at the American box office, reviving John Travolta's career and making the multiplexes safe for chronology-scrambling movies about foulmouthed gangsters making unlikely pop-culture references and groping toward a state of grace. (Unfortunately, that became a formula too.) In 1993, Tarantino was filming *Pulp Fiction;* the same year, sensing a tidal change in taste without really understanding it, Disney acquired Harvey and Bob Weinstein's Miramax, the production company behind Tarantino.

Dazed and Confused, Richard Linklater's pitch-perfect comedy about the last day of school in a Texas town in 1976, didn't do as much box office, but it laid out a new, looser way forward for movie comedies, and launched the careers of a large ensemble cast, including Matthew McConaughey, Ben Affleck, Parker Posey, and Milla Jovovich.

By 1993, River had been acting long enough—over a decade since he showed up at the *Seven Brides for Seven Brothers* ranch—that he was a seasoned veteran. But he was young enough that he was in a good position to surf the wave of generational change washing through Hollywood. He was, for example, younger than Matthew McConaughey.

Bill Clinton won the 1992 presidential election and moved into the White House in 1993. Just forty-six, he represented a new generation: the first American president born after World War II. (River served as his opening act at an early-morning campaign rally in Florida, playing music for a crowd of thousands of voters.)

Nineteen ninety-three was also the year of the first web browser, and the debut of *Wired* magazine. Culture was rapidly decentralizing, both through technology and changing taste, but the transition provoked anxiety. When Nirvana hit the top of the charts in 1992 and made the cover of *Rolling Stone,* Kurt Cobain wore a handmade T-shirt to the cover shoot. Its message: CORPORATE MAGAZINES STILL SUCK. It was a gesture born not just out of surprise that the band had catapulted from the cultural margins to the center, but out of dismay that the margins themselves had collapsed.

185

IF I HAD A HI-FI

The onetime dogfather of Gainesville was spending less and less time in Florida. After *The Thing Called Love* wrapped, he officially broke up with Solgot; they parted on amicable terms and she moved to San Francisco to work as a masseuse. While River and Mathis were smitten with each other, they didn't have the easy hippie domesticity that he and Solgot had found. One friend commented later, "I don't think their relationship would have lasted."

Some fans started making pilgrimages to Gainesville specifically to seek out River. One group of young Japanese female tourists came into a bar where River was having a beer, said a woman who was working there, and "started crying and trying to touch him. It was a weird scenario and it really freaked him out."

River considered leaving Florida, maybe giving away the Micanopy property to charity. He talked about moving to Boston, or Canada, or Athens, Georgia—he had spent time there playing music and hanging out with Michael Stipe. What kept him in Gainesville was Aleka's Attic.

With enough time to recover from the shock of the Island rejection, River had thrown himself back into his music. Violist Tim Hankins and bassist Josh McKay were gone, having started a new group. River didn't replace Hankins, but he recruited Sasa Raphael, a friend of Joaquin's, to play bass. With Rain and drummer Josh Greenbaum, they all went into the Pro Media Recording Studio in Gainesville. River paid for the studio time, and for the services of Grammy-nominated recording engineer Mark Pinske (a Frank Zappa veteran).

The sessions, costing thousands of dollars a week, happened sporadically for over a year whenever River was in Gainesville, ultimately adding up to about three months in the studio. Before River had to start filming *Dark Blood,* he made a final monthlong push, wanting to complete enough material for an album.

"River was in charge of everything," Pinske said. "Whatever River wanted, we did. He was a workhorse. He'd want to go, go, go, and sometimes we'd get past the point of no return."

Recording would typically last from noon until 6 A.M. the following day. After eighteen hours, River would collapse, sometimes falling asleep in his clothes, cradling his guitar. Heart made a daily appearance with health drinks and vegetarian platters, helping to keep everyone's strength up for the marathon sessions.

River kept writing song after song—after he finished each one, he would declare, "It's brilliant, brilliant." If anyone offered him advice or suggestions, he would blow them off, saying he didn't want to compromise the original idea. During the course of the sessions, he got a staggering ninety songs down on tape, but many of them were unpolished. River would quickly lose interest in fleshing out his material—he always had another song he wanted to get down.

"We were in overdrive," Raphael said. River experimented with unusual sonic ideas, such as doing vocals through a long tube or recording windshield wipers in the parking lot and incorporating the rhythm into a song.

Studio owner Dave Smadbeck, who was also working on the sessions, advised River that he needed more focus, with no effect. "He was being so creative that it was just one raw piece after another," he said. "He just had to get it out at any cost."

John had come up from Costa Rica to visit the family. He tried to be at every session, but didn't have the stamina for River's relentless pace. One time, when River found his father asleep on the studio couch, he positioned a microphone near his mouth to record his snores. Turning on his video camera to capture the scene, he then "interviewed" John. He would ask his father various questions—and each time, in response, John would snore. River and Joaquin were both helpless with laughter; when John woke up, he thought it was funny, too, and watched the video over and over. Neither father nor son could fix the other's problems, but they could take pleasure in each other's company.

The tracks, compiled after River's death and leaked under the title *Never Odd or Even* (also sometimes called *Zoo*), showcased the strengths and weaknesses of Aleka's Attic. On the positive side, the band was in sync; Sasa Raphael proved to be an inventive bassist; Rain Phoenix had a lovely, warm voice, and got most of the lead vocals. On the negative side, the tracks felt more like sketches than actual songs. Some of them were extremely short— "Scales & Fishnails" was just forty-eight seconds long—and would have benefited from choruses, bridges, and other fundamentals of songwriting. When River didn't write a melody or a hook, the band either noodled pleasantly or settled into a languorous groove. In person, River's charisma (even with his hair over his face) was sufficient to make up for these flaws, but without his physical presence, Aleka's Attic was just another pretty good local band not ready to go nationwide.

The best song was "Note to a Friend." "My days are heavy / Of the inside of your denial," River and Rain harmonized, transforming surreal gloom into a pretty melody, while River did some open-chord strumming. Their voices blended and separated with the ease that came after years of playing together. It sounded lovely, but at seventy-two seconds, it also sounded like the introduction to an unwritten song.

River's preferred mode of lyric writing was to string together evocative non sequiturs: "Let's start with nothing," "Backwards motion, all fall down," "Don't want to hear from your satellite." He had grown fond of palindromes (phrases that have the same letters when read backward): *Never Odd or Even* was one, as were the song titles "Dog God" and "Senile Felines." A palindrome promises the ability to reverse time: to return to your youth with the knowledge of how to survive it or to bring your childhood innocence into the present day. River could do those things in music, if nowhere else.

188

FIRST NIGHT AT THE VIPER ROOM

In Los Angeles, a building seems historic if it makes it ten years without being knocked down for a gas station, which made 8852 Sunset Boulevard the Stonehenge of L.A. drinking establishments. It dated back to Prohibition times, when it was a speakeasy partially owned by "Lucky" Luciano. (Since Luciano was the supreme boss of organized crime in the United States, the same could likely be said of many drinking establishments.)

In the 1940s, it was called the Melody Room, and was controlled by "Bugsy" Siegel, a childhood friend of Al Capone who became a bootlegger and hit man; he had come to Los Angeles to develop gambling syndicates, and palled around with movie stars and studio heads. He poured an enormous amount of mob money into building Las Vegas, specifically the Flamingo Hotel; in 1947, he was shot twice in the head.

The Melody Room hosted an array of cool musical acts, including Dizzy Gillespie, Esquivel, and Billy Ward and His Dominoes. Circa 1969, it was renamed Filthy McNasty's, having been bought by two German brothers who legally renamed themselves Filthy McNasty and Wolfgang McNasty. Filthy was the showman, who cruised around town in his antique hearse or his stretch limo. One bartender remembered, "On nights when a hired band failed to show, Filthy climbed onstage with his all-girl band." His big hit: "You're Breakin' My Heart, You Tear It Apart, So Fuck You."

In 1974, the British glam-rock band the Sweet had a Sunset Strip photo session for the cover of their second album, *Desolation Boulevard* (featuring the immortal "Fox on the Run"). They took the picture just outside Filthy McNasty's; the club's sign can be seen in the upper-left-hand corner of the cover.

189

In the eighties, after the McNasty brothers sold out, the bar became an anonymous watering hole called the Central. "It was a dive," said musician Morty Coyle. By 1993, the Sunset Strip had been rendered generally uncool by the lingering aroma of heavy metal and Aqua Net, but the Central was particularly low rent, with sawdust on the floor and a peanut vending machine mounted on the wall. "Anybody could get a gig there," Coyle said. "Anybody. There was a great AA meeting at the Central during the day on Mondays. It was like therapy—at the point of the problem."

The musician Chuck E. Weiss, an old drinking buddy of Tom Waits and the subject of Rickie Lee Jones's 1979 hit single "Chuck E.'s in Love," took up a weekly residency at the Central. He had been playing every Monday night for eleven years when one of the co-owners died. The remaining owner, Anthony Fox, didn't want to run the business—he had another job, and the Central was piling up bills.

Weiss alerted Johnny Depp, who had been coming to his Monday-night shows with his pal Sal Jenco. Adam Duritz, lead singer of Counting Crows, explained what went down with Depp and Jenco: "When the Central was closing down, the idea of Chuck not having a place to play was just terrible to them. So in order to keep Chuck playing and have a place for all their friends to hang out, they started the Viper Room."

Both Arnold Schwarzenegger and Frank Stallone (Sylvester's brother) made bids on the property, but Depp won out. Essentially on a lark, he put down a reported $350,000 to acquire fifty-one percent of the club's controlling company, making him CEO of "Safe in Heaven Dead." Fox retained forty-nine percent and was named vice president, drawing a salary of $800 a week; Jenco became general manager (and had a share of Depp's stake).

Depp renamed the club the Viper Room—a "viper" was 1920s drug slang for, depending on who you asked, a heroin user or a pot smoker. Depp explained the inspiration as "a group of musicians in the thirties who called themselves vipers. They were reefer heads and they helped start modern music."

The new regime tore out all the Central's decor (such as it was) and refurbished the club in basic black. It was a small space, holding about 250 patrons; the club was built into the side of a hill. The entrance was on the side street of Larrabee; after coming in, you could linger in the downstairs bar or head up the stairs to the main room, where there was a small stage and another bar. A VIP room was tucked behind one-way glass, and an exit led directly to Sunset Boulevard. One private booth was reserved for Depp and his agent, Tracy Jacobs, adorned with a sign reading DON'T FUCK WITH IT.

Depp's stated plan was to make the ambience cooler, but to maintain the Viper Room as a low-key joint where he and his friends could hang out. Like River, or Dan Aykroyd, who had opened the House of Blues on the other end of the Strip, Depp loved music—and now he had a place where he could jump onstage whenever he felt like it.

What Depp hadn't counted on was that the very fact of his owning the club would alter its status—just as in quantum mechanics, you can't observe a particle without changing its condition. "The place became a scene instantly when we opened it," Depp complained. "I never had any idea it was going to do that. I really thought it was going to be just this cool little underground place. You can't even see the place—there's no sign on Sunset. It's just a black building, and the only sign is on Larrabee: a tiny little sign, real subtle. And I figured it'd be low-key."

Of course, if Depp had *really* wanted to keep everything low-key, he wouldn't have booked Tom Petty and the Heartbreakers. The band—Gainesville's most famous residents before River Phoenix—owed Depp a favor for his appearance in the video for "Into the Great White Open," and so agreed to play a benefit on opening night. Well, all of them except drummer Stan Lynch, who had recently moved back to Florida and didn't see why he should return to L.A. for a free show.

A pissed-off Petty directed the band's management office, "Just tell Stan, 'Never mind, Ringo's going to do it.'" Within twenty-four hours, Lynch was back in town.

Depp was unaware of that drama until years later. When informed, he mused, "God, it would have been cool to see Ringo play."

Weiss was astonished at how quickly attitudes had changed toward his old haunt: "People who had never walked into the Central felt very strongly about being there." People who made it inside for the Viper Room's opening night on August 14, 1993, included Quentin Tarantino, Julien Temple, Mary Stuart Masterson, Crispin Glover, and Tim Burton.

Part of the reason the Viper Room was immediately trendy was that although the Sunset Strip was arguably the heart of Los Angeles, by 1993 it was covered in arteriosclerotic heavy-metal plaque. The eighties had made the Strip synonymous with hair-metal bands. A few of them became internationally famous (Mötley Crüe, Poison), but most had nothing more to show for their time in L.A. than some herpes sores. In 1991, when rock fans moved on to Nirvana and Pearl Jam, big hair and screeching vocals were immediately out of date. The metal party was over and "alternative" was cool.

The most storied of the Sunset Strip's rock temples was the Whisky a Go Go, right across the street from the Viper Room. "There used to be graffiti by Morrison and Hendrix on the dressing room's ceiling panels," punk-rock legend Henry Rollins said of the Whisky. "That's pretty amazing." The club opened in 1964 (there was an earlier outpost in Chicago), and with live music and dancing girls soon became the center of the L.A. rock scene. For a while, the house band was the Doors, who played dozens of shows until the night Jim Morrison blurted out "Mother, I wanna fuck you" at the climax of "The End." Since then, it had hosted everyone from Van Halen to Guns N' Roses.

On the corner of Sunset and Larrabee, sharing a physical building with the Viper Room, was a liquor store. Just down the street was Tower Records, which by 1993 had switched most of its stock from vinyl to CDs, and still provided employment opportunities for musicians who needed to pay the rent.

Close on the heels of the Tom Petty show came another impossibly hot ticket: country legend Johnny Cash had signed with Rick Rubin's American Recordings label (which had just changed its name from Def American Recordings, holding a mock funeral to bury the "Def," with Al Sharpton presiding). Cash did a solo acoustic gig on the Viper Room stage; the club was soon hailed as the hippest room in town.

The Viper Room was quickly turning into a giant VIP room, a place where on many nights the audience was more famous than the performers. The most exclusive spot within the Viper Room, unusually, was not the actual VIP room, but the club's offices, where Depp could sometimes be found. When he got bored, he would watch the Viper Room entrance through a closed-circuit TV and instruct whoever was working the door on whether to admit particular individuals to the club or turn them away.

Many of the regulars were Friends of Johnny, including actor Vincent D'Onofrio, musician Evan Dando (of the Lemonheads), the band Thelonious Monster, and rock legend Iggy Pop. By most accounts, the people working at the Viper Room were warmhearted and generally not assholes—but you might never learn that if you didn't already have some celebrity juice. The Wallflowers got a weekly gig at the Viper Room right after it opened; they didn't even have a record contract at the time. Singer Jakob Dylan said, "We just walked in, brought Sal a tape, and for whatever reason, he gave us a chance to play." It surely didn't hurt that his father was Bob Dylan.

Some nights, a limousine would shuttle select personalities back and forth between the Viper Room and a hotel room at the Chateau Marmont, on the other end of the Strip. They could do some serious drug consumption off premises, and then move the party back to the Viper Room.

By the early nineties, the L.A. music world had migrated east, to the boho district of Silver Lake, home of hipsters and adult kickball games; folkie/rapper Beck exemplified the new scene, even before he had the surprise hit single "Loser." While the Viper Room would attract rock stars looking for an intimate place to play—Lenny Kravitz and Stephen Stills both got onstage multiple times (not together)—it rarely booked musicians from the east side of town. But the club did get Beck to play—once.

George Drakoulias, a producer at American Recordings who got name-checked on the Beastie Boys' *Paul's Boutique,* remembered the show as "a very bizarre night. He did some break dancing and things like that, and people didn't know what to make of it. They just stared at him." When Beck played a solo on an electric leaf blower, Depp personally pulled the plug on him.

"Johnny lost interest in the place really quick," said one former employee. He mostly left the logistics of running the club to Jenco and dropped by when it entertained him. Sometimes at the end of the night, Depp would host a private party for his friends. Kate Moss might get behind the bar; Naomi Campbell might dance with security; Depp might have a long conversation with Chrissie Hynde about religion. On those nights, Depp had reduced the Viper Room to its essence: a party room for him and his celebrity pals.

GIVE BLOOD

After finishing the Aleka's Attic sessions, River celebrated his twenty-third birthday—on August 23, 1993—and then flew down to Costa Rica with all his siblings and his father. John was opening a vegan restaurant, but his real agenda was to get his children, especially River, to leave behind the corruption of the USA and live by the Phoenix family values again. John explained, "The idea was for them to spend more time here, helping with the cooking, making music, writing, harvesting the organic fruit, and living off the land like we used to."

John implored River to get out of the movie business before it ate him up. Eventually, River acceded, either because John had convinced him or because he was tired of arguing about it. But he had to fulfill his agreements, he told his father: he had signed contracts to appear in *Dark Blood* and *Interview with the Vampire,* and he had promised William Richert that he would be in his version of *The Man in the Iron Mask.* After he made those three films, he could quit and move down to Costa Rica.

"As it turned out," John said, "that was too many."

When River left Costa Rica, he said, "I'll see you after this movie, Dad"—a commonplace sentiment that nobody would ever have remembered if things had turned out differently.

"Well, he did," John said. "Only he was in a box."

George Sluizer, the director of *Dark Blood,* had heard rumors about River's drug use, but he didn't worry about them. "I knew of his drug habit," he said. "The actors in Hollywood, at the top level, all are, I would say, drug addicts in some way or another. I worked with Kiefer Sutherland: he was a whisky addict, two bottles a day. He wanted to compete with me: 'You drink

194

one bottle, I drink one bottle, let's see if you're drunk.' I never on set noticed that he had drunk anything—in the morning, he was sober."

Sluizer asked River to come out to the film's desert location five days before everyone else. "I wanted him to breathe the Utah air, to readjust, and let him remember the relationship we had to build for the next seven or eight weeks," Sluizer said. Those five days also provided some time for River to detox, but apparently he arrived clean and healthy.

Actor and director went hiking in the Utah mountains, bringing a few sandwiches and spending all day tramping about: breathing fresh air, they attuned themselves to the desert landscape. River was gradually submerging himself in his character. More than ever, he liked shedding the person he had become so he could transform into somebody else's invention. "That's the only time I have security," he said. "Myself is a bum! Myself is nothing!"

The movie was centered on the house of Boy, ramshackle but scenically located. Sluizer had found the location he thought was ideal visually, but it was far from any vestiges of civilization: "Maybe twenty miles from the nearest house and thirty miles from the nearest village," Sluizer said. The production staff objected—they wanted to be closer to a restaurant and a hotel, and other useful infrastructure. "I'm not an idiot," Sluizer said. "I'm not like Werner Herzog, saying, 'There's a nice tree, but it's thirty miles away,' when the same tree is one mile away. But the location was important."

Sluizer had actually worked with Herzog, the famously uncompromising German director, on his 1982 movie *Fitzcarraldo,* about a European rubber baron attempting to bring a steamer ship across land in the Peruvian jungle. The movie was originally intended to star Jason Robards and Mick Jagger, but Robards dropped out when he got dysentery, and Jagger then had to depart for Rolling Stones commitments. "All the Americans left," Sluizer said dismissively. "That's why they lost Vietnam."

Sluizer took pride in working on that movie, as he did in the documentary he made for *National Geographic* in the sixties that required him to spend five months in Siberia at temperatures reaching seventy degrees below zero (Celsius). "Very difficult, but I loved it," he said. "There's something that attracts

195

me to extreme circumstances, the opposite of the Hollywood people who are used to a swimming pool and a shower."

So Sluizer scoffed at the relatively mild deprivations of *Dark Blood;* the production booked a local motel and rented some nearby houses. Hollywood people being unable to cope with the real world is a major theme of *Dark Blood:* a Hollywood couple drive their Bentley into the desert on a second honeymoon, and get into big trouble when it breaks down. The couple, Harry and Buffy, was played by British actor Jonathan Pryce and Australian actress Judy Davis (Oscar-nominated for her work in David Lean's *A Passage to India* and Woody Allen's *Husbands and Wives*).

River played Boy, who takes them in, but develops an infatuation with Buffy, whom he recognizes from her days as a *Playboy* pinup, and becomes hostile when Harry attempts to leave. It emerges that Boy is mourning the death of his Native American wife (a motif overlapping with *Silent Tongue*). She died from cancer, a result of the fallout from the nuclear bombs the U.S. government had tested—and while Boy may be a prophet of the desert, he is also unbalanced. The movie ends in violence and fire. Harry kills Boy with an ax, and Boy's house burns down.

River revered Pryce: he had starred in River's favorite movie, *Brazil,* the absurd urban dystopia directed by Terry Gilliam (formerly of Monty Python's Flying Circus) that River had seen thirteen times. Things were tougher with Judy Davis, who was brilliant, but famously acerbic. *Dark Blood* producer Nik Powell said, "Since David Lean could not get Davis to do what he wanted her to do in his film, it is no surprise that George Sluizer had difficulties."

"We were not the best of friends, Judy and me," Sluizer said. "She made my life very tough, and I have never had to deal with a person making it so difficult." Having agreed to the script, he said, she started demanding various changes; as Sluizer told it, some were to correct what she saw as the screenplay's antifeminism while others were to cater to her vanity.

River, used to playing the peacemaker, tried to intercede between Davis and Sluizer, only to find himself the object of her scorn: she nicknamed him

"Frat Boy." When River, trying to be friendly, asked Davis when her family would be visiting the set, she snapped, "What is this, Frat Boy's question time?" She also believed River was using drugs. "I thought he was doing something when I first got there," she said. "There was one day when he came in so out of it. River said he'd had too much sodium the night before. Okay, I've never had a sodium overdose. Maybe that's exactly what they're like."

"He did not use anything during the period we were in Utah," Sluizer insisted. "I would put my hand in the fire and swear to it."

River's difficulty with the script derived from the quantity of Boy's monologues; he was having a hard time memorizing them accurately, and would sometimes flip the word order. "He had difficulty with certain lines," Sluizer said. "He asked me a few times in rehearsal if he could change the line—it's too complicated or too long. I was strict. I said, 'We've been thinking about the story and the character for two years now—we're not going to change it because you're dyslexic.' And that might hurt a little bit—I'm saying, 'I don't care if you're blind. You have to see anyway.'" Ultimately, Sluizer said, he consented to the modification of one line.

Davis's version was that River was having problems with the character: "In my opinion, that was made more difficult by the director constantly telling him how he should play it. Whether he should be angrier, loonier, whatever. It was a difficult part because it could so easily be absurd. He had most of the dialogue in the film, huge speeches; he kept trying to cut the lines down. Any change freaked the director out. River said to me one day, 'Maybe I should give up acting.'"

For the entirety of the shoot, River ate nothing but artichokes and corn: he wanted to look as if he had been living in the desert and eating insects to survive, like a modern John the Baptist. He wasn't alone in the wilderness, though; accompanying River to Utah were Samantha Mathis and his personal assistant, Abby Rude.

River was delighted to discover that the area where they were filming had a reputation as a hot spot for alien visitations. He would drop the phrase "Thanks be to UFO Godmother" into casual conversation, and tried to con-

197

vince friends that he had levitated over his bed. Sometimes he would lie down and shout, "Take me, I'm ready! What else is out there?"

Meanwhile, the tension on the set grew. Davis refused to take direction from Sluizer. In scenes with River, she would act in ways that seemed designed to break his concentration, like moving around erratically during his dialogue. "You're in this picture, so why do you have to make it so difficult for me?" River implored her. He never yelled at her, but between takes he would retreat to his trailer and play Fugazi, the hardcore band, at top volume.

"I had to sometimes say hey, a little less, because it's loud," Sluizer remembered.

"We were on this kind of inexorable journey to some disaster," Pryce said. "Every day there was some kind of difficulty." After some unseasonable rain, the remote location became muddy, with vehicles careening on the dirt roads. Once, Sluizer's director's chair went over the side of a cliff minutes after he had vacated it.

River told Pryce, "Somebody's going to die on this film."

Mathis went home, and the only phone line River could use was a party line shared by six people, making it difficult for him to call friends and unburden himself emotionally. River had been clean for almost two months without any real support system. And then one day, about five weeks into the shoot, he snapped.

A scene in the movie featured a dead snake—and when it came time to shoot the scene, River flipped out, locking himself in his trailer and refusing to come out until the production presented a death certificate for the snake.

On the phone with Iris Burton, River ranted, "Iris, they're killing snakes. They want me to work with murdered snakes. They poisoned them. Or strangled them. I don't know. They're liars—they say the snake died of old age. I don't believe it. They're liars, fucking liars, all of them. They killed the snake. *They're murderers! Murderers!*"

Once again, Burton flew to the set, complaining, "I'm not a pet coroner, for Christ's sake!" The desert shoot concluded without further incident. At River's request, Sluizer rescheduled the love scenes between Boy and Buffy for the end of the shoot. Tension was so high between River and Davis, he wanted to put them off as long as possible.

River left a message on Richert's answering machine, saying, "I'm having a hard time keeping my head above water in this crazy business."

The production moved briefly to New Mexico, and then headed to Los Angeles for its final two weeks, to shoot interiors and close-ups in a studio. River caught a cold and wasn't needed for a night shoot in New Mexico; Sluizer gave him permission to head back to L.A. a day early. Bidding Sluizer farewell, River told him, "I'm going back to the bad, bad town."

PART SIX

"I DON'T WANT YOU TO DIE"

78

THE BAD, BAD TOWN

River came to Los Angeles for the last time on Tuesday, October 26, 1993. He didn't stay at his usual hotel, the St. James's Club—the *Dark Blood* production booked him a room at the elegant, Japanese-themed Hotel Nikko. After two months of staying straight on a stressful movie, River took the opportunity to cut loose, and promptly started a drug binge.

He managed to make a lunch appointment the next day with Iris Burton, who was still trying to sell him on the virtues of doing *Safe Passage*. River unenthusiastically agreed to meet with director Robert Allan Ackerman, who could fly in from London, where he was directing a play. When he saw Chris Snyder at Burton's office, River apologized for calling in the middle of the night and swearing at him. They hugged; River was so skinny, Snyder could feel his skeleton.

"He looked like a corpse," Snyder said. "His skin was pasty and white, almost as if he'd been ravaged by illness. His jet-black hair looked as if he cut it himself without looking in a mirror." Some of his appearance may have been attributable to playing Boy—he had dyed his hair for the part, and the artichoke-and-corn diet wasn't packing on the pounds—but not his shuffling affect.

River returned to the Hotel Nikko, and his old habits.

4:30 P.M., FRIDAY, OCTOBER 29: *Safe Passage* director Robert Allan Ackerman, having spent all day flying from London to Los Angeles, had cleared customs and was on his way to the Hotel Nikko to meet with River. That's when River called Snyder. Barely coherent, he whispered into the phone, "Chris . . . I can't . . . the . . . meeting. You have to . . . cancel."

Snyder tried to stave off disaster, getting Nikko room service to send a large pot of coffee to the room of "Earl Grey." Hollywood indulged substance abusers so long as they still showed up for work—if people found out that River was missing meetings because he was drunk or stoned, he'd be virtually unemployable.

Snyder patched in Burton and Heart so they could hear River's condition, and they gently persuaded him to take a shower and drink the coffee before Ackerman showed up. After River hung up, they agreed that Burton would supervise River on the *Dark Blood* set the following day, while Heart would fly into L.A. on Sunday. As Snyder remembered it, he told them, "This can't go on."

SATURDAY, OCTOBER 30: RIVER SHOWED up on time for work, but looked exhausted, as if he had pulled an all-nighter. He had taken a Valium to bring himself down for work. "He was not one hundred percent in control of his body movements," Sluizer said. "But there was no problem with his acting and so there was no reason for me to interfere." Burton didn't show up to supervise him.

The scenes that day were set in Boy's underground fallout shelter, which he had decorated like a religious shrine, with candles, used paperbacks, and handcrafted wooden dolls. Boy gives his visitors a tour; he and Buffy have both consumed datura (an herb with hallucinogenic effects similar to peyote). "Magic's just a question of focusing the will," Boy tells her while Harry's out of the room. "You don't get what you want because you're lucky. You get it because you *will* it." And they kiss by flickering candlelight.

Davis had told River that she wouldn't be taking peyote to prepare for the scene; she said that he agreed.

3:30 P.M.: LUNCHTIME. RIVER AND Sluizer discussed their plans for the following day: Sunday, a day off from shooting. They agreed to meet at 10:30 A.M. to go over the scenes for the coming week. After that, River had a 2 P.M. meeting scheduled with Terry Gilliam, the genius director behind *Brazil.* Pryce had arranged it, and River was almost vibrating with excitement at the prospect of meeting one of his heroes.

4:30 P.M.: RIVER AND DAVIS returned to the fallout shelter. In their second scene, Boy explains how he has created an archive of human knowledge that can be passed down after a nuclear holocaust: "Took a few thousand years just to invent the alphabet! All gonna be flushed down the john. An entire civilization."

The stage directions in James Barton's screenplay say, "He looks deep into her eyes, grasps her hand like a rope."

Then Boy tells Buffy, "I don't want you to die!"

She assures him, "Nobody's going to die."

205

When they finished the scene, Sluizer called "cut," but cinematographer Ed Lachman accidentally kept the camera running until the film ran out. Power was cut to the klieg lights, but there was just enough illumination from the candles that the final feet of film in the reel captured River in silhouette.

"He came up to the camera and became total blackness, because he covered up the lens," Lachman said. "It was like he created an image of his nonexistence."

79

VIPER HEROIN X

6 P.M., OCTOBER 30, 1993: Sluizer wrapped the *Dark Blood* shoot for the day. River lingered for about an hour, hanging out and helping the crew take down the lights. Lachman had grown accustomed to River volunteering: a week before, in New Mexico, the cinematographer had been schlepping a large number of equipment cases out of his hotel room. He came out into the hallway and shouted, "Can someone help me with my gear?"

A minute later, River knocked on his door.

"River, what are you doing here?" Lachman asked.

"I came to help you," River said simply, proposing to violate both union rules and the star-power hierarchy of a movie shoot.

"I didn't mean you!" Lachman said.

"Why can't I help ya?" River asked.

7 P.M.: RIVER TOOK A limousine back to the Hotel Nikko, where Rain (now twenty) and Joaquin (who had turned nineteen two days earlier) were waiting in his room. They had flown into town so they could audition to play River's on-screen siblings in *Safe Passage*. If either of them got the part, it would be the first time River got to act with a family member since "Backwards: The Riddle of Dyslexia," nine years earlier.

Mathis was also there, soon joined by River's assistant Abby Rude and her husband Dickie. They ordered room service, cranked up the music, and started to party. Abby Rude went down the street to buy a bottle of Moët champagne. When a room-service waiter arrived with some vegetarian snacks, the music was so loud, they almost didn't hear him knocking. The waiter wheeled in the food, and saw a room in disarray. River was dancing by himself, spinning in the middle of his room.

10 P.M.: AFTER A LONG day, and a largely sleepless night, River was exhausted. He called his friend Bradley Gregg, with whom he had acted in three movies (*Explorers, Stand by Me,* and *Indiana Jones and the Last Crusade*) to let him know that he wouldn't be able to attend the birthday party the next day for Gregg's young son. River was ready to collapse, but Joaquin and Rain had just arrived: they wanted to go out and enjoy a Saturday night in Los Angeles.

Prince had recently opened an outpost of his Glam Slam nightclub in downtown L.A., while the Auditorium on Hollywood Boulevard was hosting a "ska-lloween skankfest." But Joaquin wanted to check out the Viper Room, where Flea and Johnny Depp were going to be playing together in a version of Depp's band P. The club had been open for two and a half months.

The hitch: Joaquin and Rain were underage, meaning they couldn't get in without an adult escort, ideally a celebrity, so that whoever was working the door would turn a blind eye. Mathis agreed to take them, and they called downstairs for a car. River would stay behind, as would the Rudes.

While Mathis, Rain, and Joaquin were waiting at the elevator, River changed his mind—either because he wanted to keep partying or because he was falling into his usual paternal role, taking care of his younger siblings. He ran down the hall, shouting, "I'm coming, I'm coming!" River grabbed his guitar, planning to get onstage with his old friend Flea, and they rode the elevator down.

As Mathis and the three Phoenixes left the Hotel Nikko, Sluizer was arriving in his car. He saw them and called out to them, "Have a good time," but didn't think they heard him.

10:30 P.M.: HALLOWEEN WAS OFFICIALLY the next day, but since it was Saturday night, adult costume parties were in full swing. River was dressed casually, in dark brown pants and Converse All Star sneakers. The quartet headed for a party they had heard about in the hills of Hollywood, at the house of twin actors. Also at the party: Leonardo DiCaprio, two weeks away from his nineteenth birthday, dressed up as "Johnny Hollywood," a generic hipster actor with a leather jacket and his hair slicked back. "It was dark and everyone was drunk," DiCaprio said. "I was passing through crowds of people so thick, it was almost like two lanes of traffic." Then he spotted River.

"When I was eighteen, River Phoenix was far and away my hero. Think of all those early great performances: *My Own Private Idaho, Stand by Me.* I always wanted to meet him," DiCaprio said. And now he was right next to him. "I wanted to reach out and say hello because he was this great mystery and we'd never met and I thought he probably wouldn't blow me off because I'd done stuff by then that was probably worth watching." (*This Boy's Life* had come out six months prior; *Gilbert Grape* had wrapped but wouldn't be released until December.)

"Then I got stuck in a lane of traffic and slid right past him," DiCaprio lamented. "He was beyond pale—he looked white." Before he could circle back around to talk to his hero, River had vanished into the Hollywood night.

12:27 A.M., OCTOBER 31: CARRYING his guitar, River arrived at the Viper Room's front door on Larrabee Street and secured entrance for his party. He got stamped with a red star on the back of his right hand, and went into the club. River mingled in the crowd, finding his old friends from the Red Hot Chili Peppers: Flea and John Frusciante (who had quit the band a year and a half earlier). Flea informed River that he wouldn't be able to play with P that night. The group was already cramming too many musicians onto the tiny Viper Room stage: Depp, Flea, Sal Jenco, Gibby Haynes, Al Jourgensen of Ministry, and on keyboards, Benmont Tench of Tom Petty and the Heartbreakers.

Disappointed but unfazed, River returned to the table where Mathis, Rain, and Joaquin were sitting. "I'll sing at the table," he told them, and prepared to stand on a chair and improvise a song.

12:40 A.M.: P TOOK THE stage. Jourgensen was wearing a floppy cowboy hat; Haynes had removed his shirt and scrawled on his belly with Magic Marker. Depp had an effete pageboy haircut—an artifact of filming *Ed Wood* with Tim Burton. Benmont Tench proved to be the musical spine of the

band; Haynes, on lead vocals, amused himself with fart jokes and demands
for vodka and bourbon.

12:45 A.M.: A GUITARIST FRIEND of River's came over to his table, holding a cup. "Hey, Riv, drink this—it'll make you feel fabulous," he told him.
River didn't know what was in it, but since he had taken this friend to rehab
twice, he could guess that it wasn't ginger ale. Being the sort of person who
would jump off cliffs to travel through clouds, River downed it in one gulp.

In the drink was a dissolved speedball: a mixture of cocaine and heroin.
The heroin circulating in L.A. that fall included a particularly potent variety of Persian Brown. River immediately felt unwell. "What did you give
me? What the fuck is in it?" he shouted. To calm himself and his system
down, River took some Valium—which didn't seem to do the job. Soon
he had vomited on himself and the table. He then slumped in his chair,
unconscious.

This was the crucial moment. River was clearly not in good shape, but
the Cedars-Sinai hospital was only one mile away. If an ambulance had been
called right then, he might have been saved. But he also would have become
a tabloid sensation, with his wholesome granola image destroyed. And he had
survived other scary drug episodes before. So Mathis made a phone call—but
it was to Abby Rude back at the Hotel Nikko.

"Sam called and said she was really scared. She said River had just keeled
over," Rude remembered. "We said we'd be right over to help."

An actress in the Viper Room remembered that night as having been a
good time, before everything went wrong. She noticed there was some com-
motion in a corner of the room, but "figured some guys were having a brawl or
somebody was getting sick. I kept seeing Samantha running back and forth
and back and forth, and she looked really worried."

The actress grabbed Mathis and said, "Hey, Sam, what's up? What's
wrong?"—but Mathis couldn't even speak.

12:55 A.M.: RIVER JERKED AWAKE and asked to go outside to get some fresh air. He had trouble walking, and fell to the floor. Joaquin assured everybody that he was fine, and helped his brother past the stage where P was playing, through the back door and onto the Sunset Boulevard sidewalk.

Across the street at the Whisky, there was a triple bill in progress featuring the Pies, from Liverpool. Milling outside the Viper Room were young people dressed in costume: witches, harlequins, somebody in a Louis XIV getup. Nobody noticed a young man with dark hair stumbling into the night air.

1 A.M.: MOMENTS AFTER RIVER stepped outside, he collapsed onto the sidewalk. Photographer Ron Davis was outside the Viper Room, hoping to get a picture of the Chili Peppers when they left the club. Rain flipped River's body over, and Davis recognized him immediately. (In a rare example of paparazzi restraint, Davis did not take any pictures that night.) River started having violent seizures, his whole body shuddering and flopping on the pavement.

210

"No one was doing anything," Davis said. "They were all standing around like deer caught in headlights." He saw Mathis leaning against the wall, futilely banging her head. Rain sat on River's chest, trying to restrain his body. They were young and terrified.

Two girls in witch costumes walked past the scene. One of them said to the other, "Oh God. Gross."

Christina Applegate came out of the club, saw what was happening, and walked away. On the corner, she started crying.

A Viper Room doorman came outside, surveyed the situation, and told Joaquin, "You need to call 911."

"He's fine, he's fine," Joaquin said while his brother thrashed around.

Across the street, the manager of the Whisky a Go Go, Sean Tuttle, saw something was happening at the Viper Room, but classified it as a typical Saturday night: "It looked like a normal occurrence."

Inside the Viper Room, completely unaware of what was happening outside its walls, P played a country-flavored song called "Michael Stipe," about celebrity and feeling out of place at glitzy parties in the Hollywood Hills. Spookily, it mentioned River by name: "I finally talked to Michael Stipe / But I didn't get to see his car / Him and River Phoenix / Were leaving on the road tomorrow."

1:09 A.M.: EACH SEIZURE LASTED about twenty seconds. River's arms would flail around, while his knuckles and the back of his head kept smacking against the pavement. Davis started hoping for more seizures—they were evidence that River was still alive.

1:10 A.M.: JOAQUIN CALLED 911, frantic but trying to keep it together as his beloved brother passed away before his eyes.

"It's my brother. He's having seizures at Sunset and Larrabee. Please come here," Joaquin begged.

"Okay, calm down a little bit," the dispatcher replied.

Moments later, Joaquin said, "Now I'm thinking he had Valium or something. I don't know." His voice cracked with anguish. "Please come, he's *dying*, please."

1:12 A.M.: AN ACTRESS ON the scene remembered, "Outside there was a crowd of people, and I saw him—lying flat, totally ghostly white. It didn't really look like him. He had, like, this dark hair, this totally pasty complexion, and he was panting and sweating. He was convulsing. People were trying to splash water on his face and move his head and get his tongue out of his mouth. He was kind of changing colors, and his eyes were all dilated and open, and it was really scary. I kept hearing from people, 'Wow, it's River, it's River.' You don't think it's going to happen. One minute you're on top of the world and the next minute you're gone—you're gone and nobody can help you."

1:14 A.M.: A TEAM OF four paramedics arrived in a fire truck and immediately went to work. "We found him pulseless and not breathing," stated Captain Ray Ribar. "We went into our cardiac arrest protocols. CPR was immediately started, along with airway breathing and circulation. Then we went into our advanced life support, which is a paramedic operation."

Some of the bystanders said that drugs had been involved; somebody mentioned "speedballing." The paramedics injected River's heart with a medication called Narcan, designed to counteract the effects of narcotics, and began chest compressions. "However, his heart was in a flatline—clinically dead," said Ribar. "We stabilized him the best we could and prepared him for transportation."

While the paramedics worked, Abby and Dickie Rude arrived. Dickie said, "It was a terrifying shock to see your best friend lying on the sidewalk with paramedics standing over him, and a crowd of people dressed up in Halloween costumes."

"It was the classic cocaine overreaction," Ribar said. "It just nails some people and stops the heart."

1:25 A.M.: P FINISHED THEIR set and walked off the stage. One of the bouncers told them that a friend of Flea's was having a seizure on the sidewalk. Flea and Depp went out the door to see River—whom Depp didn't recognize—with his shirt and jacket stripped off, being worked on by the paramedics.

Depp stood there, unable to do anything, hoping everything would be okay. He didn't recognize Mathis either, but he told her, "If there's anything we can do, if you need a ride to the hospital?" She politely declined his offer.

Flea wanted to ride in the back of the ambulance with River. He was allowed to come along, but only in the front seat. He hopped in.

1:31 A.M.: THE AMBULANCE LEFT for the one-mile drive to Cedars-Sinai hospital. Ribar didn't know who his patient was, but one of the other paramedics did: "I could hear him saying, 'Come on, River, you can make it.'"

1:34 A.M.: THE AMBULANCE ARRIVED at Cedars-Sinai Medical Center. River's skin was turning blue but his body was still warm. He had been in full cardiac arrest for at least twenty minutes, but the emergency room doctors labored mightily to pull him back into the land of the living, opening his chest to massage his heart, hooking him up to a respirator, even inserting a pacemaker. Nothing worked.

1:51 A.M.: DR. PAUL SILKA officially pronounced River Jude Phoenix dead.

R.I.P. RJP

Iris Burton got a phone call summoning her to Cedars-Sinai. She identified River's corpse, and then collapsed, a sobbing mess. When Mathis arrived, she also insisted on seeing the body; a nurse took her to where it lay in the emergency room.

All through the night, people got woken up with news of the tragedy: friends, family, producers, executives. One person who couldn't be reached right away was Heart: she was already on the first flight out of Gainesville, on her way to Hollywood to help River with his problems before it was too late. Once she arrived at the hospital, Burton left, crying so hard that she burst a blood vessel in her nose. Heart wanted to take possession of River's body, but was told that the autopsy would have to happen first. The Phoenix family all flew home to Florida the same day, before they could be questioned by an L.A. homicide detective.

Eleven years earlier, comedy superstar John Belushi had died from an overdose while speedballing, on the other end of the Sunset Strip, in a bungalow at the Chateau Marmont hotel. Cathy Smith, the woman who provided him with the drugs and helped inject him, ended up pleading guilty to involuntary

213

manslaughter and serving fifteen months in prison. But the Phoenix family (and Mathis) ducked questions from the police department, not wanting to see anyone prosecuted for River's death by misadventure. "The bottom line was the family didn't want anyone to go to jail who was participating with River in ingesting the drugs," said L.A. homicide detective sergeant Mike Lee. "They said if it was an overdose of drugs, then so be it."

Sometime after 3 A.M. on October 31, Depp found out that the kid who had collapsed on his doorstep was dead—and that it had been River Phoenix. He hadn't known River well, but he was shocked. Depp closed the Viper Room for the next ten days. That patch of sidewalk outside his club's back door quickly drew crowds anyway: news crews getting footage of the Viper Room's exterior, and mourners leaving flowers and scrawling memorials to River on the club's wall and door. Depp later offered to take the door off its hinges and send it to the Iris Burton Agency; they gave him the Florida address of the Phoenixes instead.

In the newspapers, the story of River's death played alongside obituaries of the Italian director Federico Fellini (*La Dolce Vita*, *8½*), who had died in Rome the same day, at age seventy-three. But although Fellini had half a century and five Oscars on River, he didn't have a younger brother pleading with 911. The tape of Joaquin's call went into heavy rotation on TV news and tabloid shows—the worst moment of his young life was when most Americans first heard his voice.

The *Dark Blood* cast and crew showed up at the studio on Monday, not that there was any way to keep working. Jonathan Pryce said a few words in memory of River, and asked everyone to join hands in a circle. They did, except for Judy Davis. "I didn't want to hold hands," she said. "I don't believe in spirits passing, but I didn't have a choice, so I wished that I'd not gone into the studio. I don't like to be forced to be dishonest. I think it has to be remembered in the midst of all this that he was twenty-three, and he made the choice."

River was cremated in a blue coffin, wearing an Aleka's Attic T-shirt, with the long hair he had cut off for *Dark Blood* laid next to him as a ponytail. The night before the cremation, somebody with access to the funeral home took a picture of his body and sold it to the *National Enquirer*.

On November 12, about a hundred guests went to Micanopy for a memorial service, held under a large oak tree on the Phoenix property. Neighbors walked over; Dan Aykroyd and Keanu Reeves came in limousines. Flea and Michael Stipe were in attendance, as were Martha Plimpton, Suzanne Solgot, and Samantha Mathis. Heart tracked down Father Stephen Wood, who had helped her family get out of Venezuela; he was doing missionary work in Mexico. She paid for his plane ticket to Gainesville and he helped officiate.

Heart gave a eulogy for the child she had thought would change the world, talking about River's life and how, even in death, he touched her: "When the sun shines I see River, when I look in someone's eyes and make a connection, I see River. To have death transformed into another way to look at life is his huge gift."

The mourners took turns remembering River. "He was my brother and I loved him a great deal," Stipe said. "It was just an awful, awful mistake. We fed off each other and learned a lot from each other."

Ethan Hawke copped to how he had been in awe of River, and then asked whether the people in attendance would learn anything from his death.

John kept interjecting wisecracks that made many of the guests uncomfortable.

As the residents of Camp Phoenix took turns speaking, the tenor shifted: River's pure soul was too good for this world, they said, and so he had progressed to a higher state of being. (Essentially the same message that had so infuriated Judy Davis, but at greater length and without the hand-holding.) Or as Solgot summarized it: "River's in heaven, blah blah blah, it was his time, blah blah blah."

The sentiment began to rankle some of those in attendance. Bradley Gregg—father of the child whose birthday party River didn't attend on October 31—shouted, "River didn't have to die to be free!"

Later, the perspicacious Martha Plimpton observed, "You would have thought he was ninety and had died in his sleep. The people who were saying this felt tremendous guilt that they had contributed to his death." She wasn't any happier about how his death was being discussed outside Micanopy: "He's already being made into a martyr," she complained. "He's become a metaphor for a fallen angel, a messiah. He was just a boy, a very good-hearted boy who was very fucked up and had no idea how to implement his good intentions. I don't want to be comforted by his death. I think it's right that I'm angry about it, angry at the people who helped him stay sick, and angry at River."

Two weeks later, there was another memorial service, this one on the Paramount lot in Los Angeles, with about 150 of River's show-biz colleagues in attendance. Before it started, they milled around outside, smoking cigarettes and gossiping about Hollywood casting, as if it were just another movie screening. The list of speakers was star-studded: Sidney Poitier, Rob Reiner, Jerry O'Connell, John Boorman, Christine Lahti, Peter Bogdanovich, and Helen Mirren. When it was Heart's turn, she related a vision she had: that River hadn't wanted to be born, preferring to stay with God in heaven. God had convinced him to go, and they haggled over how long, settling on twenty-three years.

After a moment of silence, Jane Campion, the director of *The Piano*, stood up and announced that earlier that year, her infant son had died when he was only thirteen days old, and that although she hadn't known River, she had come to the service in search of some solace and understanding. Heart stepped off the stage and gave Campion a hug.

Not to be outdone, Peter Bogdanovich's wife, Louise Stratten, stood up and said, "Peter and I adopted this stray cat that came around the house every day." They believed, she explained, that the spirit of her sister (murdered Playmate Dorothy Stratten) lived in that cat.

The testimonials continued: people who had known River intensely and briefly, all talking about how he had touched their lives. Then John Boorman, sitting in a corner, spat out a question: "Is there anybody here who can tell us why River took all those drugs?"

The room fell silent. Heart looked shocked; River's younger sisters, Liberty and Summer, left the room in protest. Mathis, who had been silent until then, tried to answer the question: "River was a sensitive," she said gently. "He had so much compassion for everyone and everything that he had a weight on his heart."

In December, Christina Applegate found her own way of memorializing River: at a Studio City theater, she starred in an antidrug performance piece based on witnessing his death. While a song called "Junkie" played, she writhed on the stage.

81 BROKEN DREAMS

While Hollywood agents mouthed pieties of sorrow, some of them smelled chum in the water. River's in heaven, blah blah blah—but that meant there were vacancies to be filled in movies here on earth, especially in *Interview with the Vampire,* which now needed a new interviewer—and quickly. The interview scenes had already been held to the end of the shoot so River could finish making *Dark Blood.*

It was an ideal gig: a quick, lucrative job in a classy movie that looked like it would be a hit. Christian Slater got the role, but recognizing the gruesome situation, donated his paycheck to two of River's favorite charities, Earth Save and Earth Trust. *Interview with the Vampire* proved to be a respectable success: apparently audiences liked watching a vision of Hollywood stars who couldn't die and looked young forever, even if River Phoenix wasn't one of them.

Safe Passage filled the role of the son with Sean Astin, fresh off the success of *Rudy.* Some other films got shelved permanently: without River to wear the gorilla suit, Allan Moyle couldn't imagine making *Morgan.* Similarly, Agnieszka Holland abandoned *Jack and Jill,* and Gus Van Sant never revived his Andy Warhol movie.

John Malkovich didn't want to play Verlaine without River as Rimbaud, and dropped out of *Total Eclipse;* director Volker Schlöndorff followed. The project was taken over by (coincidentally) Agnieszka Holland, who cast Leonardo DiCaprio as Rimbaud and David Thewlis as Verlaine; the film was released in 1995. In 2008, Van Sant finally made *Milk,* his award-winning Harvey Milk biopic. Sean Penn starred instead of Robin Williams, while the role of Cleve Jones, which Van Sant had earmarked for River, was taken by Emile Hirsch, who was just eight years old when River died.

The movie that was the most problematic was the one River had been in the middle of, *Dark Blood.* Sluizer had completed about eighty percent of the shooting schedule, with roughly eleven days to go—not very many, except that they would have included crucial interior scenes and close-ups of River. With CGI in its infancy, a special-effects solution wasn't feasible. The missing pieces were too big to edit around. And nobody had the stomach to start over with a new actor in the role of Boy.

As was customary, the film had been insured against a disaster like this; CNA International Reinsurance made the unusual but appropriate call to abandon the picture. They paid off the movie's investors and ended up as the legal owners of *Dark Blood,* not to mention 1,500 pounds of 35mm film. Some of the filmmakers were glad to put the tragic episode behind them. *Dark Blood* producer Nik Powell said, "For me, the most respectful thing was to close it, not attempt to finish it, and let bygones be bygones."

The insurance company then sued River's estate for about $5.5 million, arguing that by "taking illegal drugs, River J. Phoenix deprived the parties to the contract of his services, and he therefore breached his obligation/duty." The crux of the argument was that River had lied when he attested during his insurance-required medical exam that he didn't use drugs. The lawsuit kept River's estate tied up in probate until 1997, when it was finally dismissed.

In 1999, Sluizer found out that the insurance company was going to dispose of the *Dark Blood* footage, believing it was of no value. Sluizer liberated the reels of films from the storage facility, with the consent of the claims adjuster—when they couldn't find a key, they had to break open a lock. "I call it saving, not stealing," Sluizer said. "Morally, I was saving important material. If you go to the Guggenheim and it's a fire and you save a painting, you're not stealing a painting—you're saving it."

82
NEVER GONNA WITHER

As he would have wanted, River lived on in song. Friends recorded tributes to him: Flea's composition "Transcending," found on the Red Hot Chili Peppers' *One Hot Minute* album, includes the lyrics "Smartest fucker I ever met" and "I called you hippie, you said fuck off." Michael Stipe was so shattered by River's death that he found himself unable to write songs for five months. When he recovered, R.E.M. made the classic *Monster,* which they dedicated to River; the song "Bang and Blame" had backing vocals by Rain. (Behind the scenes, Stipe bought the rights to the Aleka's Attic recordings from Island.)

219

There was also a slew of songs about River by musicians who didn't know him well, or at all, including Natalie Merchant, Rufus Wainwright, Belinda Carlisle, the Cult.

When River died, it was generally assumed that he would become the "vegan James Dean"—a star even better remembered in death than in life, a potent symbol of youthful talent and beauty snuffed out at an early age. Instead, he faded in people's memories.

Partially, this is because of the idiosyncrasies of River's filmography: of his four great films, two (*Dogfight, Running on Empty*) are basically forgotten, while *My Own Private Idaho* is well-regarded but rarely seen (there's no easy way to edit it down to make it palatable on basic cable). *Stand by Me* has become an enduring classic, but River was so young in the movie, it can be hard to connect his performance to the man he became.

The other reason River didn't become more iconic in death: on April 5, 1994, only five months after River died, Kurt Cobain shot himself in the head and became the symbol of snuffed potential. Apparently the nineties had room for only one angel-faced blond boy, too pained by the world to live in it.

Ever since River died, his absence has reverberated through Hollywood, and not just in growing awareness of veganism and rain forests. Leonardo DiCaprio played so many parts that River originally intended to do, it's hard not to wonder which roles River might have beaten him out for, had he stayed alive and healthy. Steven Spielberg commented, "When I finally worked with Leonardo DiCaprio on *Catch Me If You Can,* he reminded me of River. Not only do they look alike, their approach to acting, to their art, is very similar." Would River have starred in *Titanic,* and found himself transformed into a global superstar? Might he have one day vanished into the role of a plantation owner for *Django Unchained?* Would River and DiCaprio have acted opposite each other as doppelgangers in *The Departed?*

220

Or perhaps River and Van Sant would have forged a long-term collaboration, the way DiCaprio did with Martin Scorsese and Depp did with Tim Burton. As it happened, the first film Van Sant made after River died was *To Die For,* which featured Joaquin in his breakout role (a disturbed teen who is seduced by a local newscaster and gulled into killing her husband). It was Joaquin's first movie in six years; he had been spending a lot of time with his father in Costa Rica, but after River's death, he found himself thrust into his brother's role as the family breadwinner, if not its missionary.

While Joaquin chose different roles than his brother probably would have—based on their physical types, if nothing else—his career successfully balanced art films (*The Master*) with popcorn movies (*Gladiator*), a path that River had tried to walk himself. The movie that obviously echoed Joaquin's own life was *Walk the Line:* he played country singer Johnny Cash, who saw his beloved brother die in front of him. But the film that actually seems to draw from the Phoenix family's experience is *I'm Still Here,* the fake documentary Joaquin made with his brother-in-law Casey Affleck (his *To Die*

For costar, who married his sister Summer) and released in 2010 to general confusion.

River never had a ludicrous beard or a meltdown on David Letterman, but like Joaquin in *I'm Still Here,* he chafed at the self-important rituals of the acting life, and wanted to trade it all in for music (Joaquin's version of this impulse in *I'm Still Here* was making a rap album). The movie begins with all five Phoenix children performing on the streets of Los Angeles and ends with a choice that River never made, although Costa Rica was open to him: leaving the United States behind and heading into the jungle.

River had a boyish face—and not just because he made the majority of his movies when he was a teenager. Leonardo DiCaprio has maintained the same youthful quality as an adult, giving the impression of having baby fat, even in his late thirties. That look was ascendant in the early nineties, as teenage pinups reliably turned into movie stars. Nineteen ninety-seven proved to be a watershed year for the look: it was when *L.A. Confidential* came out, making a leading man out of Russell Crowe, who was praised as a sweaty Australian throwback to an era of real men, not a pretty boy like DiCaprio, Depp, or Jared Leto. The praise was often couched as a commercial analysis—where would Hollywood find its new leading men and action heroes?—but had a whiff of homophobia to it nevertheless.

Film actors know that youthful glamour will fade—there's a reason that Hollywood plastic surgeons stay busy. River couldn't have predicted that at age twenty-seven, his physical appearance would be going out of fashion. If he had maintained his acting at a high level, however, his talent and star power would likely have trumped the zeitgeist.

If he had triumphed over his addiction-prone genes, River would have celebrated his forty-third birthday in August 2013. It's not hard to imagine him as an actor with dozens of movies of all stripes behind him, a powerful performer in full command of his craft. Sluizer said, "His heart went a little more to music than acting, but probably he was more gifted as an actor. He was an actor who had so much appeal for an audience, film would have carried him on."

221

83

ECHO #5: MONTGOMERY CLIFT

Alive, River was frequently compared to James Dean; after the two actors were united by a young death, the link seemed to be mandated by federal statute. But a more telling comparison may be Montgomery Clift, the 1950s Hollywood icon who was Dean's hero. (Dean wasn't just inspired by Clift, he was obsessed—he tracked down the actor's unlisted phone number and kept calling him.)

When Clift was just eight years old, in 1928, his family left the United States for three years—in his case, it was a moneyed tour of Europe, with trips to the Louvre and St. Moritz. The roots of his performing life began on that journey, with an outing to the Comédie-Française and a short play that the precocious Clift wrote and performed, about a sixth-century king of France and his conversion to Christianity.

Back in the States, Clift entered professional show business via advertising: he appeared in print ads for Arrow shirts and Steinway pianos. He became a working actor as a teenager, appearing on Broadway at age fourteen in the play *Fly Away Home*. Regularly cast in the theater, he found it difficult to adjust to conventional schools or to make friends his age.

Actress Anne Baxter remembered Clift as "hyperenergetic, hyper-sincere." In 1948, he made the move from Broadway to Hollywood, appearing opposite John Wayne in the western *Red River* and starring in *The Search* in an Oscar-nominated performance as a U.S. Army engineer helping a young concentration-camp survivor find his mother. Clift became a teen idol, but made his disdain for Hollywood widely known and received publicity for his unconventional ideas and his dirty T-shirts.

The lives of River and Clift did not run on perfectly parallel tracks, of course. Clift lived almost twice as long, had much more classical education, and was a closeted homosexual. His most intense screen partnership was with Elizabeth Taylor, with whom he starred in *A Place in the Sun, Raintree County,* and *Suddenly, Last Summer.* Although they were close friends and Taylor reportedly would have happily married him, Clift's homosexuality meant that they would never register for wedding gifts. The analogue to Taylor in River's life was Keanu Reeves, a dark-haired beauty who proved to be his most passionate on-screen romantic foil; their heterosexual bent hindered any real-life love affair.

Clift specialized in beautiful martyrs. His most famous performance was in *From Here to Eternity* (1953), as Private Robert E. Lee Prewitt, a top-notch Army bugler who is tormented by his company when he refuses to box for them. The script, set in Hawaii in the months before the Pearl Harbor attack, verged on the melodramatic, but Clift made Prewitt a vivid character: passionate, proud, wary, wounded. His rawest moment comes in a flash of sympathy, when he tells his love interest (Donna Reed), "Nobody ever lies about being lonely."

223

In 1956, driving home from a party at Elizabeth Taylor's house, Clift smashed his car into a telephone pole. He survived, but the left side of his face was largely paralyzed, and he was never the same. He became addicted to alcohol and pills, turning into the sad, dissolute figure the Clash sang about on their song "The Right Profile": "He said, 'Go out and get me my old movie stills' / 'Go out and get me another roll of pills' / 'I'm shaking, but I ain't got the chills.'" And then there's nothing but anguished sputtering.

Clift lived for a decade after his accident, and remained photogenic enough to keep working: he made half of his seventeen movies in that time. (Eight before the accident, eight after, and one, *Raintree County,* that was filmed both before and after.) If Clift had died that night, he might have become mythologized as one of the heroic victims he played so often on film. Instead, he faded away gradually, becoming pathetic rather than tragic.

Ultimately, alternate histories and other what-if stories are just guesses. People wish that River's narrative had a different ending: he survives his bad night at the Viper Room, but the experience scares him straight and he matures into one of our finest actors. But he might have kept using drugs instead, making himself gradually unemployable. Or he might have gotten clean and then had a relapse months later that killed him. He could have had a car crash of his own, or abandoned acting for environmental activism. Cheating death doesn't guarantee a happy ending—it just gives you a chance to add another chapter to your story.

84 CLOSING TIME AT THE VIPER ROOM

Sometimes, when Samantha Mathis turned on the television and flipped around, she'd stumble on one of River's movies: there he'd be, young and alive. "I'm grateful to be able to see him like that," she said, "but at the same time it is very odd and I'm never quite sure how to explain my emotions." Mostly, she tried to get on with her life, even as she carried around her loss and her horror. The lesson she took from River's death was to be more selfish: since life is fleeting, don't waste it with the wrong people. Mathis worked steadily, appearing in *Little Women, The American President,* and *Broken Arrow.* And improbably, she started hanging out at the Viper Room.

Some friends of River's won't even say the Viper Room's name. Although Mathis described her visit on Halloween in 1993 as "ultimately not a joyous experience," she decided that the club itself wasn't responsible for River's death, even indirectly by creating a libertine environment. "The way the public perceived it was unfortunately out of everyone's control," she said.

Mathis and her friend Tracy Falco, a studio development executive, shared a little house nearby that their friend Adam Duritz (of Counting Crows) jokingly called "the hillside manor." They found themselves at the center of a bohemian social circle: people would come by their house, stay up late, and drink a lot of red wine.

"We were all just twenty-three or so and we had all these wonderful friends—people were in town making music or doing things," Falco remembered fondly. "We always said that we should have had a sign-in book at the house those two years, because at one time or another I think every actor in Hollywood traveled to our house."

Their living room was one center of gravity for that crowd, which included old friends of River like Michael Stipe; another was the Viper Room. "It was kind of a given that no matter where we went, we'd end the night at the Viper Room," Mathis said. "The doors would always be open to us. We would arrive, and Sal would call Damiano's Pizza, and we'd order fifteen pizzas and sit around and talk and smoke cigarettes and wind down the evening."

In 1996, Mick Jagger and Uma Thurman went to the Viper Room together, catching a Wallflowers show from a corner booth. Photographer Russell Einhorn spotted them in a full-on makeout session, what he described as "a real hot, heavy kiss, like in some film with the stars overacting—and he had his hands all over her. His leg was cocked over hers." Unable to resist the opportunity, Einhorn fished a camera out of his pocket and took a picture.

As soon as the flash went off, Einhorn was tackled by Jagger's bodyguard and slammed to the ground. The camera fell out of his hand; Einhorn was restrained by Viper Room security while Jagger's people found it and removed the film. Einhorn was ejected from the Viper Room and banned for life.

Einhorn then sued both Jagger and the Viper Room for damages (the confiscated photograph was his property, and a valuable item). Jagger reportedly settled for $350,000 to avoid testifying in court; he was married to Jerry Hall at the time, although she filed for divorce shortly after the story made headlines. The Viper Room fought the suit, but lost at a jury trial in 1998 and had to pay Einhorn $600,000—putting a rather precise price tag on the cost of their mission to create a safe space for celebrities.

In 2000, Depp (through his lawyers) attempted to buy out Anthony Fox, who had sold him fifty-one percent of the Viper Room ownership back in 1993; relations between them had been strained for years, ever since Fox's weekly stipend of $800 had been suspended. During negotiations to acquire the other forty-nine percent, Fox discovered that the licensing rights to the Viper Room had been transferred to another legal entity, Trouser Trumpet, which was owned by Depp and Jenco. Fox sued.

In December 2001, Fox suddenly disappeared, never to be heard from again. He left behind a sixteen-year-old daughter named Amanda and a few thousand dollars in his bank account. Foul play was suspected. "Maybe it's the curse of the Viper Room," speculated David Esquibias, one of Fox's lawyers.

Even with Fox mysteriously gone, the lawsuit continued, with Fox's daughter, Amanda, as the beneficiary. In February 2003, Los Angeles Superior Court Judge Allan Goodman made a temporary ruling extremely unfavorable to Depp, stating, "The facts establish persistent and pervasive fraud and mismanagement and abuse of authority" and that "Defendant Depp breached his fiduciary duties to the corporation and to Fox as the plaintiff-shareholder and failed to exercise any business judgment."

Depp initially appealed, but eighteen months later, he quietly relinquished his shares to Amanda Fox (who promptly cashed out, selling the club). A press release didn't mention the ongoing legal mess, but rather blamed the "bad memories" of River's death and the continued presence of "death tourists" who still came to the patch of sidewalk where River had died. Depp had been living in France with model/singer/actress Vanessa Paradis and their children for some years; the Viper Room hadn't been his personal rec room for a long time.

85 BLOOD ON THE TRACKS

After River's death, a devastated Sluizer moved back to Europe. He mostly split his time between Amsterdam and France, and kept making movies, just not for Hollywood studios—one was even in Portuguese.

"I had the *Dark Blood* material for years," Sluizer said. "But I had no desire to look at Judy Davis—I can say I was traumatized by her. That's my sense of humor: I don't think I was traumatized, but irritated. I didn't want to see her, because she made me suffer so much, in so many nasty little things. And I was doing other movies, so it took time."

Sluizer acquired the footage in 1999, but had trouble finding an institution to house it and grew frustrated at how film preservation had turned into a 9-to-5 bureaucracy rather than a passion. Then he read a newspaper article about a film museum in Kabul, Afghanistan. Movies were illegal under Taliban rule, so the curators had to keep the museum completely concealed—hiding art carried a death sentence. "I said, 'God, these people, they put their life at stake for film?' I like that," Sluizer chortled. He wrote them a letter asking if they would store the raw *Dark Blood* footage for him. He never heard back, which he conceded might have been for the best, given that it was wartime: "It would have been lying in Afghanistan, while everybody was shooting each other."

Then Sluizer almost died. On Christmas Day of 2007, he was on vacation with his family in the foothills of the French Alps when he collapsed: he had suffered an aortic dissection, meaning that the tissue inside his body's largest artery had torn, which often leads to fatal blood loss. After a five-hour ambulance ride, Sluizer was in a cardiovascular hospital, where he received life-saving surgery.

"Normally, within five minutes you're dead," he said. But at age seventy-five, Sluizer had been given some extra time. During an arduous year of physical therapy, during which he had to relearn how to sit, how to stand, how to walk, he made a resolution: he didn't know how much time he had left alive, but he would finish *Dark Blood*. "I had to finish the creative work which hundreds of people had done together," he said, "so that it would be there for anyone who wanted to see it."

Sluizer struggled with the question of how to work around the missing footage—include animation?—but after months of tinkering, landed upon a simple solution. Where necessary, Sluizer would narrate in a gravelly voiceover, summarizing the content of missing scenes. (Early on, he considered asking Joaquin, but the Phoenix family made it clear they had no interest in getting involved.)

Sitting in the living room of his Amsterdam apartment in 2013, with two canes by his chair, a white-haired Sluizer served a visitor fresh herring and bread, and outlined his plans for the movie: play it at various film festivals and then consider the possibility of wider distribution. That would require negotiating with the insurance company—although Sluizer absconded with the physical film, he didn't control the underlying rights.

Sluizer discussed how the character of Boy had a degree of fanaticism that was almost totally opposite to River's own nature. "He had contrasts," Sluizer said. "It's not so simple as people think—a 'nice boy.' He was as complex as we all are, or maybe even a little more so because of his life. His mother taught him, more or less, everything, and he never had the privilege of being surrounded by a class. He never went to school. I do think that makes a difference—you might be hated by everyone in your class, you might be loved, but because there are a lot of people around, you're in a solidarity situation. So River's mind is a little different."

Although there are some obvious holes in the footage, the final cut of *Dark Blood* hangs together remarkably well. Pryce and Davis skillfully portray a couple on the rocks, barely concealing their hostility with acidic banter. The southwestern landscape is gorgeous. But the reason anyone is watching is to see River Phoenix, to witness his final performance as a desert mystic savant, to get one last glimpse of him as a living twenty-three-year-old.

River gives an unvarnished but magnetic performance. He looks as if he's emerging from a cocoon after a century-long slumber, gazing at the world with curiosity and taking pleasure in the simple actions of moving his limbs. Watching it in the context of River's life, it's inspiring and heartbreaking. Inspiring because of the distance between River's work here and the sluggish performance he gave in *The Thing Called Love*: this movie documents an actor who got clean and was rediscovering his gift. Heartbreaking for exactly the same reasons: knowing that he was pulling himself together makes his Viper Room overdose that much more of a senseless waste.

After a lifetime of providing for his family and being anointed as the savior of the planet, River had given himself an extended vacation from responsibility—a delayed childhood, but with adult vices. If it had gotten out of control, that didn't mean he was on an inevitable junkie journey to a young death. River had spent some time wandering around, but he was ready to come out of the desert.

At the end of *Dark Blood,* Boy lies dead, a victim of his own obsession and of a money-counting representative of Hollywood wielding an ax. The house he built with love and care is in flames, burning bright as the picture fades to black.

EPILOGUE

When River died, in 1993, the rules of Hollywood and pop culture were in flux: what was once marginal and avant-garde had become wildly successful and commercial.

In 1995, Leonardo DiCaprio appeared in two movies that had been attached to River: *Total Eclipse* and *The Basketball Diaries*. After burnishing his reputation with Baz Luhrmann's hit version of *Romeo + Juliet*, DiCaprio became one of the most famous people in the world by starring in *Titanic*, the first movie ever to gross a billion dollars at the box office. As DiCaprio grew into baby-faced adulthood, the Hollywood studios sussed out the new terrain of commercial movies, and became steadily more reliant on "tentpole" series, comic-book movies, and other entertainments squarely aimed at male teenagers. DiCaprio sidestepped them, specializing in classy big-budget movies that assumed the audience had something resembling an attention span: *Catch Me If You Can, Inception, Django Unchained, The Great Gatsby*. He also achieved his boyhood dream of working with Martin Scorsese, the two of them making four films together (*Gangs of New York, The Aviator, The Departed, Shutter Island*). DiCaprio had the true measure of Hollywood power: the de facto ability to green-light any movie he wanted. As Jeff Robinov, president of the Warner Bros. movie division, said, "I don't know of a movie that Leo wanted to make that hasn't been made."

Sean Astin took over the *Safe Passage* role that River never played, and then kept working steadily. His role as Samwise Gamgee in the *Lord of the Rings* trilogy (2001–2003) let him continue his habit of starring in one iconic film project every decade, following *The Goonies* in 1985 and *Rudy* in 1993. After pinch-hitting for River in *Interview with the Vampire,* Christian Slater appeared in nearly fifty movies over the following twenty years, some successful, many totally obscure. There appeared to be no unifying theme or purpose to them other than Slater's name usually being above the title.

Ethan Hawke, along with director Richard Linklater and actress Julie Delpy, made a sublime trilogy of relationship dramas across eighteen years: *Before Sunrise, Before Sunset,* and *Before Midnight.* "Shit, man, this might be our life's work," Hawke said. He also wrote two novels, was nominated for an Academy Award for playing a rookie cop opposite Denzel Washington in *Training Day,* had impressive stage turns at Lincoln Center in Shakespeare and Stoppard plays, and, despite his best efforts to avoid publicity in the tabloids, received saturation coverage when his marriage to Uma Thurman broke up. Across the decades, he remained committed to the artistic ideals that he was formulating when he was a teen acting opposite River in *Explorers:* "Theater is not a stepping stone," he said. "Independent cinema is not a stepping-stone. I bump into a lot of young actors who are interested in it as a stepping-stone, and it really pisses me off. Big movies aren't a stepping-stone to another movie. Do what you're *doing.* You are your actions, and thinking motivates your actions. That's why you have to be so careful what you think about."

Michael J. Fox followed his eight seasons on *Family Ties* with four on the political sitcom *Spin City,* leaving the show in 2000 when his Parkinson's disease worsened. Through talent and force of will, Tom Cruise remained one of the biggest movie stars on the planet, starring in *Jerry Maguire, Eyes Wide Shut,* and the *Mission: Impossible* films, to name a few. He continued to approach his career like a military strategist, but as his box-office returns declined, his support of Scientology became more vocal. He also jumped up and down on Oprah Winfrey's couch.

Gus Van Sant had a breakthrough hit in 1997 when he directed *Good*

Will Hunting, the film written by and starring Matt Damon and Ben Affleck. The year after that, Van Sant made his biggest career misstep: the remake of *Psycho* starring Vince Vaughn, Julianne Moore, and Anne Heche. Since then, he has careened from classy commercial films (*Finding Forrester, Milk*) to experimental cinema, sometimes starring amateur actors (*Gerry, Elephant*). "I've always held on to the idea that with any setting and character, if you execute the film correctly, and it's an enthralling movie experience, that the rest would just fall into place, that the setting and character won't matter," he said, looking back at his career. "Now I'm realizing that there are other ways to think about what you're doing, other more accommodating ways to think about what subjects you're choosing. To be less defiant makes more sense now than it did before."

William Richert never directed another studio film after *A Night in the Life of Jimmy Reardon,* although he did helm a low-budget version of *The Man in the Iron Mask.* He also sued the Writers Guild of America for credit on the movie *The American President* and the TV show *The West Wing,* unsuccessfully arguing that Aaron Sorkin had drawn on a screenplay of his called *The President Elopes.*

Wil Wheaton matured into a geek icon, writing a popular blog and several volumes of memoirs. He also played a vindictive version of himself in a recurring role on *The Big Bang Theory.* Corey Feldman battled his addictions and became most prominent as a generic celebrity on reality shows such as *The Surreal Life.* Jerry O'Connell dropped a lot of weight, became a regular on the TV show *Sliders,* and married Rebecca Romijn.

The Butthole Surfers had a name so obscene they were sometimes referred to as the "Buttonhole Surfers" by squeamish newspapers, but in 1996, they had a bona fide hit single, proving that the music-world rulebook had been discarded. The slurry, hypnotic "Pepper," with a refrain of "pouring like an avalanche / coming down the mountain," received substantial pop airplay and hit number one on *Billboard*'s Hot Modern Rock Tracks. After that hit, and an extended dispute with their record label, the Surfers released just one more album.

233

The Red Hot Chili Peppers replaced guitarist John Frusciante with Dave Navarro of Jane's Addiction; he lasted for one album, the successful yet not well-liked *One Hot Minute.* After the other band members parted ways with Navarro, they recruited a cleaned-up Frusciante to rejoin the group. Frusciante bore the marks of his addiction: his arms were covered with abscesses, making them look as if they had been badly burned. (He was taught to shoot up by people who didn't really know how, and the abscesses didn't deter him from his habit.) "I love everything that I felt on drugs, but I can do more justice to those feelings by trying to re-create them with my music," he said. "A couple of years ago, I could only make people feel sad. That was the only ability I had. So it means everything to me to be able to sit down and sing and play guitar and make whoever I'm with feel good." Frusciante made three more albums with the Peppers—*Californication, By the Way,* and *Stadium Arcadium*—before quitting the band again. When the group went on hiatus, Flea played in various side projects (including Atoms for Peace with Radiohead singer Thom Yorke) and went back to school to study music composition.

Brad Pitt was at the apex of the most famous love triangle of the twenty-first century, dropping Jennifer Aniston for Angelina Jolie in what became a multiyear tabloid theatrical. He seemed like the least interesting member of that threesome—for the story to have legs, Pitt needed to be portrayed as lacking agency, to be terrain fought over by two women rather than an adult making decisions. The hubbub obscured that Pitt was staying on top of Hollywood while making a minimal number of popcorn movies. His performances weren't eccentric or flashy. Pitt's preferred MO was to serve as an engaging, upright presence in what turned out to be a darker, weirder movie than audiences might have expected: *Fight Club, Inglorious Basterds, Babel, Burn After Reading.*

Aside from hanging out at the Viper Room, Samantha Mathis was a working actress, with credits ranging from *American Psycho* to *Curb Your Enthusiasm.* Suzanne Solgot studied belly dancing, got married, and had two kids. She practiced alternative healing, employing massage and the Reiki technique. Martha Plimpton shuttled between the stage, movies, and TV, before anchoring the Fox sitcom *Raising Hope* as a scabrous grand-mother. "It's a crazy thing, you know, when kids become actors," she said, looking back. "Very often, their parents or whoever aren't interested in what their kids are learning while they're doing it. They're interested in what their kids are *getting* . . . Cuteness doesn't last."

R.E.M. drummer Bill Berry had a brain aneurysm onstage in Switzer-land in 1995, and quit the band two years later; after some soul-searching, the other three members continued without him. R.E.M. released seven studio albums between River's death in 1993 and the band's dissolution in 2011—their sales gradually diminished (as they did for just about everybody in the music business), but most of the albums were pretty great.

Before he died, River introduced Michael Stipe to Sandy Stern, who had produced Mathis's film *Pump Up the Volume.* Stern and Stipe became partners in Single Cell Pictures, and produced some excellent left-of-center movies, in-cluding *Being John Malkovich, Velvet Goldmine,* and *Saved!* Stipe spent more time in Los Angeles, and on R.E.M.'s 1996 album *New Adventures in Hi-Fi,* sang the gorgeous, elegiac "Electrolite," about standing in the Hollywood Hills gazing at the twinkling nighttime lights of L.A. "Twentieth century go to sleep," he sang, in a loving elegy for show business, and for the whole world. "Stand on a cliff and look down there / Don't be scared / You are alive," he counseled, echoing River's monologue when he stood over the foggy ravine outside William Richert's house.

After an extended separation, John and Heart Phoenix officially split up about three years after River died. John returned to Florida and worked as an organic farmer, while Heart married Jeffrey Weisberg. She also led gender workshops and eventually founded the River Phoenix Center for Peacebuild-ing. River's sister Liberty worked at the River Phoenix Center as office man-ager, taught midwifery, worked as a Realtor, and, after the tragic death of a young son that she attributed to toxic outgassing, opened the nontoxic Indigo Green Building Supply Store.

Summer Phoenix told a British newspaper that changing the world had gone by the wayside for her. "Nah, it's not about that now," she said. "Now

I just want to act." Summer appeared in a dozen movies through 2004, plus nearly as many TV roles, but stopped acting after she became a mother; she and her husband, actor/director Casey Affleck, had two sons and she opened a vintage store called Some Odd Rubies.

Rain Phoenix starred in the video for R.E.M.'s "At My Most Beautiful," playing a harried cellist auditioning for the band. She also toured with the Red Hot Chili Peppers as a backing vocalist on the tour for *One Hot Minute,* and had her own band, called Papercranes. For a while, all three Phoenix sisters were members of a new-wave band called the Causey Way. The group's gimmick: a (fictional) cult that decided to spread the word through music.

"Of course there is a sadness with not seeing him in the physical world, but everything I do, he is part of," Rain said of River. "Through my music, I am forever able to stay connected to my brother. We are always infinitely collaborating in spirit."

Joaquin Phoenix became one of the most intense actors in film, receiving Oscar nominations for his glowering performances in *Gladiator, Walk the Line,* and *The Master,* despite expressing contempt for the Academy Awards and all they represented. "I think it's total, utter bullshit, and I don't want to be part of it," he said. "It's a carrot, but it's the worst-tasting carrot I've ever tasted in my whole life." Joaquin fiercely guarded his privacy but denied reports that he had a breakdown while filming the scene in *Walk the Line* where, playing Johnny Cash, he can't prevent the death of his older brother. "I don't need to pull from my experience for a character, and I've never understood why actors would, except for lack of ability, imagination, or research," he said. "Suggesting that I would use this personal part of my life for a fucking movie . . . it kind of makes me sick." He added: "The press has kind of imposed upon me the title of Mourning Brother, and because I haven't been vocal about it, the assumption is that I'm holding on to this shit that's just not there."

Johnny Depp maintained his alliance with Tim Burton; after *Edward Scissorhands,* they made six more films together, from *Ed Wood* to *Dark Shadows.* Aside from his work with Burton, Depp kept making anticommercial

236

choices, playing a Victorian police inspector in *From Hell* with Albert and Allan Hughes, a fugitive accountant in *Dead Man* with Jim Jarmusch, and a jailed transvestite in *Before Night Falls* with Julian Schnabel. In 2003, he had an antic turn as Captain Jack Sparrow in *Pirates of the Caribbean: The Curse of the Black Pearl,* basing his performance on Keith Richards and Pepe Le Pew. After the movie became a surprise blockbuster, finally elevating Depp to the top of Hollywood's A-list, he made three sequels and cashed a check for playing opposite Angelina Jolie in the international thriller *The Tourist.* But he maintained his status as the major star most willing to put on his crazy hat for movies—literally, with his role as the Mad Hatter in *Alice in Wonderland.*

"I don't think anybody's necessarily ready for death," Depp reflected. "You can only hope that when it approaches, you feel like you've said what you wanted to say. Nobody wants to go out in mid-sentence."

ACKNOWLEDGMENTS

Thank you to everyone who helped with this book, or who just made the world a better place during those interludes when I came up for air. When you're on an overcaffeinated book-writing odyssey, you want excellent people to be in the boat with you, in case it takes ten years to get back to Ithaca.

I am extremely lucky to be working with the brilliant editor Carrie Thornton, who is filled with wisdom and talent the way a Russian nesting doll is filled with more nesting dolls. Thanks to all her fellow superstars at It Books, especially Kevin Callahan (whose enthusiasm made this book possible), Brittany Hamblin, Heidi Lewis, Julia Meltzer, Trina Hunn, Elissa Cohen, Shannon Plunkett, Cal Morgan, and Lynn Grady. Thanks also to Laura Wyss and Martin Karlow. And a special salute to Amanda Kain, who designed the beautiful cover of this book before I finished writing it. On more than one late night, the cover was highly motivating: I wanted to write a book that would live up to it.

My agent, Daniel Greenberg, routinely brings keen intelligence, good humor, and elite ninja skills to bear on my behalf: a thousand thank-yous to him and his associates at Levine Greenberg, especially Monika Verma and Tim Wojcik.

In the Venn diagram with two circles, one of which is "awesome people" and the other is "my friends," I am extremely fortunate that they have such a huge overlapping area. I am particularly in the debt of four people who read this book when it was just a raw manuscript; all provided sage counsel and useful reality checks. Bill Tipper is the guy you want by your side when you're on top of a mountain (and not just because he brings snacks). Steve Crystal is formerly my roommate, currently a Hollywood power player, and always a mensch. Nina Blackwood is a VJ goddess and one of the kindest people I know. Rob Sheffield is my friend, my inspiration, and a man who can lead a crowd of strangers in a sing-along version of "Build Me Up Buttercup."

Thank you, Julie Farman, for your essential assistance in locating celebrities and their publicists. Thank you, Molly Ker Hawn, for your invaluable genealogy skills. Thank you, Abby Royle, for crackerjack transcription. Thank you, Tim Atkinson, for letting me drag you out to the Viper Room when you were in town to hang with Lemmy. Thank you, Marjorie Ingall, for timely *Sassy* help. Thank you, Katie Hollander, for your talented navigation of the art world.

Thank you for your help, guidance, and courtesy, Jennifer Keishin Armstrong, Diedrich Bader, Rob Brunner, Steve Crystal, Flea, Stacey Grenrock-Woods, Sal Jenco, Melissa Maerz, Morgan Neville, Eddie Schmidt, John Vlautin, Marc Weidenbaum, Hillary Wendroff, and Moon Zappa. And an extra-special thanks to Sebastian Bach.

I am full of gratitude to everyone who consented to an interview with me, some in recent months, some years before I knew I was going to write this book: Richmond Arquette, Gus Brandt, Kim Buie, Johnny Depp, Joe Dolce, John Frusciante, Ethan Hawke, Rose McGowan, Frank Meyer, Heart Phoenix, William Richert, Ione Skye, George Sluizer, and anonymous sources.

I spent most of the nineties working at *Details,* which proved to be the best possible training ground I could have hoped for. This book has let me revisit that era, so I want to salute all my twelfth-floor coworkers who inspired me, then and now, especially James Truman, David Keeps, Joe Levy,

Joe Dolce, Michael Caruso, John Leland, Pat Blashill, Caren Myers, Michael Dolan, Jeanie Pyun, Tommy Dunne, Ilsa Enomoto, Lisa Steinmeyer, B. W. Honeycutt, Lisa Murray, Markus Kiersztan, Francesca Castagnoli, Rob Tannenbaum, William Shaw, Mim Udovitch, and Chris Heath.

My *Rolling Stone* colleagues are basically the Avengers of the magazine world, and I'm always psyched to get into the quinjet with them. I am in awe of the superpowers of Will Dana, Nathan Brackett, Sean Woods, Jonathan Ringen, Peter Travers, Simon Vozick-Levinson, Christian Hoard, Andy Greene, Alison Weinflash, Coco McPherson, Jodi Peckman, Jason Fine, and the god of thunder, Jann Wenner.

In New York, I salute James Hannaham, Brendan Moroney, Brian Smith-Sweeney, Sabrina Smith-Sweeney, Emily Nussbaum, Clive Thompson, Chris Kalb, Ben Smith, and Chris Molanphy; in Los Angeles, David Handelman, Syd Sidner, Leah Lehmbeck, Jason Lehmbeck, Nettie Neville, Philip Farha, Meryl Emmerton, Christine Street Gregg, David Gregg, Martha Quinn, Julie Heimark, Peter Heimark, Hillary Seitz, Brenna Sanchez, and Travis Barker; in Evanston, Megan Kashner, Trina Whittaker, Zane Kashner, and Tessa Kashner.

Much love to my far-flung family, especially my parents, my brothers Julian and Nick, my Aunt Lis, and my cool Texas in-laws, Alex and Cynthia and Big Al. And even more love to my sons, Strummer and Dashiell, who are too young to read this book now, but who may pull it off the shelf someday. And infinite amounts of love to my wonderful wife, Jen Sudul Edwards, who offered trenchant commentary on my early drafts, provided emotional support when I was wrestling with the manuscript, kept the household running when I was wandering around pulling out my hair, and, as always, inspired me to achieve things that I didn't know I was capable of doing.

Finally, thanks to River Phoenix for all the cool things he did; I'm sorry I never got to meet him. "Love conquers all," River said once. "Even the assholes that don't want it."

241

BIBLIOGRAPHY

Rachel Abramowitz, Peter Biskind, Veronica Chambers, John Clark, Christopher Connelly, Joan Goodman, Nancy Griffin, Charlie Holland, Eliza Bergman Krause, John H. Richardson, Fred Schruers, "A Brief Life," *Premiere,* March 1994.

Christopher Andersen, *Mick: The Wild Life and Mad Genius of Jagger,* Gallery Books, 2012.

Michael Angeli, "Young Man River," *Movieline,* September 1991.

Isis Aquarian with Electricity Aquarian, *The Source: The Untold Story of Father Yod, YaHoWa13, and the Source Family,* Process Media, 2007.

Simon Banner, "Vegetarian of Love," *SKY Magazine* (UK), October 1990.

Sheila Benson, "From Hubris to Good Humor: 'The Mosquito Coast,'" *Los Angeles Times,* November 26, 1986.

Lisa Bernhard, "Let It Flow," *Rolling Stone,* October 17, 1991 (issue no. 615).

Louis Black, "Dogfight," *Austin Chronicle,* March 27, 1992.

Iain Blair, "The Rise of River Phoenix," *Chicago Tribune,* March 27, 1988.

——, "River Phoenix—Rising Fast," *Playgirl,* August 1988.

Peter Bogdanovich, "River Remembered," *Premiere,* January 2001.

Patricia Bosworth, *Montgomery Clift: A Biography,* Harcourt Brace Jovanovich, 1978.

Blanche McCrary Boyd, "Ahead of the Pack," *Premiere,* April 1988.

Rob Brunner, "The Strange Saga of River Phoenix's Final Film," *Entertainment Weekly,* September 28, 2012.

Grace Catalano, *River Phoenix: Hero & Heartthrob,* Bantam, 1988.

James D. Chancellor, *Life in the Family: An Oral History of the Children of God,* Syracuse University Press, 2000.

Randi Sue Coburn, "Marines at Their Best," *Premiere,* October 1991.

Jenny Cooney, "Their Own Private Idaho," *Empire* (UK), April 1992.

Lena Corner, "Rain Phoenix's Unusual Childhood," *Guardian* (UK), July 8, 2011.

Peter Cowie, *World Cinema: Diary of a Day,* Overlook, 1995.

Joe Dolce, "River's Edge," *Details,* November 1991.

Nina J. Easton, "For Tim Burton, This One's Personal," *Los Angeles Times,* August 12, 1990.

Roger Ebert, "Running on Empty," *Chicago Sun-Times,* September 23, 1988.

——, "The Thing Called Love," *Chicago Sun-Times,* January 21, 1994.

Mark Ebner, "Snake Pit on Sunset!," hollywoodinterrupted.com, March 1, 1999.

Daniel Mark Epstein, *Sister Aimee: The Life of Aimee Semple McPherson,* Harcourt Brace Jovanovich, 1993.

Tad Friend, "River, with Love and Anger," *Esquire,* March 1994; also available on byliner.com as "The Short, Happy Life of River Phoenix."

Ilene Froom, " 'Rock Against Fur' Concert," available on myriverphoenixcollection.com, 2002.

Cal Fussman, "What I've Learned: Johnny Depp," *Esquire,* January 2008.

——, "10 Essential Lessons from Leo DiCaprio," esquire.com, 2010.

Oliver Gettell, "River Phoenix's Final Film, 'Dark Blood,' Finally Comes to Screen," *Los Angeles Times,* February 14, 2013.

Ryan Gilbey, "The Lost Boy," *Guardian* (UK), October 23, 2003.

John Glatt, *Lost in Hollywood: The Fast Times and Short Life of River Phoenix,* Donald I. Fine, 1995.

Owen Glieberman, "My Own Private Idaho," *Entertainment Weekly,* October 11, 1991.

Todd Gold, "Spotlight: Samantha Mathis," *Us Weekly,* May 15, 2000.

Nigel Goodall, *Johnny Depp: The Biography,* Blake Publishing, 1999.

David Greene, " 'Stand by Me': A Love Letter to Childhood Innocence," radio segment on *All Things Considered* (archived on npr.org), August 6, 2011.

Gayle Guthman, "The Big Top Comes Down, but Memories of the First Hernando Fiesta Will Linger," *St. Petersburg Times,* May 1, 1979.

——, "The Phoenix Children, River and Rain, Are Natural Musicians," *St. Petersburg Times,* May 19, 1979.

Christopher Hampton, "The Long Brief Encounter," *Sunday Telegraph* (UK), April 6, 1997.

David Handelman, "Gus Van Sant's Northwest Passage," *Rolling Stone,* October 31, 1993 (issue no. 616).

Aljean Harmetz, "Up and Coming: Leonardo DiCaprio," *New York Times,* December 12, 1993.

Will Harris, "Random Roles: Martha Plimpton," *Onion A.V. Club,* April 3, 2012.

Ethan Hawke, "I Am Ethan Hawke—AMAA [Ask Me Almost Anything]," reddit.com, posted June 5, 2013.

Chris Heath, "Johnny Depp: Portrait of the Oddest as a Young Man," *Details,* May 1993.

——, "The Next Big Thing," *Empire,* April 1994.

Phyllis Heller, "This Butt's for You," *Spin,* June 1986.

Hermann Hesse (as translated by Hilda Rosner), *Siddhartha,* Bantam, 1971.

Bill Higgins, "The L.A. Riots at 20: Edward James Olmos Remembers 'All-Out War' in Hollywood," *Hollywood Reporter,* April 27, 2012.

Hal Hinson, "Little Nikita," *Washington Post,* March 18, 1988.

Barney Hoskyns, *Montgomery Clift: Beautiful Loser,* Grove Weidenfeld, 1992.

Shawn Hubler and Steve Hochman, " 'Designer Drug' Enters Hollywood's Fast Lane," *Los Angeles Times,* November 3, 1993.

Rebecca Johnson, "Young Man River," *Mademoiselle,* August 1993.

Iain Johnstone, *Tom Cruise: All the World's a Stage,* Hodder & Stoughton, 2006.

Celeste Jones, Kristina Jones, and Juliana Buhring, *Not Without My Sister,* HarperElement, 2007.

Tom Junod, "The Moment Leonardo DiCaprio Became a Man," *Esquire,* May 2013.

Dave Kehr, "Kasdan Goes Slumming in 'I Love You,' " *Chicago Tribune,* April 6, 1990.

Christina Kelly, "Does River's Dog Eat Meat?: And Other Burning Questions," *Sassy,* October 1989.

——, "I Saw River Phoenix Brush His Teeth," *Sassy,* June 1991.

Rita Kempley, "Sneakers," *Washington Post,* September 9, 1992.

Dana Kennedy, "River's Edge," *Entertainment Weekly,* November 12, 1993.

Peter Keough, "Youthful Idealism Keeps River Phoenix Running," *Chicago Sun-Times,* September 25, 1988.

Anthony Kiedis with Larry Sloman, *Scar Tissue,* Hyperion, 2004.

Steve Kokker, "Cry Me a River," *Face,* October 1995.

Richard Kozar, *Michael J. Fox,* Chelsea House Publishers, 2000.

Eric Larnick, " 'Stand by Me' at 25—The Stars' Oral History of Their Beloved Classic," moviefone.com, March 25, 2011.

Don Lattin, *Jesus Freaks: A True Story of Murder and Madness on the Evangelical Edge*, HarperOne, 2008.

Barry C. Lawrence, *In Search of River Phoenix: The Truth Behind the Myth*, Wordsworth, 2004.

Shelley Levitt, "River's End," *People Weekly*, November 15, 1993.

Sidney Lumet, *Making Movies*, Vintage, 1996.

Andrew MacDonald, "River Deep," *Face*, July 1989.

Janet Maslin, "The Screen: Explorers," *New York Times*, July 12, 1985.

——, "'Running on Empty,' A Family Underground," *New York Times*, September 9, 1988.

Todd McCarthy, "Review: 'Silent Tongue,'" *Variety*, February 3, 1993.

Cole McFarland, "Phoenix Rising," *Animals' Voice Magazine*, February 1989.

Carey McWilliams, *Southern California: An Island on the Land*, Peregrine Smith, 1973.

Denis Meikle, *Johnny Depp: A Kind of Illusion*, Reynolds & Hearn, 2004.

Holly Millea, "Ghost in the Machine: Now You See Johnny Depp, Now You Don't," *Premiere*, February 1995.

Henry Miller, *The Time of the Assassins: A Study of Rimbaud*, New Directions, 1949.

Elvis Mitchell, "Joaquin Phoenix," *Interview*, October 2012.

Marc Mohan, "Interview: Gus Van Sant on 'Promised Land' and More," *Oregonian*, December 22, 2012.

Andrew Morton, *Tom Cruise: An Unauthorized Biography*, St. Martin's Press, 2008.

Nardwuar the Human Serviette, "Nardwuar the Human Serviette vs. Corey Feldman," *Skratch*, July 1999.

Tom Nordlie, "The Girls in the Band," *Gainesville Sun*, July 1990; archived on web page http://web.uflib.ufl.edu/Staff/d-harris/chix.html for "The Fabulous Mutley Chix."

247

James Robert Parish, *Gus Van Sant: An Unauthorized Biography,* Thunder's Mouth, 2001.

Susan Peters, "One Big Hippy Family: River Phoenix and Company Move into Hollywood," *Life,* August 1987.

Nathan Rabin, "Interview: Wil Wheaton," *Onion A.V. Club,* November 20, 2002.

Susan Reed, "The Child of Flower Children, Actor River Phoenix Rises from a Strange Past to Blossom in *Stand by Me,*" *People,* September 29, 1986.

Janet Reitman, *Inside Scientology: The Story of America's Most Secretive Religion,* Houghton Mifflin Harcourt, 2011.

David Rensin, "The Us Interview: River Phoenix," *Us,* September 1991.

J. W. Rinzler, *The Complete Making of Indiana Jones: The Definitive Story Behind All Four Films,* Ebury, 2008.

Roberta and David Ritz, "Strange Days," *Us,* October 1995.

Cecil M. Robeck Jr., *The Azusa Street Mission & Revival,* Nelson Reference & Electronic, 2006.

James E. Rogan, *Rough Edges: My Unlikely Road from Welfare to Washington,* William Morrow, 2004.

Henry Rollins, foreword to *Straight Whisky: A Living History of Sex, Drugs, and Rock 'n' Roll on the Sunset Strip* by Erik Quisling and Austin Williams, Bonus Books, 2003.

Reid Rosefelt, "Remembering River," *Elle,* February 1994.

Dario Scardapane, "Lost Boys," *Us,* November 1991.

Richard Schickel, "Depp Charge," *Time,* March 3, 1997.

Susan Schindehette, Lyndon Stambler, Johnny Dodd, Lorenzo Benet, Joanna Stone, "High Life," *People,* January 17, 1994.

Mary Shedden, "River Phoenix's Estate Sued over Film Roles," *Gainesville Sun,* July 12, 1994.

Gini Sikes and Paige Powell, "Boy Meets Boy," *Interview*, November 1991.

Sean Smith, "Coming Attractions," *Newsweek*, August 28, 2005.

Chris Snyder, *Hunting with Barracudas: My Life in Hollywood with the Legendary Iris Burton*, Herman Graf, 2009.

John Stark, "Kids for Sale: Stage Parents, Agents, Overachieving Tots—How Hollywood Urchandises Its Youngest Stars," *People*, November 12, 1984.

Douglas Thompson, *Leonardo DiCaprio*, Berkley Trade, 1998.

Stephen Tobolowsky, "Memories of the *Sneakers* Shoot," Slate.com, September 10, 2012.

Peter Travers, "Dogfight," *Rolling Stone*, November 14, 1991 (issue no. 617).

Kenneth Turan, "Reverence Runs Deep in 'River,'" *Los Angeles Times*, October 9, 1992.

Mim Udovitch, "Ethan Hawke," *Details*, March 1994.

——, "Tarantino and Juliette," *Details*, February 1996.

Leslie Van Buskirk, "Johnny Depp: The Us Interview," *Us*, February 1994.

Gus Van Sant, *Pink*, Nan A. Talese, 1997.

Polly Vernon, "Summer Time," *Guardian* (UK), February 14, 2004.

John Voland, "River Phoenix: Running on a Full Set of '60s/'80s Ideals," *Los Angeles Times*, September 7, 1988.

Barry Walters, "Interview: Christopher Owens," emusic.com, January 15, 2013.

Ruth Wangerin, *The Children of God: A Make-Believe Revolution?*, Praeger, 1993.

Lord Justice Sir Alan Hylton Ward, Children of God Judgment ("W 42 1992 in the High Court of Justice, Family Division, Principal Registry in the Matter of ST (A Minor), and in the Matter of the Supreme Court Act 1991"), as hosted on xfamily.org, May 26, 2005.

Bernard Weinraub, "Death of River Phoenix Jolts the Movie Industry," *New York Times*, November 2, 1993.

Debra Blake Weisenthal, "River on the Rise," *Vegetarian Times,* March 1988.

Vicki Woods, "Tofu Guys Don't Eat Meat," *Vogue,* May 1990.

Lawrence Wright, *Going Clear: Scientology, Hollywood, and the Prison of Belief,* Alfred A. Knopf, 2013.

Dan Yakir, "River Phoenix, Nature Boy," *SKY Magazine* (UK), July 1989.

——, "A Hero by Any Other Age," *Starlog,* October 1989.

Blaine Zuckerman, "Rose McGowan: I Escaped a Cult," *People,* September 5, 2011.

NOTES

W hile this book isn't meant to be a scholarly tome, I want readers to be able to check out its sources—so each quotation in the main text gets a citation in the following notes, referring to the book or magazine in the bibliography from where it came (or to an interview that I conducted). Where it seems particularly illuminating, I also provide references for other information. I refer consistently to River's mother below as Heart Phoenix, because that was the name she was using when I interviewed her.

I am in debt to all my sources, but I am particularly grateful for the biographers of River who came before me, especially Tad Friend, John Glatt, Barry C. Lawrence, and Roberta and David Ritz, and to Chris Snyder for his very entertaining book about working with Iris Burton. If you are interested in more information on any particular chapter, pursue the notes: wanting to know more about the history of Southern Californian religions, for example, will take you to Carey McWilliams's book. But if you want to read just one other piece of writing about River Phoenix, I recommend you track down Michael Angeli's 1991 profile from *Movieline,* which is a vivid portrait of River living in Florida just before the release of *My Own Private Idaho,* full of talent and charm. (Compiling the bibliography was bittersweet because of all the great magazines that aren't around anymore, especially *Movieline, Premiere, The Face,* and *Sassy.*)

251

INTRODUCTION

"I think he was the best": Heath (1994). "River was one of those people": Hawke. "He was the kind of guy": Wade Evans, as quoted in Friend. "His eyes made him": Friend. "He had very long hair": Abramowitz et al. Patricia Arquette: author interview with Richmond Arquette (2013). "there was a specific road": Van Buskirk. "The guy was having a good time": Millea.

PART ONE

1. SKYLARKING

Author interviews with William Richert (2013) and Ione Skye (2012).

2. THE SEARCHERS

"I just wanted to be loved": author interview with Heart Phoenix (1997). "I wasn't thrilled": Glatt. "I ran away from home": Glatt. "It's very interesting": Catalano. "gift from God": Glatt. "I just instantly saw," "Maybe you didn't need": Boyd. "We were flower children": Reed. "They were a rather strange lot": Lawrence. "The river has taught me": Hesse. "three and a half hours": Lawrence. "When the baby came out": author interview with Heart Phoenix (1997). "The book *Siddhartha* talks about": Lawrence. "Why don't you receive me?": Guthman (May 19, 1979).

3. DEAR GOD

"There will be no billion-dollar tax bill": Reitman. Details of Miscavige lifestyle: Reitman, Wright. Aimee Semple McPherson: Epstein. History of California cults: McWilliams. Pentecostal movement: Robeck. The Source Family: Aquarian with Aquarian.

4. ONE NIGHT AT THE VIPER ROOM

"Would you give me," "I can get": Ebner.

5. SUFFER THE CHILDREN

"One dark night": Chancellor. "come-union": Ward. "Christian sex cult": Glatt. "It was not until I kicked over": Chancellor. "We have a sexy God," "revolutionary sexual freedoms": Ward. Treatment of the children of the Children of God: See, for example, Jones, Jones, and Buhring. "There was a big effort": Walters. "Like most cults, you were cut off": Zuckerman. "When I was five": author interview with Rose McGowan (2007). "Their whole thing": Zuckerman. After River's family left the Children of God, the cult changed its name to the Family.

6. FOLLOW THE LEADER

Used stereos and TV sets: Lattin. "We'll blow like Krakatoa": Chancellor. Drunk cowboys shooting: Wangerin. Rain's birth date has sometimes been erroneously reported as being in March 1973, but the November 21, 1972, date is correct according to the "Texas Birth Index 1903–1997" provided by the Texas Department of State Health Services. "We moved around a *lot*": Keough. "Archbishop of Venezuela and the Caribbean": Some sources have the title as "Archbishop of South America"; John may have had both titles at various points. "The kids grew up going out": Boyd. "They were devoted parents": Ritz and Ritz. "We did it because we needed money": Catalano. "It was what God told them": Lawrence. "I've been through some pretty desperate times": Catalano. "What greater way": Chancellor. "The guy running it got crazy": Glatt. "He may have been a sexual pervert": Glatt. "They tried to evangelize and entertain": Lawrence. "I got the feeling": Ritz and Ritz. "While they were definitely poor": Lawrence. "When a journalist would come": Author interview with George Sluizer (2013). "Is there anything you did": Dolce. Glatt printed an expanded version of the exchange that included River saying, "I didn't want those young vaginas and different body parts that were in my face to make me perverse when I was older." After the interview was printed, River claimed he had been joking. "Yes, yes, yes": Lawrence. "Happy? Well, it was interesting": Blair (August 1988).

7. ANOTHER NIGHT AT THE VIPER ROOM

"You know, these people sure do party strange": author interview with Richmond Arquette (2013).

8. MEAT IS MURDER

"An airplane is not the only way": Lawrence. "the crew discovered us": Angeli. "These weren't bad people": Kelly (1989). "It was the first time that I really saw": Weisenthal. "I tell my kids to celebrate the Earth": Author interview with Heart Phoenix (1997). "ultravegetarianism": Friend. "It was hard to give up dairy": Weisenthal. "Every child starts out loving animals": Kelly (1989). "Vegetarianism is a link to perfection": Weisenthal. "Hello, I'm River Phoenix": PETA PSA and outtakes available online on sites including YouTube.

PART TWO

9. BACK IN THE U.S.A.

"companies paid people's families": Friend. "that he never really got its logic": Friend. "When I was in first grade": Glatt. "Ask your father": Peters. "generic items you'd find": Angeli. "We all look completely different": Yakir (July 1989). "We never treated them like children": MacDonald. "The youngest gets to yell the loudest": MacDonald. "They were really trippy": Lawrence. "They were the best clothes": Glatt. Joaquin as X-Men fan: Snyder, who learned of Joaquin's long-running appreciation of the mutant superheroes when the actor was up for the role of Wolverine in the X-Men movie (Dougray Scott had to pull out due to his role in *Mission: Impossible II,* but Hugh Jackman hadn't yet been cast). "We all wanted to be entertainers": Angeli. "Those girls were moving": Guthman (May 1, 1979). "Except a man be born again": the line is from John 3:3. "independent missionaries," "I hope to be famous," "This was an 8-year-old talking": Guthman (May 19, 1979). "They answered": Angeli. "Things went wrong": Glatt. "We'd roll into gas stations": Glatt.

10. JOHNNY CAME FROM MIAMI F-L-A

All quotations from author interview with Johnny Depp (2007).

11. SHOW-BIZ BABIES

"I put a bowl of fruit": Lawrence. "We were really naïve": Glatt. "We schlepped forever": Angeli. "When they went to L.A.": Lawrence. "So what's been the happiest day of your life?" (and ensuing dialogue): author interview with Heart Phoenix (1997). "I'm a groomer": Stark. "Throw a white sheet": Snyder. "Kids are pieces of meat": Stark. "Commercials were too phony for me": Glatt. The video of the Phoenix kids in yellow tank tops can be seen in the opening minutes of *I'm Still Here,* the fake Joaquin Phoenix documentary (2010) directed by Casey Affleck.

12. LET'S WORK

"What are your goals?": Kozar. "I averaged about four hours": Kozar. "Laser Head": Morton.

13. THE MAGNIFICENT SEVEN

"He came in with that": Glatt. "I just leaped": Glatt. "He would burst out crying": Glatt. The dinnertime scene is from the pilot episode of *Seven Brides for Seven Brothers.* "a sad little child": Lawrence.

14. TV EYE

"kind of dreary": Peters. "River was very much part": Glatt.

15. ECHO #1: *SURVIVING*

All dialogue from *Surviving,* also known as *Surviving: A Family in Crisis* and *Tragedy.*

16. UNMAPPED TERRITORY

"I got a thrill": Glatt. "I saw him practicing": Hawke. "River had to do the most acting": Ritz and Ritz. "Although River liked to be cool": Glatt. "It was the longest shoot": Ritz and Ritz. "We competed": Ritz and Ritz. "Getting laid was a major goal": Glatt. "River had a very doctrinaire": Glatt. "naïve pretentiousness": Ritz and Ritz. "River didn't have a lot of material knowledge": Glatt. "Television wasn't really": author interview with Heart Phoenix (1997). Three Stooges: Lawrence. "We got along exceptionally": Lawrence. "Are you going to be famous?" and ensuing conversation: Ritz and Ritz. "One day, John showed up": Ritz and Ritz, relating a story from an anonymous source. "It's charmingly odd": Maslin (1985). "I believe it is profoundly negative": Ritz and Ritz. "He would send me into fits of envy": Udovitch (1994). "My biggest fear": author interview with Ethan Hawke (2004). "I would have really liked": Udovitch (1994). The Looney Tunes cartoon that Hawke remembered (mostly accurately) was "Show Biz Bugs," starring Bugs Bunny and Daffy Duck. Determined to outdo Bugs on a vaudeville stage, Daffy drinks "a generous portion of gasoline," nitroglycerine, "a goodly amount of gunpowder," uranium-238, and then swallows a match. He explodes, to massive applause. "They loved it! They want more!" Bugs tells him. As a ghostly Daffy floats off this mortal plane, he says, "I know, I know, but I can only do it once."

17. IF THE SKY THAT WE LOOK UPON SHOULD TUMBLE AND FALL INTO THE SEA

"I kind of limped in": Lawrence. "He was a young James Dean": Larnick. "And River was cool": Greene. "He was so professional": Larnick. "Whenever we saw each other on auditions": Larnick. "The other guys dared me to do it" and ensuing dialogue with Kiefer Sutherland: Yakir (July 1989). "There was no alcohol": Lawrence. "Kids never got along with me": Lawrence. "We both coughed a lot": Nardwuar the Human Serviette (actually his legal name—he's a Canadian music obsessive and oddball but effective celebrity interviewer). "Sex was nearly all": Lawrence. "It was a beautiful experience": Glatt. "A very strange experience": Glatt. "WELL IT HAPPENED": Glatt. "Is there a moment": Lawrence. "it took him a while": Glatt. "Personally, I didn't think": Glatt.

18. ECHO #2: *STAND BY ME*

"sad and weird and eerie": from Rob Reiner's commentary track on the

DVD of *Stand by Me (Special Edition)*, Sony Pictures Home Entertainment, 1986.

19. YOUNG HOLLYWOOD 1985

"Yertle the Turtle": Kiedis. "Michael Stipe / despite the hype": Heller.

20. FAMILY AFFAIR

Financial details: Lawrence. All dialogue from "My Tutor," the seventh episode of the fourth season of *Family Ties*.

21. TILT-A-WHIRL

"We partied all day": Glatt. "River looked very unsure": Glatt. "the devil's dandruff": Angeli.

PART THREE

22. SMALL-TOWN HOLLYWOOD

"Our neighborhood": author interview with Ione Skye (2012).

23. WELCOME TO THE JUNGLE

"There's a boy on this tape": Catalano. "I finally said to myself": Catalano.

24. ECHO #3: *THE MOSQUITO COAST*

"I knew that character": Glatt. "Paul Theroux didn't steal": Angeli.

25. JUNGLE BOY

"It was very hot": Lawrence. "In a matter of months," "But the more he stepped": Rosefelt. "River Phoenix was born to movies": Glatt. "In his position": Lawrence. "There are a lot of people": Rosefelt. "I wondered if there was something strange" Rosefelt. "I was a curious kid": Rosefelt. "With a young person": Glatt. "He'd stuff himself": Glatt. "It was like living": Blair (August 1988). "I've been so much more": Boyd. "The character's just so weird":

Harris. "But we couldn't stand each other": Reed. "I knew what it was like": Harris. "Martha Plimpton was his first": Ritz and Ritz. "I learned that even among": Lawrence. "Half the conflict of the film": Benson. "It just feels so good": Glatt.

26. LAST YEAR AT THE VIPER ROOM

All quotations from Ebner.

27. HIS NAME IS RIO AND HE DANCES ON THE SAND

"one of the most exciting": Reed. "Because he made such an impact": Lawrence. "After *Stand by Me* came out": Glatt. "That room was filled with kids": Abramowitz et al. "They teach you how to pose": Woods. "I like girls who are so natural," "It's a great feeling": Glatt. "It's like there's a grandstand": Voland. "He told me that he had to get up": Rosefelt. "Yo, Mama-jama": Reed. "That's been a lot of fun": Blair (August 1988). "His parents saw him": Friend. "It was something like": Glatt.

28. MARTHA MY DEAR

"River went off": author interview with Ione Skye (2012). "I loved him for that": Friend.

29. COMING OF AGE STORY

"and he was completely surrounded by light," and following dialogue between River and Richert: author interview with William Richert (2013). "intelligent teenage comedy": Lawrence. "In three months": author interview with William Richert (2013). "I could get away with a lot": Boyd. "How many blow jobs": Author interview with William Richert (2013). "very party atmosphere": author interview with Ione Skye (2012). "The most out-of-control thing": Glatt. "Don't tell anybody," "Like, yeah, I'm going to call": Glatt. "I'm the monogamous type": Glatt. "You were listening to the ultimate makeout record," "I remember thinking": author interview with Ione Skye (2012). "She seemed to be in charge": Glatt. "I wrote that back": author interview with William Richert (2013). "Where do I cry," "Not in this one": author interview with William Richert (2013). "He was very powerful": author interview with Ione Skye (2012). "and his handwriting," "Well, I really do want to say": author interview with William Richert (2013).

30. RATTLESNAKE SPEEDWAY

"Yeah, very funny, kid": Boyd.

31. I AM AN ISLAND

"The bigger labels are supermarkets": from the Chris Blackwell biography at the Rock and Roll Hall of Fame Web site (he was inducted in 2001). "He seems like a really cool kid," "My God, he just stood out": author interview with Kim Buie (2012). "progressive ethereal folk-rock": multiple sources, including Blair (August 1988) and Yakir (July 1989).

32. YOUNG HOLLYWOOD 1987

Stealing car keys with a fishing rod: Kiedis.

33. I HOPE THE RUSSIANS LOVE THEIR CHILDREN, TOO

"I felt so out of place": Boyd. "Is River Phoenix a star?": Hinson. "I feel River Phoenix": from the Columbia Pictures press kit for *Little Nikita*. "He gave me tips about life": Glatt.

34. DINNERTIME FOR THE PHOENIX FAMILY, SPRING 1987

"Tofu cheesecake," I get to lick the bowl," etc.: Peters. *The Cookbook for the People Who Love Animals* is by Michael A. Klaper.

35. PARTY AT THE ZAPPA HOUSE

"big crush": author interview with Ione Skye (2012). "It was a really wild, eclectic mix," etc.: author interview with Frank Meyer (2012). In 1990, Nelson had a number one single with a catchy pop-metal slice of cheese, "(Can't Live Without Your) Love and Affection."

36. ECHO #4: *RUNNING ON EMPTY*

"People think the Popes": MacDonald. "There's a connection there": Voland.

37. RUNNING INTO THE SUN BUT I'M RUNNING BEHIND

"He's never studied formally": Glatt. "pianomanship": Lumet. "This feels fake to me," "River doesn't have a false bone": MacDonald. "Who's General Patton?": Abramowitz et al. "He could read and write": Abramowitz et al. Lahti's competing urges: described by her at River's memorial service, as found in Snyder. "As I got closer": Abramowitz et al. "He was leaping and jumping": Abramowitz et al. *Running on Empty* actually contains footage of River executing one of those leaps, awkwardly but joyfully, roughly fifty-eight minutes into the movie: it's a shot in the sequence where River and Plimpton are walking by the shore.

38. EXT. PHILLIPS HOUSE

"I think of the roles I've played lately," River said to John Voland of the *Los Angeles Times,* "the one in *Running on Empty* shows the direction I want to head in: on the leading edge *out* of the teen years."

PART FOUR

39. MAKING PLANS FOR RIVER

"My father is worried": Blair (August 1988). "I'm against the nuclear arms race": Yakir (July 1989). "the gods of the oceans": McFarland.

40. FOOD FOR LIFE

"I like to pretend," etc.: Boyd.

41. CAMP PHOENIX

"River had his own way": Glatt. Details on mortgage: Lawrence.

42. SONGS IN THE ATTIC

"Gainesville is your basic college town": Angeli. "He came in one day": Glatt. "I don't know if the superior being": Peters. "I'm usually wary": Glatt. "worst song": Boyd. "Needed: bass guitarist": Lawrence. "It wasn't just the music": Glatt. "I've got more of a musician's build": Yakir (July 1989). "I've been doing that": Glatt. "I thought these tight": Glatt. "Aleka is a poet-philosopher": Glatt.

43. ORANGES AND LEMONS

"airplane crash": Boyd. "the great Babylon": Glatt. "The Devil is so pretty and tempting": Boyd. "We had five million talks": Friend. "You have to remember": Glatt. "He really liked": Friend.

44. A NIGHT IN THE LIFE

Editing of *Jimmy Reardon:* author interview with William Richert (2013). "a painful, enormously moving drama": Ebert (1988). "outstandingly well": Maslin (1988). "While the film": a review and synopsis from *Time Out London,* credited to "EP" and archived on the timeout.com Web site. "I'm not sure I was even": Blair (March 1988). "I chose the role": Lawrence. "It didn't turn out": Blair (March 1988). "Let's not even think": Boyd.

45. WHY DID IT HAVE TO BE SNAKES?

Campanaro's house: Glatt. "Harrison came out": Lawrence. "It would have been lying": Yakir (October 1989).

46. BOTH OF THEM ARE BONY

All quotations from author interview with Ione Skye (2012).

47. OUR BAND COULD BE YOUR LIFE

"I thought they were a little amateurish": Glatt. "Three years ago": Froom. "Oh, my baby," "Holy shit": Glatt.

48. ROLLING ON THE RIVER

"It's an official bonus": from the press conference at the 1989 Oscar nominees' lunch (as found on YouTube). Wanting to hug Kline: Glatt.

49. WE ARE ALL MADE OF STARS

"If you really want to kick my ass": Glatt, quoting tutor Dirk Drake.

50. ALONE WE ELOPE

"It was kind of a private thing": Lawrence. "When we split up": Friend.

51. YOUNG HOLLYWOOD 1989

"It makes you realize": Levitt. "I was still the jealous": Kiedis. "I went out and bought": Goodall. "I fuck animals," etc.: Heath (1993).

52. WHIP IT

"We'd practice for six or eight months," "We were all kind of at the mercy": Lawrence. "Tracey and I clicked": Banner. "He's like my older brother": Sikes and Powell. "You could have gotten ten times": Lawrence, quoting Danette Staatz. "strangely timid": Kehr. "You can't just wake up," "Devo is bouncing": Yakir (October 1989). "He said the best actors": Rensin. "He is a wonderful actor": Lawrence.

53. HOW DO YOU SAY GOOD NIGHT TO AN ANSWERING MACHINE?

"Hello, Bill": as found in Lawrence.

54. SENSES WORKING OVERTIME

"Hey, Riv!": Woods. "number 89, Tofu Yum-Woon-Sen": Lawrence. "The nicest, most unassuming guy": author interview with Gus Brandt (2013). "They came back eight times": Angeli. "humorous noise," "When you're a Mutley Chick": Nordlie. "I'm not that guy," "He was very private": Friend. "Mrs. Phoenix, she'll take care of it": Lawrence, from an interview with landlady Melanie Barr. "River had a little too much": Glatt. "People look at you": Woods. "Klingons," "the tofu mafia": Friend. "We cut down an area": Woods.

55. SEMPER FI

"I had one foot out the back door": Coburn. "When we first got to Seattle": Abramowitz et al. "twigs and bark": Coburn. "River was the head": Abramowitz et al. "I like the character": Glatt. "Hug a tree": Abramowitz et al. "Okay, it's 2. A.M.," "Yeah. We felt good," and subsequent conversation: Coburn. "I realized, the way he's playing that character": from the commentary track on the 2003 *Dogfight* DVD. "By trying to be": Black. "What could have been": Travers. "I anticipated River": Lawrence. Surprisingly, *Dogfight* was adapted as an off-Broadway musical, which received good notices and played at the Second Stage Theater in New York City for two months in 2012. If you're curious, the show has an original cast album, with songs by Benj Pasek and Justin Paul such as "Come to a Party."

263

56. INT. STILL LIFE CAFÉ

For an excellent in-depth discussion of *Dogfight* and close readings of the performances in it, check out the conversation between Sheila O'Malley and Matt Zoller Seitz at http://www.sheilaomalley.com/?p=33135.

57. THE FIRST CUT IS THE DEEPEST

"a combination of a dog": author interview with Johnny Depp (2003). "auteur hag": Schickel. "If it's something that I do": author interview with Johnny Depp (2003). "I'm a dumbass and I poisoned myself": author interview with Johnny Depp (2007).

58. THE GOLDEN AGE

"After *Dogfight*": Glatt. "One day, you just wake up": Angeli.

PART FIVE

59. THE BOTTOM OF THE BOTTOMLESS BLUE BLUE BLUE POOL

"The camera was this little machine": Handelman. "We were excited": Sikes and Powell. "They probably felt the risk": Parish. "This will get me off the cover": Glatt. "I think maybe he had feelings": Glatt. "If he loved somebody": Friend. "It's a big fat pederast," "No no no, Bill," and ensuing story of Richert taking the role: author interview with William Richert (2013). "sort of a fusion-funk," "River would just start playing": Glatt. "a definite pick-up": Glatt. "But after we agreed": Glatt. "I'm so lonely!": Parish. "I remember thinking": Lawrence. "Imagine, I had to find out": Snyder. "I'm River Phoenix": Glatt. "Quite honestly": Scardapane. "It's as much about gays": Rensin. "I didn't have to suck dick": Parish. "Just think, Keanu," "He scolded": Sikes and Powell. "This is the best part": Lawrence. "I love you, and you don't have to pay me'—I'm so glad I wrote that line": Lawrence. *Pink:* River was recast as the gregarious storyteller "Felix Arroyo, a young and talented spokesman and informmercial [sic] presenter." *Arroyo* is Spanish for a dry creek, a type of river, while "Felix" is a consonant away from Phoenix. "I was hoping," "Okay, then": Parish.

60. YOUNG HOLLYWOOD 1991

"your average, no-depth, standard kid": Harmetz. "It got to the point": Kiedis. "I figured that was as far": Rabin. "an evil version of Tracy and Hepburn": Goodall. "biggest cock in Hollywood," "Eggs, hash browns": Meikle.

61. PSIONIC PSUNSPOT

"research": Glatt. "You're my best friend": author interview with William Richert (2013). "The hardest drink": from an unbylined essay ("River Phoenix: Talent, Looks, a Bright Future—and a Fatal Drug Cocktail") in *Gone Too Soon*, a special edition of *People* published in December 2007. "He liked red wine": author interview with Ione Skye (2012). "We had the same heroin dealer": author interview with anonymous source (2012). "Here's a kid": Lawrence.

62. YOU'RE WHERE YOU SHOULD BE ALL THE TIME

"Having a movie star": Glatt. "I just have to tell you": author interview with Kim Buie (2012). "She has a very flat stomach," Kelly (1991). "I'm kinda like Gainesville's godfather": Bernhard. Canaries and other household details: Angeli. "It sucks and it kinda doesn't suck": Angeli. "River and Sue never took baths": author interview with William Richert (2013). "the same threadbare print shirt," "Jesus, River," "No, man": Angeli. "that never came to fruition": Glatt. "River loved nothing better": Ritz and Ritz, quoting an anonymous "music-business friend." "During one of our conversations": Glatt.

63. THE REFRIGERATOR PARABLE

"I want to make $1 million": Friend. "River realized that his family's ideas": Friend, quoting "one close friend." "all sorts of homeless kids": MacDonald. "I've lost a lot of checks" and following conversation between River and Richert: author interview with William Richert (2013). "I get offered a lot of stuff": Glatt. "me and about a thousand other guys": Angeli. "He knew ways to get in": author interview with William Richert (2013). "Phoenix's slightly anonymous quality": Glieberman. (He gave the movie an A-minus.) "I have lied and changed": Levitt, quoting an interview with French journalist Jean-Paul Chaillet. "River walked into the room," "How are you," "Not too bad": Glatt.

64. ACROSS THE WAY

"I'm not against gays," "I thought you liked that," "Shut up": Lawrence, quoting the January 23–30, 1982, issue of *City Limits* (London). "God, the physical sensation": Cooney. The best introduction to the history of homosexuality in Hollywood is probably *The Celluloid Closet,* either the 1981 book by Vito Russo or the 1995 documentary film directed by Rob Epstein and Jeffrey Friedman.

65. THAT NIGHT AT THE VIPER ROOM

"I like to masturbate": author interview with Richmond Arquette (2013).

66. SATIATE LACK

"I just did not feel": Glatt. "It sounded like a bad teen comedy": Tobolowsky. "We'd think": Lawrence. "Just complete, absolute, total irreverence": Abramowitz et al. "He makes very quirky choices": Glatt. "It turned out that my voice": Glatt. "In hindsight, I'm not sure": author interview with Kim Buie (2012). "furious about the glamour," "Don't worry, I have the fear": Glatt. "He was 100% different": Glatt. "River had a strong passion": Glatt. "entertaining time-waster": Kempley. "I play this cyberpunk nerd": Lawrence.

67. THE MOVIES OF RIVER PHOENIX, RANKED BY AMERICAN BOX OFFICE

All data from boxofficemojo.com.

68. COWBOY MOUTH

"Imagine me being the one": Abramowitz et al. "He looked upon me": Abramowitz et al. "You know, I think," "No, I'm his real": author interview with William Richert (2013). "Sam was, in my opinion": Abramowitz et al. "I'd never had an actor say": Abramowitz et al.

69. BURN HOLLYWOOD BURN

The 1992 riots in Hollywood: Higgins. "Joaquin had drawn Satan": author interview with William Richert (2013). "I'm a minor, stupid talent": Johnson. "River would just bullshit": Glatt. "Nobody knew it was him": author interview with William Richert (2013).

70. MANY RIVERS TO CROSS

"I met with River a few times": Gilbey. "Conditioned to ecstasy": Miller. Making of *Total Eclipse:* Hampton. "He didn't want me nagging him": Friend. "He was hanging around with people": Lawrence. "It was a formal affair": Kennedy. "his language had become": Friend. **"What would those** twelve-year-old girls": Friend. "He fooled a lot of people": Friend. "a frantic phone call," "I don't even eat meat," and ensuing conversation: Ritz and Ritz.

71. THE LAST PICTURE

"This script really isn't ready," "the guy who directed that picture": Bogdanovich. "Iris had called in": Snyder. "Silence": Bogdanovich. "It's one thing to be the star": Abramowitz. "Well, be sure and cast me": Bogdanovich. "The first take was River": Snyder. "River was wandering around," "been into drugs," "didn't cause me another problem": Bogdanovich. "What am I supposed to do?": Snyder. (Bogdanovich claimed that Burton stayed in Nashville "a day or two.") "Samantha managed a pretty impassive": Bogdanovich. "River was determined." "River's face was contorted": Glatt. "I knew maybe there were problems": Abramowitz et al. "No one wanted to confront him": Snyder. "a painful experience": Ebert (1994).

72. YOUNG HOLLYWOOD 1993

Van Sant on River's cameo in *Even Cowgirls Get the Blues:* Lawrence. "the breakthrough performance of the decade": Thompson. "I knew it was awful": Thompson. "Johnny was pretty unhappy": Thompson. "spelled u-r-i-n-e": Meikle. "career-making": Turan. "I can't do this anymore," "I don't know if it was a combination": Kiedis.

73. TONIGHT'S THE NIGHT

"I'm here because my manager": Glatt. "was wearing those flared-out hippie pants": Schindehette et al. "Earl Grey": Schindehette et al., password confirmed by Snyder. "Hey, is anyone there?": Schindehette et al. "When you do blow": Ritz and Ritz. "That's what they'll take you out in": Schindehette et al. "People say it's an amino acid": Hubler and Hochman. "I tried it once": Hubler and Hochman. "The real drug of choice": Schindehette et al. "a really cute boy": interview segment in the "River Phoenix" episode of the *Final 24* television show, first broadcast in 2006. "I'd rather you just point a gun," "That's the end of the drugs": Glatt. "When my next two films are released": Snyder. "a bizarre, meandering and finally, maddening mystical oater": McCarthy. (*Oater* is *Variety* argot for "western.") "You've had that script for a month," "Samantha said it was great," "I think Samantha wants": Snyder. "Do you have any idea," "I don't want to work," and subsequent conversation: Snyder. "You know, Bill, I'm working": author interview with William Richert (2103). "He was sweating, drunk, tired, very beautiful": Cowie. *Safe Passage:* Snyder. *Noah:* author interview with William Richert (2013). *By Way of Fontana:* Friend. "River didn't ask the waiter": author interview with George Sluizer (2013). "I told the director": Snyder.

74. I'M IN A TRANSITIONAL PERIOD, SO I DON'T WANT TO KILL YOU

"Basically, that whole Touchstone formula": Udovitch (1996).

75. IF I HAD A HI-FI

"I don't think their relationship": Glatt (quoting William Richert). "started crying and trying": Glatt, quoting Rachel Guinan. "River was in charge": Glatt. "It's brilliant": Glatt. "We were in overdrive": Lawrence. "He was being so creative": Glatt.

76. FIRST NIGHT AT THE VIPER ROOM

Early Viper Room history: Meikle. "On nights when a hired band": Rogan. That bartender, James E. Rogan, later became a Republican member of the U.S. House of Representatives for two terms and. as of 2013, is serving as a judge on the Superior Court of California. "It was a dive": Ebner. "When the Central was closing down": Ebner. "a group of musicians," "The place became a scene": Meikle. "Just tell Stan," "God, it would have been cool": from *Runnin' Down a Dream,* the 2007 documentary on Tom Petty directed by Peter Bogdanovich. "People who had never walked": Ebner. "There used to be graffiti": Rollins. "We just walked in": Ebner. "a very bizarre night": Ebner. "Johnny lost interest": author interview with anonymous Viper Room employee (2012).

77. GIVE BLOOD

"The idea was for them": Glatt. "I'll see you after": Glatt. "Well, he did":

Glatt. "I knew of his drug habit": author interview with George Sluizer (2013). "That's the only time": Glatt. "Maybe twenty miles": author interview with George Sluizer (2013). "Since David Lean": Lawrence. "We were not the best of friends": Sluizer. "What is this, Frat Boy's question time?": Glatt. "I thought he was doing": Abramowitz et al. "He did not use anything": Abramowitz et al. "He had difficulty with certain lines": author interview with George Sluizer (2013). "In my opinion, that was made": Abramowitz et al. Artichokes and corn: author interview with William Richert (2013). "Thanks be to UFO Godmother," "Take me": Friend. "You're in this picture": Glatt. "I had to sometimes say": author interview with George Sluizer (2013). "We were on this kind of inexorable journey," "Somebody's going to die": Abramowitz et al. "Iris, they're killing snakes," "I'm not a pet coroner": Snyder. "I'm having a hard time": author interview with William Richert (2013). "I'm going back": Glatt.

PART SIX

78. THE BAD, BAD TOWN

"He looked like a corpse": Snyder. "Chris . . . I can't": Snyder. "This can't go on": Snyder. "He was not one hundred percent": Glatt. All *Dark Blood* dialogue is quoted from shooting script by James Barton ("Fifth Draft B," dated September 16, 1993). "He came up to the camera": Lawrence.

79. VIPER HEROIN X

"Can someone help me," "I came to help you," and following dialogue: Abramowitz et al. "I'm coming": author interview with William Richert (2013). "It was dark": Thompson. "When I was eighteen": Fussman (2010). "I wanted to reach out": Thompson. "He was beyond pale": Fussman (2010). "I'll sing at the table": author interview with William Richert (2013). Vodka and bourbon: Lawrence, quoting Pleasant Gehman. "Hey, Riv, drink this": author interview with William Richert (2013). "What did you give me?": Glatt. "Sam called and said": Glatt. "figured some guys," "Hey, Sam, what's up?" : Abramowitz et al. "No one was doing anything": Lawrence. "Oh, God. Gross": Glatt. "You need to call," "He's fine": Lawrence. "It looked like a normal occurrence": Levitt. "Michael Stipe" appeared two years later on P's eponymous album. "It's my brother" and other 911 conversation: public record transcribed by multiple sources, including Weinraub. "Outside there was a crowd": Abramowitz et al. "We found him pulseless": Lawrence. "speedballing": Glatt. "However, his heart": Lawrence. "It was a terrifying shock": interview segment in the "River Phoenix" episode of the *Final 24* television show, first broadcast in 2006. "It was the classic cocaine overreaction": Lawrence. "If there's anything we can do": Van Buskirk. "Come on, River": Lawrence. Time of death: River's autopsy report. Some times are precise in this chapter; for example, the ones logged by medical professionals. Some of them are the best approximations available, especially given the chaos at the Viper Room that night. The people closest to River that night have never spoken publicly about what happened on the evening of his death, but in the immediate aftermath, William Richert discussed it with Samantha Mathis, and his information proved invaluable when sorting through conflicting versions of events.

80. R.I.P. RJP

Events at the emergency room: Snyder. "The bottom line was": Glatt. "I didn't want to hold hands": Lawrence. "When the sun shines": Friend. "He was my brother": Friend. "River's in heaven, blah blah blah": Friend. "River didn't have to": Friend. "You would have thought": Friend. "Peter and I adopted": Snyder. "Is there anybody," "River was a sensitive": Friend.

81. BROKEN DREAMS

"For me, the most respectful thing": Brunner. "taking illegal drugs": Shedden. "I call it saving": Gettell.

82. NEVER GONNA WITHER

"When I finally worked": Rinzler. "His heart went a little more to music": author interview with George Sluizer (2013). Two lesser-known but moving musical tributes to River are "River" by Versus and "River Phoenix" by Japanther.

83. ECHO #5: MONTGOMERY CLIFT

Part of the reason for Clift's enduring mythic power may be his friendship with Taylor; after he died, she kept talking about him in interviews (in striking contrast to River's family and friends). "hyperenergetic, hyper-sincere": Hoskyns. "Nobody ever lies about being lonely": frequently misquoted as "lied." "The Right Profile": found on the Clash's album *London Calling* (1979 [UK]/ 1980 ([USA]). The song's chorus features the line "That's Montgomery Clift, honey," and the lyrics are rife with biographical details, including a verse on his car crash. The "roll of pills" lyrics appears to come from Patricia Bosworth's biography and refers to a thousand Seconals. The title refers to the undamaged side of Clift's face.

84. CLOSING TIME AT THE VIPER ROOM

"I'm grateful to be able": Lawrence. "ultimately not a joyous experience": Ebner. "the hillside manor": Ebner. "We were all just twenty-three": Ebner. "It was kind of a given": Ebner. "a real hot, heavy kiss": Andersen. "Maybe it's the curse": Meikle. "The facts establish": Meikle. "bad memories": Meikle.

85. BLOOD ON THE TRACKS

"I had the *Dark Blood* material": author interview with George Sluizer (2013). "Normally, within five minutes": Brunner. "He had contrasts": author interview with George Sluizer (2013).

EPILOGUE

"I don't know of a movie": Junod. "Shit, man," "Theater is not a stepping-stone": author interview with Ethan Hawke (2004). "I've always held on to the idea": Mohan. "I love everything that I felt on drugs": author interview with John Frusciante (2000). "It's a crazy thing": Harris. "Nah, it's not about that now": Vernon. "Of course there is a sadness": Corner. "I think it's total, utter bullshit": Mitchell. "I don't need to pull from my experience": Smith. "I don't think anybody's necessarily ready": Fussman (2008).

PHOTOGRAPHY CREDITS

Title page photograph and part opener photograph: © by Lance Staedler/ Corbis Outline.

Page 1: © by Steve Schapiro/Corbis.

Page 2: (top) Dianna Whitley_Shooting Star™; (bottom) Stephen Ellison_Shooting Star™.

Page 3: (top) © by Columbia Pictures/courtesy of Everett Collection; (bottom) © by Warner Bros./courtesy of Everett Collection.

Page 4: Nancy Ellison/Polaris.

Page 5: (top) Photofest; (bottom) Ron Galella/Getty Images.

Page 6: (top) Photograph by Moviestore Collection/Rex/Rex USA; (bottom) photograph by Moviestore Collection/Rex/Rex USA.

Page 7: (top) Steve Eichner/WireImage; (bottom) © by Paramount/courtesy of Everett Collection.

Page 8: © by MR Photo/Corbis Outline.